ALMOST HEAVEN

published by

THE JUNIOR LEAGUE OF HUNTINGTON, WEST VIRGINIA

"The purpose of the Junior League is exclusively educational and charitable, and is to promote voluntarism, to develop the potential of its members for voluntary participation in community affairs, and to demonstrate the effectiveness of trained volunteers."

Proceeds from the sale of this cookbook go to all community projects of the Junior League of Huntington, West Virginia.

D1275739

1

Goodtime DESIGN, Inc.

Copies of **ALMOST HEAVEN** may be obtained by writing **ALMOST HEAVEN,** Junior League of Huntington, 617 Ninth Avenue, Huntington, West Virginia 25701.

KANSAS CITY
PRESS, INC.

Printed by
Kansas City Press, Inc.
Olathe, Kansas

COOKBOOK ACKNOWLEDGEMENTS

Steering Committee

Co-Chairmen............................. Nancy Dewhurst Hanshaw
Theo Wallace Tippett
Category Coordinator ....Margaret Dodge Wolfe
Promotion and Publicity .... Peggy Massey Baker
Patricia Prichard Crews
Secretary .... Sally Herr Lowe
Treasurer .... Joyce Sullivan Ey
Executive Liason............................ Judy Varnum Ketchum

Category Chairmen

Alicia Allen Adams
Mary Lou McDonald Anton
Teri Mulholland Bergin
Harriette Matthews Cyrus
Margaret Manly Graddy
Susan McCray Hage
Linda Hatten
Marcia Heckman Hatten

Jane Yates Hess
Mary Harvey Wilson Midkiff
Mary Witten Neal
Rebecca Warden Offutt
Sharon Noe Peoples
Donna Lycan Stark
Brandon Brossy Vaden
Dixie Hudson Wilson
Janet Dorado Yost

Marketing Committee

Sue Ellison Jennings
Edna Fattaleh Meisel

Mary Jo Miller
Jimelle Walker Bowen

Typist .... Anita Murrell Smith
Introduction .... Rebecca Fletcher Kinsey
Cover Concept .... Jimelle Walker Bowen
Cover Design and Illustrations ....Ken Halstead
Goodtime DESIGN, Inc.

3

Members of the Junior League of Huntington and their friends who have contributed recipes to ALMOST HEAVEN are:

Helen Dale Acker
Wynn Wygal Adam
Alicia Allen Adams
Patricia Parker Agee
Alice Groverman Ainslie
Charlotte Garred Aldridge
Helen Allen
Mary Armstrong Allen
Doris Bailey Andrews
Mary Lou McDonald Anton
Peggy Massey Baker
Anna Louise Smith Basarich
Maxine Plumley Baur
Mary Plyde Marsh Bell
Patricia Anne Woody Belshe
Teri Mulholland Bergin
Virginia Wardrup Berner
Mary Beth Eddy Biederman
Elsa Biern
Wilma Huntley Biggs
Sally Worley Blankenship
Susie Block
Sally Lester Bogers
Barclay Lytton Bolen
Clara Tebay Boso
Jimelle Walker Bowen
Suzi Hersh Brodof
Lori Rebecca Brodof
Nannette Brossy
Peg Church Brown
Catherine Peter Bryan
Nancy Cooper Burkhardt
Peggy Goode Burton
Lillian Helms Buskirk
Rose Anton Cancro
Barbara Honaker Carter
Meredyth Myers Champ
Marjorie Swan Chellis
Nancy Chandler
Rebecca Herdman Christian
Margaret Benjamin Clanton
Anne Gilmore Conaty

Eleanor Wolfe Conaty
Kay Karraker Cook
Betty Steele Coster
Paul Coster
Sandra Smith Coster
Michele Prestera Craig
Catherine Gwinn Crews
Patricia Prichard Crews
Joanne Crumbley·
Sharon Shingleton Curnutte
Harriette Matthews Cyrus
Mary D'Allessandro
Pattie O'Malley Damron
Pauline Allport Danner
Huldah Parrish Daugherty
Lucy H. Dawson
Jane Belcastro D'Egidio
William N. Denman
Cynthia Cunningham Dennis
Betty Galloway Devine
Karen Fischman Dicker
Margaret White Dillard
Jane Adams Dingess
Joan Middleton Dodge
Jean Fowler Doyle
Sally Fletcher Duncan
Judy Stewart Eblin
Katherine Sedgeman Elias
Pam Ison Eller
Lucile Hayes Elmore
Mary Elizabeth Reaser Emmons
Joyce Sullivan Ey
Terry Edwards Fattaleh
Anita Gardner Farrell
Ellen Feiss
Geoffrey Fennessey
Connie Ferguson
Julie Houchin Ferguson
Katherine Peyton Forbes
Mary McClain Frazier
Gayle Fritz
Jerri Cyrus Gainer

4

Rebecca McCray Gallagher
Mary Plymale Garst
Margaret Manly Graddy
Jane Gessel Graham
Jacqueline Wagers Green
Debbie Little Greenstein
Guyan Golf and Country Club
Kitty Allport Hage
Susan McCray Hage
Jean Atkinson Hamilton
Katherine Noel Hanshaw
Nancy Dewhurst Hanshaw
Vicki Kidd Hanshaw
Cherry Martin Harrison
Linda S. Hatten
Marcia Heckman Hatten
Virginia Pollitt Hatten
Ann Margaret Moore Havens
Julie Ducharme Haynes
Patricia Pennock Henry
Jane Yates Hess
Anni Hite
Gretchen Hite
Mary Whitaker Hite
Lucile Huff Holswade
Polly Holway
Linda Chandler Hood
Barbara Hemphill Hopta
Nancy Herring Humphrey
Sue Hilliard Humphries
Yvonne McCormick Hurry
Betty J. Jackson
Barbara Raynes James
Elizabeth Wilkinson Jennings
Sue Ellison Jennings
Lilly Gade Johnson
Fern Porter Jones
Judy Varnum Ketchum
Betty Sue Hayden Kinzer
Christine Theus Kluemper
Ann Peoples Krieger
Patricia Hardy Lansaw
LaPola's, Hilton Head, South Carolina
Dorothy Leukart
LeAnn Dodd Litton

Marsha Roberts Logan
Hilda Sheets Long
Robin Peck Mahaffey
Pola Svingos Maniskas
Jane Brown Manning
Janet Selvey Marple
Christine Owens Maynard
Jennie Lawton McAllister
Guida Mae McCray
Gail Ann McCray
Betsy Keadle McCreight
Jean McNeer McCurry
Carol Bowling McDonald
Chris Dwight McDonald
Louise Rettenmaier McDonald
Marion Keay McGinnis
Moira Richardson McGrath
Beverly Castle McKinney
Julienne Shinn McNeer
Elizabeth Kinser Meek
Edna Fattaleh Meisel
Mary Harvey Wilson Midkiff
Betty Ann Sheets Miller
Carol Devine Miller
Ming's Restaurant
Marsha Rucker Mohr
Karen Lieving Morrison
Susan Harwood Morton
Marilyn McGinnis Murdock
Bertha Brewer Narozniak
Margaret Moore Neal
Mary Witten Neal
Martha Ann Neale
Nancy Patricia Neale
Barbara Martin Neighborgall
Ellen Clark Nelson
Rebecca Ann O'Conner
Alice Dickinson O'Malley
Rebecca Warden Offutt
Rosa Henni Ore
Catherine Owens
Marge Owens
Jane Holswade Pancake
Jane Hurt Patterson
Lucille Bowes Peake

Betty Chadwick Peck
Betty Duncan Peck
Sharon Noe Peoples
Sally Perinoni Pettit
Susie Stapleton Points
Pia Sinka Porter
Deborah England Prestera
Mike Prestera
Helen Gwinn Prichard
Helen Hamill Proctor
Jean Ramsey
Virginia H. Ranson
Rebecca Bastinelli Ray
Kay Williams Rente
Louise Rettenmaier
Rocco's Ristorante
Ann Wolfe Rowe
Georgann Hartman Ruby
Martha Bohart Rummell
Barbara Hall Russo
Ann Davies Sammons
Elza H. Saunders
Virginia Cohagen Schmidt
James L. Seaton
Janet Reese Seitz
Jewel Plymale Shingleton
Mary Lind Hagan Smart
David Smith
Day Doughty Smith
Harriet Thomas Smith
Kenneth Smith
Pat Slack Smith
Pauline Reffeitt Smith
Mabel Godby Smith
Becky Williams Smythe
Betty Jo Thomas Smythe
Ann Logan Speer
Charlene Gallagher Sprouse
Susan McAllister Sprouse
Donna Lycan Stark

Gail Queen Stephenson
Myra Seese Stewart
Martha Stone
Carol Morgan Taylor
Anita Thomas
Betty Bolling Tippett
Theo Wallace Tippett
Anne Burns Todd
Belinda Edwards Trainer
Leslie Triplett
Brandon Brossy Vaden
Ann Van Voris
Betty Jane Nelson Vinson
Cherry Skinner Vinson
Annette Vickers Walker
Sara Allen Walsh
Martha Johnson Warren
Sandra Fawn Warzin
Karen Price Watson
Julia Dickinson Watts
Elmira Weston
Nell Woodall Wharton
Mary Berner Whitten
Betsy Holtzmuller Wilson
Dixie Hudson Wilson
Kim Adams Wilson
Margaret Phillips Wilson
Jessie Dorey Wise
Elizabeth Penick Withers
Betty Merrill Wolfe
Frances Maude Wolfe
Margaret Dodge Wolfe
Martha Cobb Woodward
Ellen Harris Wotring
Melanie Sayegh Wotring
Myra Snyder Wright
Janet Dorado Yost
Helen Young
Jean Zbailey
Janet Bressler Zettle

TABLE OF CONTENTS

INTRODUCTION

When the song "Country Roads" became popular, a lot of people suddenly began to sing the praises of our Mountain State. To those of us who live, work and raise families here, however, the words "Almost Heaven" were nothing new, for that's the way we've always felt about West Virginia. The saying proud Mountaineers have about West Virginia being the most northern of the southern states, most southern of the northern states, most western of the eastern states, and most eastern of the western states surely placed it somewhere in the heart of the country.

Come follow our soaring balloon and discover that from the very essence of luxury and culture in our historic areas and cities, to the wild, natural beauty of our hills and streams, West Virginia is, indeed, **ALMOST HEAVEN**. Heavenly, too, are the recipes we've collected, tested and present here....as rich and varied as our heritage. Welcome to our mountain homes and to **ALMOST HEAVEN**.

Appetizers

BLACK WATER FALLS

APPETIZERS

ALMOND CHEESE FINGERS

Preparation: 30 to 40 minutes   *Can do ahead*   *Yield: 6 dozen*
Freeze: 30 to 40 minutes   *Can be frozen*
Cook: 10 minutes

6 slices bacon, fried and crumbled
1 (2 ¾ ounce) package chopped sliced almonds
2 teaspoons Worcestershire sauce

½ pound sharp grated Cheddar cheese
1 cup mayonnaise
1 loaf thin sliced white bread

Combine bacon, almonds, Worcestershire sauce, Cheddar cheese, and mayonnaise. Cut off crust on bread. Spread mixture on bread and cut into strips. Freeze strips on cookie sheets. When strips are frozen, remove from cookie sheets and seal in an airtight container in freezer. When ready to serve, remove from freezer, place strips on cookie sheets. Bake at 400° for 10 minutes.

Note: Double this recipe and bake only the number needed. Handy for "drop-in" company.

ALMOND AND WINE STUFFED MUSHROOMS

Preparation: 20 minutes   *Can do ahead*   *Yield: 8 to 12 servings*
Cook: 5 minutes

24 to 36 medium-sized mushroom caps, washed and dried
½ cup margarine
⅓ cup bread crumbs

Dash of oregano
½ cup chopped almonds
½ cup red wine or sherry
1 envelope onion soup mix
Grated Parmesan cheese

Cut stems from mushrooms and chop. Melt margarine and add mushroom stems, bread crumbs, oregano, chopped almonds, wine and onion soup mix. Mix well. Fill each cap with a rounded teaspoon of mixture. Sprinkle with Parmesan cheese. Place mushrooms 4 inches from broiling unit. Broil 5 minutes.

HINT: *Spread a whole wheat wafer with herb cheese and top with a slice of olive. Broil until bubbling - serve.*

10

ASPARAGUS ROLLS

Preparation: 25 minutes   *Can do ahead*   *Yield: 24 servings*
Cook: 12 minutes

12 slices white bread, crusts
  removed
1 (8 ounce) container whipped
  cream cheese with chives
8 slices bacon, cooked and
  crumbled

24 fresh asparagus spears,
  partially cooked (or canned
  asparagus, drained)
¼ cup melted butter or
  margarine
Grated Parmesan cheese

Preheat oven to 400°. After removing the crusts, use a rolling pin to flatten each slice of bread. Combine cream cheese and bacon, stirring well. Spread bread with cheese mixture covering to edges. Place 2 asparagus spears, in alternate directions, on each slice of bread; roll up, and place seam side down on a greased baking sheet. Brush each generously with butter and sprinkle with grated Parmesan cheese. Cut each roll in half. Bake for 12 minutes.

BACON-CHEESE FINGERS

Preparation: 25 minutes   *Can do ahead*   *Yield: 30 appetizers*
Cook: 10 minutes

1 cup shredded Swiss cheese
8 slices bacon, cooked and
  crumbled
3 to 4 tablespoons mayonnaise
1 tablespoon grated onion

½ teaspoon celery salt
10 slices day-old sandwich
  bread, crusts removed and
  cut into thirds

Preheat oven to 325°. Combine Swiss cheese, bacon, mayonnaise, onion and celery salt; blend well. Spread cheese mixture over each piece of bread. Place on ungreased baking sheet. Bake for 10 minutes.

HINT: *To keep avocado dip from darkening, bury one of the avocado pits in the dip. Remove just prior to serving.*

APPETIZERS

BACON WRAPS

Preparation: 20 to 25 minutes
Cook: 2 hours

Butter flavored rectangular
  crackers

Grated Parmesan cheese
Bacon slices, cut in half

Preheat oven to 225°. Take each half slice of bacon and lay flat. Lay one cracker on top in center of bacon so that bacon can wrap around cracker. Pour Parmesan cheese in center on cracker. Wrap bacon around cheese and cracker carefully. Lay cracker on ungreased cookie sheet, ends of bacon down. Bake for 2 hours.

Note: Can use small bread sticks instead of crackers.

PETITE BROCCOLI QUICHE

Preparation: 45 minutes
Cook: 25 minutes

Yield: 2 dozen

1 (3 ounce) package cream
  cheese
½ cup butter
1 cup flour
5 ounces frozen chopped
  broccoli, thawed

1 cup shredded Swiss cheese
½ cup half and half
3 eggs
1 teaspoon salt

Preheat oven to 400°. Combine cream cheese, butter and flour in a bowl. Blend well. Chill. Shape into 24 1-inch balls. Place in ungreased miniature muffin tins. Press against bottom and sides. Drain broccoli well. Into each muffin cup spoon 1 teaspoon broccoli and top with Swiss cheese. In a small bowl mix cream cheese, eggs and salt. Spoon about 1 teaspoon egg mixture into each. Bake for 25 minutes.

HINT: *Chilling raw vegetables in juice of dill pickle jar makes a crunchy low cal snack.*

12

BLACK BEAUTIES

Preparation: 30 minutes   *Can do ahead*   *Yield: 24 appetizers*
Bake: 10 minutes

24 pitted ripe olives   **Bacon**
¼ to ½ pound Gruyere cheese

Preheat oven to 400°. Drain olives. Cut small pieces of cheese and stuff into olives. Cut bacon slices into thirds. Wrap olive with bacon, making certain that the olive hole is covered. Secure with toothpick. Bake in 400° oven until bacon is crisp, 10 minutes or longer. Serve immediately.

AMARETTO CHEESE BALL

Preparation: 10 minutes   *Can do ahead*   *Yield: 1 cheese ball*
Stand: overnight

1 (8 ounce) package cream   **¼ cup Amaretto**
** cheese**   **½ cup blanched sliced almonds**

Soften cream cheese. (Let come to room temperature or place in microwave for 1 minute on medium power.) Mix Amaretto, cream cheese and half of the almonds. Shape into ball and use the remaining almond slivers to cover the cheese ball. Refrigerate overnight before serving to enhance flavor. Serve with slices of apples and pears. Remember to use lemon juice on fruit slices to keep them from turning brown.

BAKED BRIE

Preparation: 5 minutes
Cook: 15 to 20 minutes

1 whole Brie round (any size)   **Butter or margarine**
Blanched almonds

Preheat oven to 300°. Place cheese on ovenproof serving dish. Dot with butter and sprinkle almonds over top. Bake for 15 minutes. Place under broiler until almonds brown. Serve with French bread or unsalted crackers.

APPETIZERS

CHEESE-STRAWBERRY RING

Preparation: 20 minutes   *Can do ahead*   *Yield: serves 20*
Stand: 2 to 3 hours

1 pound sharp Cheddar
  cheese, grated
1 cup chopped pecans
1 cup mayonnaise
½ cup grated green onion
Dash of salt

Dash of pepper
Dash of cayenne pepper
1 (12 ounce) jar strawberry
  preserves or red or green
  pepper jelly

Combine Cheddar cheese, pecans, mayonnaise, green onions, salt, pepper and cayenne pepper. Refrigerate. Before serving, form into a ring mold and put strawberry preserves or jelly in the middle. Serve with crackers. Decorate with sprigs of parsley.

OLIVE ROQUEFORT CHEESE BALL

Preparation: 15 minutes   *Yield: 1 to 2 cheese balls*
Stand: several hours

12 ounces cream cheese
¼ pound butter
1 triangle (1 ¼ ounce)
  Roquefort cheese
½ cup chopped green olives

1 to 1 ½ tablespoons finely
  minced onion
Salt
Pepper
Chopped pecans or parsley
  flakes

In a mixing bowl, soften cream cheese, butter and Roquefort cheese. Mix well with an electric mixer. Add olives, onions, salt and pepper to taste. Chill. Form one large or two small cheese balls and roll in chopped pecans or parsley flakes. Refrigerate

HINT: *Make dips a day ahead for full flavor.*

SMOKY SALMON CHEESE BALL

Preparation: 20 minutes   *Can do ahead*   *Yield: 1 cheese ball*
Stand: 1 hour

1 (1 pound) can salmon (red preferred), drained and flaked with bones and skin removed
1 (8 ounce) package cream cheese, softened
1 tablespoon fresh lemon juice
2 teaspoons grated onion
1 teaspoon prepared horseradish
¼ teaspoon salt
¼ teaspoon liquid smoke
3 tablespoons minced fresh parsley
½ cup chopped pecans

Combine salmon, cream cheese and seasonings. Chill at least one hour. Form into ball; roll in mixture of chopped pecans and parsley. Serve with crackers.

CHEESE ROSETTES

Preparation: 30 to 60 minutes

¼ cup salted butter
½ cup hot water
½ cup flour
¼ teaspoon salt
¼ teaspoon sugar
2 eggs
½ cup grated imported Swiss cheese (Gruyere)
½ cup finely diced imported Swiss cheese
½ teaspoon Tabasco

Preheat oven to 375°. Combine the butter and hot water and place them over burner. When the butter is melted and the water is boiling, add the flour, salt and sugar and stir with a wooden spoon until the mixture leaves the sides of the pan and forms a ball in the middle of the pan. Remove from the pan and continue beating or place in electric mixer. Add eggs, one at a time, and continue beating until the dough is waxy and smooth. Blend in grated and diced cheese and Tabasco. Fill a pastry bag with paste. Bag should be fitted with a large rosette tube. Force the paste into a ring or into individual rosettes on a greased cookie sheet. Bake until well puffed and browned or until the paste no longer tears. Serve warm.

HINT: *Always serve cheese at room temperature.*

APPETIZERS

CHEESE STUFFED MUSHROOMS

Preparation: 20 minutes   *Yield: 4 to 6 servings*
Cook: 6 to 8 minutes

3 slices bacon, cooked   ⅛ teaspoon salt
  and crumbled   12 medium-sized mushroom
⅓ cup shredded sharp   caps, washed and dried
  Cheddar cheese   ¼ cup melted butter <u>or</u>
½ teaspoon chopped chives   margarine

Combine bacon with cheese, chives and salt. Dip mushroom caps in butter or margarine and place on cookie sheet or broiler pan. Fill each cap with a rounded teaspoon of bacon-cheese mixture. Place tops of mushrooms 4 inches from broiling unit and broil 6 to 8 minutes.

CHICKEN DRUMMETTES

Preparation: 30 minutes   *Can do ahead*   *Yield: 50 appetizers*
Stand: overnight
Cook: 1 ½ hours

25 chicken wings   1 teaspoon garlic powder
1 cup soy sauce   1 teaspoon ginger
1 cup orange marmalade   1 teaspoon pepper

Cut chicken wings in half and cut off small extension on one side. Place wings in a 9 x 13 inch pan. Mix marinade: soy sauce, orange marmalade, garlic powder, ginger and pepper; pour over chicken wings. Let stand in refrigerator overnight. Turn wings. Preheat oven and bake at 300° for 1 ½ hours.

BACON AND TOMATO SPREAD

Preparation: 30 minutes   *Can do ahead*   *Yield: 2 cups*
Stand: 1 hour

1 (8 ounce) package cream
  cheese, softened
2 teaspoons prepared mustard
½ teaspoon celery salt
6 slices bacon, cooked and
  crumbled

1 medium tomato, peeled,
  seeded and finely chopped
¼ cup finely chopped
  green pepper
Fresh vegetables for dipping

Stir together cream cheese, mustard and celery salt. Stir in bacon, tomato and green pepper. Cover and chill. Serve with vegetables.

CHUNKY VEGETABLE DIP

Preparation: 10 minutes   *Can do ahead*   *Yield: serves 10*
Stand: 2 to 3 hours

8 ounces commercial
  sour cream
¼ cup chopped tomato
¼ cup chopped avocado

1 (6 ounce) package Italian
  salad dressing mix, dry
1 tablespoon mayonnaise
1 tablespoon lemon juice
¼ teaspoon Tabasco

Mix all of the ingredients and chill. Serve with raw vegetables.

CRAB DIP

Preparation: 15 minutes   *Can do ahead*   *Yield: serves 6*
Stand: 2 to 3 hours

1 cup mayonnaise
2 teaspoons lemon juice
1 teaspoon dry mustard
1 teaspoon Worcestershire
  sauce
⅛ teaspoon hot pepper sauce

2 teaspoons minced onion
2 teaspoons minced celery
2 teaspoons minced green
  pepper
1 can (7 ½ ounce) crab, cartilage
  removed

Blend all ingredients well and chill. Serve with potato chips, corn chips or wheat crackers.

APPETIZERS

DILL DIP

Preparation: 10 minutes   Can do ahead   *Yield: 2 cups*
Stand: 1 hour

8 ounces commercial sour
   cream
1 cup mayonnaise
1 teaspoon Beau Monde
   seasoning

3 tablespoons instant minced
   onion
3 tablespoons chopped parsley
1 tablespoon dry dill weed

Combine all the ingredients, mixing well. Chill. Serve with fresh vegetables or potato chips.

HOT CRAB FONDUE

Preparation: 20 to 30 minutes   *Yield: serves 10*

2 (8 ounce) packages cream
   cheese
16 ounces frozen Alaskan King
   crab, thawed
¼ cup light cream

½ teaspoon Worcestershire
   sauce
¼ teaspoon garlic salt
¼ teaspoon cayenne pepper
¼ to ½ cup sherry for flavor

Put cream cheese in top of double boiler and stir until smooth. Add remaining ingredients and heat through. Stir as needed to blend well. Serve hot in fondue pot or chafing dish, with chunks of crusty French bread on the side. If mixture thickens while standing, stir in more cream.

MRS. RUMMELL'S SPINACH DIP

Preparation: 15 minutes   *Yield: 6 to 8 servings*
Stand: 6 to 8 hours

1 (10 ounce) package frozen
   chopped spinach, thaw and
   squeeze out all liquid
1 ½ cups commercial sour
   cream
1 envelope Knorr vegetable
   soup mix

1 cup mayonnaise
4 chopped green onions
1 (8 ounce) can water chestnuts,
   drained, sliced and quartered

Mix all the ingredients well and refrigerate 6 to 8 hours.

Note: Serve in a hollow bread round.

18

GUACAMOLE SUPREME

Preparation: 20 to 30 minutes   *Yield: 10 to 15 servings*

3 ripe avocados, mashed
Juice of ½ lemon
4 ounces cream cheese,
  softened
Dash of garlic salt
Dash of ground pepper
1 tablespoon mayonnaise

¾ cup chopped green onion
2 cups grated sharp Cheddar
  cheese
2 cups shredded lettuce
2 medium sized tomatoes,
  chopped
Taco chips or corn chips

Squeeze lemon over the mashed avocados. Add the softened cream cheese, garlic salt, ground pepper, mayonnaise and mix well. Spread the mixture on a dinner plate or a serving platter. Top mixture with green onions, grated Cheddar cheese, shredded lettuce and the chopped tomatoes. Put taco chips around edges of the dip.

ZUCCHINI DIP

Preparation: 45 minutes   *Can do ahead*   *Yield: 6 to 8 servings*
Cook: 15 minutes

1 cup diced zucchini
1 tablespoon chopped onion
¼ teaspoon minced garlic
¼ teaspoon salt
¼ teaspoon paprika
⅛ teaspoon pepper or cayenne
⅛ teaspoon basil

4 ounces cream cheese, cubed
  and softened
¼ teaspoon Worcestershire
  sauce
½ teaspoon lemon juice
¼ teaspoon seasoned salt
Paprika and minced parsley
  for garnish

Combine zucchini, onion, garlic and seasonings. Cover and simmer for 15 minutes or until soft. Cool and purée in blender or food processor. Add cream cheese and blend. Season with lemon juice, Worcestershire sauce and seasoned salt to taste. Chill. Sprinkle with paprika and fresh parsley before serving.

APPETIZERS

EGG ROLLS WITH SWEET AND SOUR SAUCE

Preparation: 2 hours   *Yield: 40 egg rolls*

1 (1 pound) can bean sprouts
3 tablespoons peanut oil,
  divided
2 cups chopped raw chicken
  and/or pork
1 tablespoon rice wine or pale
  dry sherry
1 tablespoon soy sauce
2 (6 ounce) bags frozen baby
  shrimp

½ teaspoon sugar
1 to 2 cups chopped mushrooms
2 cups chopped celery
2 tablespoons salt
1 tablespoon cornstarch
  dissolved in 2 tablespoons
  water
1 package egg roll wrappers
Peanut oil

Crisp bean sprouts in water in refrigerator for 30 minutes. Drain. Add 1 tablespoon oil to wok and stir fry chicken or pork until it changes color. Add wine, soy sauce, shrimp, sugar and mushrooms. Stir fry until shrimp turns pink. Mix well; set aside in separate bowl. Add 2 tablespoons oil to wok and stir fry celery for 5 minutes. Add salt and bean sprouts mixing well. Return chicken (pork) shrimp mixture to wok with celery and bean sprouts. Cook until the liquid begins to boil. Remove all liquid leaving only 2 to 3 tablespoons. Add cornstarch that has been dissolved in water to wok mixture. Stir well until mixture is coated in light glaze. Place 1 to 2 tablespoons of mixture in egg roll wrapper. Fold and seal with water. Deep fry in peanut oil until a golden brown. Serve with hot mustard or sweet and sour sauce.

SWEET AND SOUR SAUCE

1 ½ tablespoons cornstarch
½ cup brown sugar, firmly
  packed
12 ounces pineapple juice

½ cup vinegar
1 tablespoon soy sauce
1 to 2 tablespoons orange
  marmalade

Mix the cornstarch and brown sugar blending well until all cornstarch is dissolved. Add pineapple juice, vinegar, soy sauce and orange marmalade. Cook over medium heat stirring constantly until mixture boils. Serve when sauce thickens and darkens.

EGGS AND CAVIAR

Preparation: 30 minutes   *Yield: 8 to 10 servings*
Stand: overnight

½ cup butter, softened   1 teaspoon lemon juice
¼ to ½ cup mayonnaise   ½ teaspoon salt
6 hard boiled eggs, chopped   1 cup commercial sour cream
½ cup chopped green onions   1 (6 ounce) jar caviar

Blend butter and mayonnaise well. Add eggs, onions, lemon juice and salt. Mix well. Line a small bowl with plastic wrap. Pack mixture firmly into bowl and chill overnight. When ready to serve, unmold onto serving platter and peel off plastic wrap. Frost evenly with sour cream and top with caviar. Serve with party rye rounds.

Note: Red caviar can be substituted for the holidays.

MAKE AHEAD HOLIDAY MINCE-MEATBALLS

Preparation: 30 minutes   *Can do ahead partially*   *Yield: 6 dozen*
Cook: 12 to 14 minutes   *Can be frozen*

2 eggs, beaten   1 pound lean ground beef
⅓ cup fine dry bread crumbs   1 (22 ounce) can mincemeat pie
1 (2 ¼ ounce) can deviled ham   filling
1 pinch of dry mustard   ⅓ cup apple juice
½ teaspoon salt   1 tablespoon vinegar

Preheat oven to 375°. Combine eggs, bread crumbs, deviled ham, dry mustard and salt. Add ground beef and mix well. Shape mixture into 6 dozen tiny meatballs. Line meatballs in a shallow baking pan and bake for 12 to 14 minutes or until done. Remove from the pan, cover and chill (or freeze). When ready to serve, combine the pie filling, apple juice and vinegar in a large saucepan. Heat until bubbling. Add meatballs and heat through. Serve in a chafing dish. Keep warm. Add additional apple juice if the sauce becomes too thick.

APPETIZERS

HAM-FILLED MUSHROOM CAPS

Preparation: 40 minutes   *Can do ahead*   *Yield: 3 dozen*
Cook: 10 minutes
Bake: 10 minutes

1 pound small whole
  mushrooms
¼ cup butter
2 cups ground cooked ham
½ cup commercial sour cream

2 tablespoons minced chives or
  green onions
6 pitted ripe olives or
  minced parsley

Remove stems from cleaned mushrooms and chop finely to make 1 cup. Lightly cook mushroom caps in melted butter. Arrange in buttered baking pan. Mix together ham, sour cream, chives and 1 cup chopped mushroom stems. Stuff mushroom caps with mixture. Bake in a 350° oven for 10 minutes. Garnish, if desired, with sliced olive wedges or minced parsley.

PARMESAN CHICKEN NUGGETS

Preparation: 35 minutes   *Yield: 14 to 16 servings*
Cook: 20 minutes

7 to 8 whole chicken breasts,
  boned and skinned
2 cups fine dry bread crumbs
1 cup grated Parmesan cheese
1 ½ teaspoons salt

4 teaspoons dried whole thyme
4 teaspoons dried whole basil
1 cup butter or margarine,
  melted

Preheat oven to 400°. Cut chicken into nugget sized pieces. Combine bread crumbs, cheese, salt, thyme and basil; mix well. Dip chicken pieces in butter, and coat with bread crumb mixture. Place on a baking sheet in a single layer. Bake for 20 minutes or until done.

Note: Excellent served hot, but also very good served at room temperature.

PIMENTO-PECAN CHICKEN SALAD

Preparation: 30 minutes   *Can do ahead*   *Yield: 6 servings*
Stand: 3 hours

1 cup cooked, chopped chicken
1 tablespoon chopped onion
2 tablespoons chopped
   pimento

Dash of Tabasco
½ cup mayonnaise
1 cup chopped pecans

Combine chicken, onion, pimento, Tabasco, mayonnaise and pecans in a mixing bowl. Refrigerate at least 3 hours or overnight. Serve with wheat crackers.

SAUCY MUSHROOMS

Preparation: 30 minutes   *Yield: 24 servings*
Cook: 25 minutes
Refrigerate: overnight
Reheat: 5 to 10 minutes

3 pounds fresh mushrooms
⅔ cup soy sauce
⅔ cup Worcestershire sauce

⅔ cup butter
Juice of 3 lemons
1 clove garlic, crushed

Clean mushrooms and slice (egg slicer may be used). Combine soy sauce, Worcestershire sauce, butter, lemon juice, garlic and simmer 5 minutes. Add mushrooms and simmer 20 minutes. Cover and refrigerate overnight. To serve: reheat, transfer to a chafing dish.

SPINACH BALLS

Preparation: 30 minutes   *Can do ahead*   *Yield: 6 ½ dozen*
Bake: 20 minutes   *Can be frozen*

3 (10 ounce) packages chopped
   spinach, thawed with the
   liquid squeezed out
1 (8 ounce) package herb
   seasoned stuffing mix
2 medium onions, chopped fine

9 eggs, beaten
1 cup margarine, melted
3 ounces grated Parmesan
   cheese
1 tablespoon garlic salt
½ teaspoon pepper

Mix all ingredients well, roll into walnut-sized balls. Bake at 350° for 20 minutes. Check bottoms for doneness. Can be frozen prior to cooking.

APPETIZERS

SAUSAGE APPETIZERS

Preparation: 20 to 30 minutes　　*Can do ahead*　　*Yield: 48 servings*
Bake: 20 minutes　　*Can be frozen*

1 (8 ounce) package refrig-
　erated butterflake dinner
　rolls
½ pound hot sausage, crumbled
2 eggs, slightly beaten

1 cup cottage cheese
1 tablespoon snipped chives
Dash of freshly ground pepper
¼ cup grated Parmesan cheese

Preheat oven to 375°. Generously grease miniature muffin tins. Separate rolls into 8 sections. Press each piece between ⅛ and ¼ inch thick and fit into muffin cups. Brown sausage in small skillet, drain well. Spoon equally over dough. Mix eggs, cottage cheese, chives and pepper. Stir in Parmesan cheese. Spoon over sausage and bake about 20 minutes or until filling is lightly browned.

Note: Sausage Appetizers can be made ahead and frozen before or after baking.

SCALLOP KEBOBS

Preparation: 20 to 25 minutes　　*Do ahead partially*　　*Yield: 8 servings*
Stand: 2 to 3 hours
Grill: 12 to 15 minutes

12 strips thinly sliced bacon,
　partially cooked and cut into
　pieces same size as scallops
16 sea scallops, halved
　horizontally
16 small water chestnuts,
　halved horizontally
32 (5 to 6 inch) bamboo
　skewers

⅓ cup soy sauce
2 tablespoons rice wine vinegar
1 ½ tablespoons sugar
1 tablespoon Chinese rice wine
　or dry sherry
1 garlic clove, minced
1 teaspoon minced fresh ginger

Alternate bacon between scallop and water chestnut slices on skewer. Place in shallow dish. Combine remaining ingredients in blender or food processor and mix well. Pour over kebobs and marinate in refrigerator for 2 to 3 hours. Pour marinade off kebobs and pat kebobs dry. Grill until scallops are barely firm, about 6 minutes per side. Serve immediately.

SHRIMP MOLD

Preparation: 1 hour　　　　　　　　　*Yield: 10 to 12 servings*
Stand: 8 hours or overnight

2 packages unflavored gelatin
½ cup cold water
1 (10 ¾ ounce) can tomato soup
1 (8 ounce) package cream
　cheese
1 cup mayonnaise

1 cup halved shrimp
½ cup finely chopped onion
½ cup chopped green pepper
½ cup chopped celery
Parsley and pimento slices
　for garnish

Add gelatin to ½ cup of cold water and soak. Heat tomato soup just to boiling point, turn off heat. Add cream cheese to warm soup and beat with mixer until smooth; next add gelatin and mayonnaise, continue beating with mixer. Mixture will be creamy. Fold in shrimp, onions, green pepper and celery. Pour into 5 to 6 cup mold. Refrigerate covered for 8 hours or overnight. Before serving, put parsley and pimento slices around mold.

SHRIMP TOAST

Preparation: 20 minutes　　*Can do ahead*　　*Yield: 32 appetizers*
Bake: 10 minutes

2 green onions
1 clove garlic
1 thin slice fresh ginger
　root (optional)
1 egg white
1 ½ teaspoons cornstarch
1 ½ teaspoons dry sherry

¾ to 1 ¼ teaspoons salt
½ cup water chestnuts
½ pound medium raw shrimp,
　shelled and deveined
8 thin slices firm white bread
¼ cup soft butter

Cut onions and tops in 1-inch lengths. In food processor with metal blade, process onions, garlic and ginger root until coarsely chopped. Add egg white, cornstarch, sherry and salt and process for 2 seconds. Add water chestnuts and process with on-off bursts until coarsely chopped. Add shrimp and process with on-off bursts until finely chopped. Remove bread crusts and spread butter on both sides of each slice. Spread shrimp mixture on 1 side of each slice, then cut each slice twice diagonally to make 4 triangles. Place on a baking sheet. (Can cover at this point and refrigerate up to 8 hours.) To cook, bake at 375° uncovered for 10 minutes or until bread is toasted.

APPETIZERS

SUMMER VIDALIA SPREAD

Preparation: 20 minutes   *Can do ahead*   *Yield: 24 servings*
Stand: overnight plus several
*   hours before serving*

2 chopped Vidalia sweet onions   2 cups water
½ cup sugar   ½ cup Hellmann's mayonnaise
1 cup apple cider vinegar   ½ teaspoon dried dill weed

Chop onions. Mix sugar, vinegar and water with onions. Marinate overnight. Several hours before serving, mix mayonnaise, dill weed, well-drained onion mixture and refrigerate. Use as a spread on crackers.

Note: Celery seed may be substituted for the dill.

SWEET-SOUR SAUSAGE BALLS

Preparation: 1 hour   *Can do ahead*   *Yield: 150 appetizers*
Cook: 30 minutes plus   *Can be frozen*
*   browning time*

4 pounds bulk sausage   ¾ cup brown sugar, firmly
4 eggs, slightly beaten   packed
1 ½ cups soft bread crumbs   ½ cup white wine vinegar
3 cups ketchup   ½ cup soy sauce

Mix together sausage, eggs and bread crumbs. Using palms of hands, shape mixture into balls the size of small walnuts. Sauté in frying pan until browned on all sides; drain on paper toweling. Combine ketchup, brown sugar, vinegar and soy sauce; pour over sausage balls and simmer 30 minutes, stirring occasionally. Serve hot.

Note: This can be prepared a day or more ahead. To serve, reheat in a 350° oven for about 20 minutes. This can be frozen in the sauce.

TIROPETES

Preparation: 45 minutes   *Can do ahead*   *Yield: Serves 12 to 15*
Cook: 10 minutes   *Can be frozen*

1 (8 ounce) package cream
  cheese <u>or</u> 1 (3 ounce)
  package cream cheese and
  ⅓ pound feta cheese
3 ounces Swiss Gruyere
  cheese, shredded

1 egg
2 tablespoons chopped parsley
8 sheets filo dough (about
  14 x 20 inches)
½ cup butter, melted

Preheat oven to 375°. Cream the cream cheese and feta cheese, if used, until light and mix in Gruyere. Add the egg and beat until blended. Mix in parsley. Lay out 1 sheet of filo and brush lightly with melted butter, then cut into 3-inch wide strips about 14 inches long. Place 1 heaping teaspoon of cheese filling in one corner of a strip, fold over, making a triangle. Continue the folding, making sure the bottom edge is always parallel to the alternate side edge, until you fold over the last triangle at the end of the strip. Place on ungreased baking sheet. Repeat, until all the filling and filo are used. Bake for 10 minutes or until puffed and golden brown. After baking, they may be cooled and frozen. To reheat, place frozen pastries on baking sheet in 375° oven for 10 minutes again.

ZUCCHINI APPETIZER

Preparation: 30 minutes   *Can do ahead*   *Yield: 4 dozen*
Cook: 25 minutes   *Can be frozen*

3 cups (4 small) shredded
  zucchini
1 cup Bisquick
½ cup chopped onion
½ cup grated Parmesan cheese
2 tablespoons snipped parsley
½ teaspoon seasoned salt

½ teaspoon garlic salt
½ teaspoon oregano
Dash pepper
½ cup vegetable oil
4 eggs, slightly beaten
1 cup shredded Cheddar
  cheese

Preheat oven to 350°. Mix all ingredients. Spread in greased 9 x 13 inch pan. Bake for 25 minutes or until golden brown. Cut into 2 inch rectangles. After baking, these freeze well or may be refrigerated for 1 or 2 days.

WALNUT NIBBLES

Preparation: 15 minutes   *Yield: 2 cups*
Cook: 3 to 5 minutes

2 tablespoons margarine
½ teaspoon onion salt
½ teaspoon prepared mustard

¼ teaspoon Worcestershire
  sauce
2 cups walnut halves
⅓ cup grated Parmesan cheese

Heat margarine until melted. Stir in onion salt, mustard and Worcestershire sauce. Add walnuts, tossing lightly to coat with the seasoned margarine. Stir over low heat 3 to 5 minutes to toast lightly. Remove from heat and sprinkle with cheese, tossing lightly as cheese melts.

Beverages

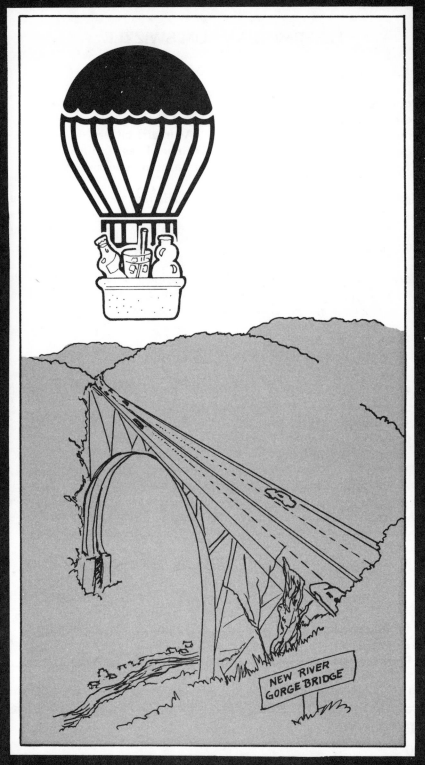

BEVERAGES

BERMUDIAN RUM SWIZZLE

Preparation: 15 minutes   *Can do ahead*   *Yield: 4 drinks or 25 drinks*

6 ounces rum
6 ounces grapefruit juice
6 ounces pineapple juice
6 ounces reconstituted frozen
  orange juice

2 ounces grenadine syrup
1 to 2 dashes Angostura
  Aromatic bitters
Orange slices, garnish
Maraschino cherries, garnish

Mix all ingredients together, except garnish. Refrigerate until ready to use. To serve, fill tall glasses ⅓ full of cracked ice and add swizzle mixture to the top. May be garnished with a thin ½ orange slice and a maraschino cherry on a toothpick.

Note: For 25 drinks increase rum, grapefruit, pineapple and orange juices to 1 quart, grenadine syrup to 1 ⅓ cups and bitters to 8 to 10 dashes. Best served in a glass, not punch bowl. Garnish as indicated.

BRANDY REFRESHER

Preparation: 10 minutes   *Can do ahead*   *Yield: 8 servings*
                              Can be frozen

1 quart coffee ice cream
1 quart vanilla ice cream

1 ounce Kahlua
6 ounces brandy

Soften the ice creams and mix together. Add Kahlua and brandy, mixing well. Freeze in a non-metallic covered container. Before serving let mixture soften until of pouring consistency. Serve immediately in sauce champagne glasses.

RITA'S BOURBON SLUSH

Preparation: 15 minutes   *Freeze: 8 hours*

1 ½ cups bourbon
1 cup sugar
1 (6 ounce) can orange juice

1 (12 ounce) can lemonade
6 cups water
2 cups fresh brewed tea

Combine all ingredients in airtight container and place in freezer. Stir with wooden spoon after 8 hours. Can leave in freezer for several days. Stir before serving.

CARIBBEAN COCKTAIL

Preparation: 5 minutes   *Yield: 1 serving*

¾ to 1 ounce gin
¼ ounce apricot brandy
3 dashes grenadine syrup

1 ½ ounces liquid whiskey sour
   mix
Ice
Orange slice, optional garnish

Put all liquid ingredients in a shaker with ice. Shake well and strain into a glass. Garnish with an orange slice, if desired.

CHRISTMAS PUNCH

Preparation: 10 minutes   *Yield: 10 to 12 servings*

1 quart cranberry juice
1 cup sugar
2 cups orange juice
1 cup pineapple juice

¾ cup frozen or fresh lemon
   juice
½ teaspoon almond extract
2 cups chilled ginger ale
1 pint pineapple sherbet

Blend cranberry juice, sugar, fruit juices and almond extract. Refrigerate covered until serving time. Just before serving, stir in ginger ale and sherbet.

CITRUS PUNCH

Preparation: 15 minutes   *Yield: 50 servings*

1 (46 ounce) can pineapple juice
3 (6 ounce) cans frozen orange
   juice concentrate
2 (6 ounce) cans frozen
   lemonade concentrate

3 or 4 cans water
5 quarts ginger ale
2 (10 ounce) packages frozen
   strawberries

Make an ice ring with 1 quart of ginger ale instead of water so punch will not be diluted. Mix pineapple juice, orange juice, lemonade and water together and chill. Add strawberries, chilled ginger ale and ice ring just before serving.

BEVERAGES

MULLED CLARET

Preparation: 15 minutes   *Yield: 5 servings*

½ cup sugar
1 ½ cups water
Peel from ½ lemon
10 whole cloves

1 stick cinnamon, broken into
  pieces
¼ cup Curacao or brandy
1 bottle Claret or other red
  table wine

Combine sugar, water, lemon peel and spices; boil for 10 minutes. Strain, add Curacao or brandy and wine. Heat gently; do not boil. Serve in mugs or punch cups. Sprinkle with nutmeg or use cinnamon sticks for muddlers.

COFFEE PUNCH

Preparation: 15 minutes   *Yield: 50 cups*

5 ounces instant coffee
1 pint hot water
1 (16 ounce) can Hershey
  chocolate syrup

1 cup sugar
1 ½ gallons milk
2 gallons vanilla ice cream

Dissolve coffee in hot water. Let cool. Add chocolate syrup, sugar and milk. Stir well. Just before serving, cut ice cream into large pieces and add to other ingredients. Add ice cream as needed to keep it well distributed.

COFFEE RUM PUNCH

Preparation: 10 minutes   *Yield: 8 to 12 servings*
Stand: 1 to 2 hours

½ gallon French vanilla ice
  cream

2 trays strong coffee ice cubes
  (crushed)
1 pint rum

Before dinner put ice cream, crushed coffee ice cubes and rum in punch bowl. After dinner, stir and serve in coffee cups, mugs or punch cups. This can be an after dinner coffee, dessert and drink all in one.

HOLIDAY EGGNOG

Preparation: 30 minutes   *Do ahead*   *Yield: 20 servings*
Chill: 1 hour

6 eggs, separated
1 cup sugar
1 ½ cups cognac or Cointreau
   or Grand Marnier

½ cup light rum
1 ½ quarts milk
3 cups whipping cream, whipped
Nutmeg

Beat egg yolks until thick and lemon colored. Add sugar gradually, beating constantly. Still beating, add brandy (can use mixture of brandy and Cointreau) and rum gradually. Chill 1 hour, stirring occasionally. Add milk slowly and fold in whipped cream and egg whites which have been stiffly beaten. Store in covered jars in refrigerator a day or so before serving to allow flavors to blend. Ladle when serving to distribute "fluff". Sprinkle with nutmeg. Keeps covered 3 plus days in the refrigerator.

SLUSHY FRUIT PUNCH

Preparation: 10 minutes   *Yield: 50 servings*

2 (6 ounce) cans frozen orange
   juice
1 (6 ounce) can frozen lemon
   juice
1 (46 ounce) can pineapple juice

1 (24 ounce) can peach nectar
1 tablespoon almond extract
1 cup sugar
2 quarts ginger ale

Mix frozen juices as directed on cans in a large container; add pineapple juice, peach nectar and almond extract. Add sugar. Freeze in carton or wide-mouth plastic containers. Remove from freezer about 2 hours before serving; slip frozen juice from carton and chip with large fork until flaky. Add ginger ale.

Note: May be frozen several weeks ahead.

GRASSHOPPERS

Preparation: 5 minutes   *Yield: 4 to 6 servings*

¾ cup green Creme de Menthe
½ cup white Creme de Cacao

1 ½ cups vanilla ice cream
8 to 10 ice cubes

Combine all the ingredients in a blender. Blend until ice is crushed and mixture is frothy. Serve in champagne glasses immediately.

BEVERAGES

PEACH SOUR

Preparation: 10 minutes   *Yield: 4 to 8 servings*

3 medium peaches, very ripe   6 ounces gin
1 (6 ounce) can lemonade   ½ to 1 tray crushed ice

Remove seed from peaches but do not peel. Cut into 3 or 4 pieces. Put into blender with other ingredients and blend.

KENTUCKY MINT JULEPS

Preparation: 5 minutes   *Yield: 1 serving*

½ ounce simple syrup (2 parts   Crushed ice
    sugar, 1 part boiling water)   Bourbon
Mint leaves and sprigs

Make simple syrup: Add 1 part boiling water to 2 parts sugar. Stir until sugar is completely dissolved; cool. Amount of syrup to prepare depends on the number of juleps desired (1 ounce boiling water added to 2 ounces sugar is enough for 4 mint juleps). Put 3 or 4 mint leaves in the bottom of a julep cup or old fashioned glass. Add 1 inch of crushed ice. Push ice down hard with the back of a spoon to bruise the mint leaves. Add 1 ounce of bourbon and ½ ounce of the cooled simple syrup. Stir. Pack the julep cup or glass to the top with crushed ice; fill with bourbon. Holding the glass by the rim, stir gently until the glass is nicely frosted on the outside. Garnish with 1 or 2 sprigs of mint. Use short straws, so that the julep can be sipped from the mint level at the bottom of the glass.

DIXIE'S ORANGE JULIUS

Preparation: 5 minutes   *Yield: 4 servings*

1 (12 ounce) can orange juice   ⅓ cup sugar
    concentrate   1 teaspoon vanilla
1 cup milk   Ice cubes
1 cup water

Put ingredients in a blender and blend until smooth. Serve immediately.

CLAIRE'S PERCOLATOR PUNCH

Preparation: 30 minutes   *Yield: 1 quart*

2 ¼ cups pineapple juice
2 cups cranberry juice
1 ¾ cups water
½ cup firmly packed brown
  sugar

3 sticks cinnamon, broken
1 tablespoon whole cloves
1 ½ teaspoon whole allspice
¼ teaspoon salt

Pour juices and water into 8 cup percolator. Place remaining ingredients in basket. Perk 10 minutes.

Note: May substitute apple juice for the pineapple juice.

PIÑATA PUNCH

Preparation: 10 minutes

1 (6 ounce) can pineapple juice
1 pint orange juice
Juice of 6 lemons
¾ cup powdered sugar

6 ounces Triple Sec or
  Cointreau liqueur
1 quart vodka
2 large bottles ginger ale

Combine ingredients except ginger ale. Pour over block of ice in punch bowl, add ginger ale, stir.

POTASSIUM HEALTH PUNCH

Preparation: 5 minutes   *Yield: serves 2 to 4*

1 (6 ounce) can frozen
  pineapple juice
2 cups orange juice

6 to 8 ice cubes, crushed
½ banana, mashed

In a blender, liquefy all ingredients. Serve immediately in chilled glasses.

ROSÉ SPARKLE PUNCH

Preparation: 15 minutes
Stand: 1 hour

Yield: 6 quarts or 20 to 24 servings

4 (12 ounce) packages frozen
  sliced strawberries, thawed
1 cup sugar
4 bottles Rosé wine

4 (6 ounce) cans frozen
  lemonade concentrate
2 (1 liter) bottles sparkling
  water, chilled

In a bowl combine strawberries, sugar and 1 bottle wine. Cover and let stand at room temperature 1 hour. Strain mixture into a punch bowl or pitcher. Add frozen lemonade concentrate, stir until completely thawed. Add remaining bottles of wine. Pour in sparkling water, add ice cubes and serve.

RUM SLUSH

Preparation: 15 minutes
Freeze: 24 hours

Yield: Serves a crowd
or will keep in freezer
for a slush a day for....

7 cups water
1 cup sugar
2 cups water
4 tea bags
1 (12 ounce) can frozen orange
  juice, undiluted

1 (12 ounce) can frozen
  lemonade, undiluted
2 cups rum, light or dark
Lemon-lime carbonated soda

Boil 7 cups water and 1 cup sugar until sugar dissolves. Brew tea bags in 2 cups water. Add to boiled sugar water and cool. Mix with frozen orange juice and lemonade and rum. This will require a very large bowl. Put mixture in freezer, covered, and stir frequently. When it is "slush" fill a tall glass 2/3 full. Add soda to fill glass.

HINT: *Top a cup of cocoa with a marshmallow rolled in cinnamon for a special treat.*

HINT: *Improve the flavor of instant coffee by gently simmering the coffee and water for 2 minutes.*

SPARKLING CHEER

Preparation: 5 minutes   *Yield: 12 servings*

1 bottle Champagne, well   1 cup apricot brandy
  chilled   ¾ cup vodka
1 quart ginger ale, well chilled

Combine all ingredients in punch bowl with ice. Stir to chill. Serve at once.

Note: Any price of liquor may be used, the taste remains the same. This recipe may be doubled or tripled depending on size of crowd.

FROZEN STRAWBERRY DAIQUIRIS

Preparation: 15 minutes   *Yield: serves 2*

1 (6 ounce) can frozen   1 (10 ounce) package frozen
  lemonade   strawberries
6 ounces of rum   Crushed ice

Empty lemonade into blender container. Use lemonade can to measure rum and add to blender. Add strawberries and blend thoroughly. Add enough ice and blend until slushy.

SUMERTIME PUNCH

Preparation: 5 minutes   *Yield: 2 ¾ quarts*

1 (6 ounce) can frozen   5 juice cans of water
  lemonade   ⅔ cups grenadine syrup
1 (6 ounce) can frozen orange   1 quart ginger ale, chilled
  juice

Mix lemonade, orange juice, water and grenadine syrup. Pour in ginger ale last. Serve over ice or in a punch bowl with ice ring and thin slices of lemon and orange.

HINT: *To remove some of the acid taste in coffee, add a pinch of salt into the basket.*

BEVERAGES

WASSAIL

Preparation: 30 minutes   *Yield: 1 gallon or 24 servings*
Stand: 1 hour

1 ½ to 2 cups sugar
1 quart water
12 whole cloves
4 sticks cinnamon
4 whole allspice

2 tablespoons chopped fresh
  ginger
3 cups orange juice
2 cups fresh lemon juice
  (6 to 8 large lemons)
2 quarts apple cider

Boil sugar and water to make a syrup, about 5 minutes. Wrap cloves, cinnamon, allspice and fresh ginger in a square of cheesecloth and secure. Add to syrup. Let stand one hour. Remove spice bag and strain. Add orange juice, fresh lemon juice and cider. Heat to barely boiling and serve.

FROSTY WHISKEY SOURS FOR A CROWD

Preparation: 5 minutes   *Yield: 16 servings*

1 (6 ounce) can frozen orange
  juice
4 (6 ounce) cans frozen
  lemonade

24 ounces rye or bourbon
Ice cubes

Reconstitute the frozen orange juice. Add the four cans of unreconstituted frozen lemonade and the four cans of liquor. Mix well. Refrigerate until ready to use. Add whiskey sours to ice in a blender. Blend until ice cubes are crushed and mixture is slushy. Serve immediately.

Note: To make 4 servings use:

1 (6 ounce) can reconstituted
  frozen orange juice

1 (6 ounce) can unreconstituted
  frozen lemonade
1 (6 ounce) can rye or bourbon

Same preparation instructions.

HINT: *Coffee will stay fresher longer if stored in the refrigerator or freezer.*

38

Soups & Sandwiches

SOUPS

CHILLED AVOCADO SOUP

Preparation: 10 minutes   *Yield: 4 to 6 servings*
Chill: 6 hours

4 avocados
1 (8 ounce) carton commercial
  sour cream
1 cup dry white wine
1 cup light cream

1 cup pineapple juice
1 tiny pinch of salt
1 tiny pinch of sugar
Julienne of apples (garnish)

Peel, pit, and purée avocados in a blender. Combine puréed avocados and all other ingredients except garnish. Chill thoroughly. Garnish each serving with small amount julienne of apples.

CHILLED CUCUMBER SOUP

Preparation: 30 minutes   *Yield: 8 to 10 servings*
Chill: 6 hours

2 cucumbers
¼ cup chopped parsley
¼ cup chopped celery leaves
2 tablespoons snipped dill
2 scallions (white part), chopped

4 cups buttermilk
2 cups commercial sour cream
2 tablespoons lemon juice
Salt to taste

Cut 8 thin slices from 1 cucumber and reserve them. Peel, seed and chop the remainder of the cucumber and another cucumber. In a blender in 2 batches or in a food processor fitted with the steel blade, purée the cucumber, parsley, celery leaves, dill and scallions with 2 cups buttermilk until the mixture is smooth. Transfer the mixture to a large bowl. Whisk in 2 cups each of buttermilk and sour cream, lemon juice and salt. Chill the soup covered, for at least 6 hours. Serve in chilled bowls and garnish each serving with a reserved cucumber slice and a sprig of dill.

Note: Dried dill weed and seed may be substituted for fresh dill.

HINT: Use vegetable juice cocktail in chili instead of tomato sauce or juice for a great flavor.

COLD GARDEN BISQUE

Preparation: 30 minutes *Yield: 6 servings*
Chill: 6 hours

2 large cucumbers, seeded, peeled
1 tomato, seeded, peeled, cut into eighths
1 onion, chopped
3 tablespoons butter
¼ cup fresh parsley
¼ cup fresh dill

½ lemon, juiced
2 cups chicken stock
1 ½ cups half and half
1 cup plain yogurt
½ teaspoon salt
1 boiled medium potato, peeled and quartered

Sauté onion and butter until tender. In food processor, purée cucumber, onion, tomato, potato, herbs and lemon juice with yogurt; add salt. Transfer to bowl or pitcher and add chicken stock and half and half. Chill well. Garnish with lemon slice and fresh dill sprig.

HOT OR COLD
CARROT AND ORANGE SOUP

Preparation: 20 minutes *Yield: 6 to 8 servings*

1 medium onion, chopped
2 tablespoons butter (if served cold, use 1 tablespoon oil instead of butter)
1 (15 ½ ounce) can carrots
2 pints chicken stock

1 (6 ½ ounce) can frozen orange juice, undiluted
Salt, pepper
1 cup half and half
Chives, chopped

Cook onion in butter (or oil) until soft, but not colored. Drain carrots and purée them with the onions in a little (1 cup or so) of the chicken stock. Return the purée to the pan and add the orange juice, seasonings and cream. Heat to just below the boiling point, adjust salt and pepper and decorate with chopped chives.

Note: Use canned carrots and orange juice for best color.

SOUPS

GAZPACHO

Preparation: 1 hour
Chill: Overnight

Yield: 2 gallons

3 garlic cloves
2 large tomatoes, skinned
1 large cucumber, peeled
1 medium onion
½ green pepper
2 (2 ounce) jars pimentos
1 (46 ounce) can tomato juice

½ cup oil
⅔ cup red wine vinegar
½ teaspoon Tabasco
2 ¼ teaspoons salt
¼ teaspoon pepper
1 cup finely chopped pepper
1 cup finely chopped celery

Mix and purée garlic, tomato, cucumber, onion, pimento and pepper with one cup of tomato juice. Mix oil, vinegar, Tabasco, salt and pepper into purée. Add balance of tomato juice. Stir in chopped celery and pepper. Chill overnight. Serve very cold.

CHILLED PEAR SOUP

Preparation: 5 to 10 minutes
Chill: 6 hours

Yield: 4 servings

1 (29 ounce) can of pears,
reserve liquid

2 to 3 tablespoons brandy

Drain pears, saving liquid. Liquefy pears in blender at highest speed. Add enough liquid (6 to 8 ounces) to make a thick soup. Add brandy to taste, starting with about 2 tablespoons. Chill until ice cold.

Note: Good before a summer salad luncheon.

RASPBERRY SOUP

Preparation: 5 minutes
Chill: Overnight

Yield: 6 servings

2 (10 ounce) boxes frozen
raspberries
1 cup plain yogurt

1 cup dry rosé wine
Fresh mint for garnish

Combine raspberries, yogurt and wine in blender. Some may wish to put through a sieve to remove seeds. Better if chilled overnight. Serve in large juice glasses or double old-fashioned glasses.

BEAN WITH BACON SOUP

Preparation: 20 minutes　　　　　　　　　　　*Yield: 3 quarts*
Soak: Overnight
Cook: 3 hours

1 pound dried navy beans
6 cups water
¼ teaspoon pepper
2 teaspoons salt
2 cloves garlic, minced
1 bay leaf
4 slices bacon

2 medium onions, finely
  chopped
1 small green pepper, finely
  chopped
½ cup finely chopped carrots
1 (8 ounce) can tomato sauce
1 teaspoon minced fresh parsley

Sort and wash beans. Cover with 2 inches water and soak overnight. Drain beans; cover with the 6 cups water. Add salt, pepper, garlic and bay leaf. Cook bacon until crisp. Reserve drippings. Crumble bacon and set aside. Add onion and green pepper to drippings and sauté until tender. Add onions, green pepper and carrots to beans. Bring to boil, cover and simmer 2 hours. Add tomato sauce and parsley to soup, cover and simmer 30 more minutes until beans are tender. Ladle into serving bowls, sprinkle with crumbled bacon.

Note: Even better the second day.

ROSY BOUILLON

Preparation: 5 minutes　　　　　　　　　　　*Yield: 4 servings*

1 (16 to 17 ounce) can tomato
  juice
1 (10 ½ ounce) can condensed
  beef broth

¼ teaspoon seasoned salt
Dash onion powder
Lemon slices for garnish

Combine all ingredients and heat. To serve, float a thin slice of lemon on top of each serving.

Note: Can also be served cold. Combine all ingredients, chill, and serve in juice glasses or small soup plates. Very refreshing before a summer dinner.

SOUPS

BROCCOLI SOUP

Preparation: 45 minutes   *Yield: 8 to 10 servings*
Cook: 30 minutes

1 large bunch fresh broccoli
1 (1 pound) bag frozen broccoli
  pieces
3 tablespoons butter
1 medium onion, chopped
1 clove garlic, finely chopped
1 medium potato, peeled and
  diced
4 cups chicken broth

2 cups half and half
½ teaspoon salt
¼ teaspoon pepper
¼ cup chopped parsley
4 cups cooked, boned white
  chicken meat
1 cup grated Monterey Jack
  cheese
1 small lemon, thinly sliced

Wash and trim fresh broccoli. Combine with frozen broccoli and steam until done. Cut fresh into bite sized pieces, separating flowerets from stems. Sauté stems in butter with onion and garlic 10 minutes stirring frequently. Add potato and broth. Bring to a boil, then simmer for 15 minutes. Add half and half, salt and pepper. Add broccoli, parsley, boned chicken and cheese. Garnish with lemon slices.

CHEESE SOUP

Preparation: 30 minutes   *Yield: 8 to 10 servings*
Cook: 30 minutes

½ cup butter
1 cup onion, diced
¾ cup diced carrots
¾ cup diced celery
½ cup flour
2 tablespoons cornstarch

1 quart chicken broth
1 quart milk
⅛ teaspoon baking soda
1 cup Cheddar cheese
Salt and pepper

Melt butter in large, heavy pot. Add onion, carrot and celery and sauté until soft. Add flour and cornstarch and stir well. Add chicken stock and milk. Stir constantly with wire whisk over medium heat until thick and smooth. Add soda and cheese. Season with salt and pepper.

Variation: This makes a delicious base for oyster stew. Add oysters and their liquid when mixture is thickened. Cook until oysters begin to curl.

NEW YEAR'S CHICKEN SOUP

Preparation: 20 minutes   *Yield: 4 servings*
Cook: 30 minutes

4 tablespoons butter
1 large onion, chopped
1 large green pepper, chopped
4 to 6 cups cooked and diced
   chicken
2 (15 ounce) cans tomatoes or
   6 to 8 frozen tomatoes
1 ½ teaspoons basil

2 to 3 quarts chicken broth
½ to 1 pound thin noodles,
   cooked according to package
   directions, drained
¼ cup minced parsley
6 dashes Tabasco
Salt to taste
Pepper to taste

Sauté onion and green pepper in butter. Add chicken, tomatoes, basil, broth, noodles, parsley and Tabasco. Add salt and pepper to taste. Simmer 30 minutes. Correct seasonings.

Note: Turkey may be used instead of chicken.

HINT: *When tomatoes are plentiful, wash, dry and freeze in plastic bags, whole. To use: Rinse under cold water - peel falls away. Add to soup, stew or make tomato sauce. Stem ends can be "fished" out as tomato cooks and falls apart.*

RUSSIAN CURRY SOUP

Preparation: 10 minutes   *Yield: 8 to 10 servings*
Cook: 3 to 5 minutes

1 (11 ¼ ounce) can green pea
   soup
1 (10 ¾ ounce) can tomato soup
2 soup cans of water
1 teaspoon curry powder

Salt and pepper to taste
2 beef bouillon cubes
¾ cup ketchup
Kitchen Bouquet to color
Lemon slices for garnish

Mix all ingredients except Kitchen Bouquet together. Heat until bouillon cubes are dissolved and soup is hot. Add Kitchen Bouquet to color - soup should be reddish-brown. Garnish each serving with a thin slice of lemon.

Note: This is a spicy soup. Use as a first course for a dinner, rather than a main course soup.

SOUPS

GREEN PEPPER SOUP

Preparation: 40 minutes
Cook: 15 minutes

Yield: 4 servings

4 large green peppers
1 large onion, chopped

2 tablespoons butter
1 pint chicken stock

White Sauce:

4 tablespoons butter
4 tablespoons flour
1 pint milk

Salt, pepper, nutmeg
Juice of ½ lemon

Remove core and seeds from pepper. Reserve one-half of 1 pepper for final step. Chop peppers and sauté with onion in butter in covered pan until soft but not browned. Blend them in the blender with a little of the stock until it is a smooth purée. Return it to soup pan with the rest of the stock and bring to a gentle boil and simmer for 10 minutes. Meanwhile, melt 4 tablespoons butter and add flour, stir until smooth. Add milk, whisking constantly. Season with salt, pepper and nutmeg, stirring until white sauce has thickened. When both pepper purée and white sauce are ready, whisk white sauce into purée. Finely chop the remaining ½ pepper; stir it into the soup and add the lemon juice.

AVGOLEMOND
(Lemon Soup)

Preparation: 45 minutes
Cook: 30 minutes

Yield: 4 servings

3 cups water
1 tablespoon instant chicken
   bouillon
¼ cup uncooked rice

2 tablespoons fresh lemon juice
2 eggs, beaten
Parsley

Heat water and chicken bouillon in 2 quart saucepan to boiling; stir in rice and reduce heat. Simmer uncovered until rice is tender, 20 to 25 minutes. Remove from heat. Stir lemon juice slowly into eggs. Gradually stir at least half the broth and rice into eggs. Mix into hot mixture in pan. Garnish with parsley.

CREOLE LIMA BEAN SOUP

Preparation: 30 minutes　　　　　　　　　*Yield: 8 servings*
Soak: Overnight
Cook: 2 ½ hours

2 ½ cups dry baby lima beans
5 cups water
3 beef bouillon cubes
1 pound lean ground beef
1 cup diced carrots
1 cup diced onion
1 cup diced celery
2 ½ cups crushed, canned
　　tomatoes

1 ½ teaspoons sugar
1 teaspoon celery salt
1 teaspoon onion salt
½ teaspoon salt
½ teaspoon pepper
¼ teaspoon garlic salt
¼ teaspoon Tabasco (optional)

Wash beans. Soak beans overnight in medium saucepan in 5 cups water. Do not drain. Next day add bouillon cubes, cover and cook over low heat for 30 minutes or until beans are almost tender. Brown ground beef in skillet until all red color is gone. Drain excess fat. Add carrots, onion and celery and sauté for 5 minutes, or until onion is translucent. Combine lima beans with their liquid, beef mixture, tomatoes, sugar, celery salt, onion salt, salt, pepper, garlic salt and Tabasco in large pot. Cover and simmer for 2 hours or until tender. Stir often to prevent sticking.

CHEESE POTATO SOUP

Preparation: 30 minutes　　　　　　　　　*Yield: 6 to 8 servings*
Cook: 45 minutes

5 pounds potatoes
2 medium onions
¼ cup butter
1 teaspoon seasoning salt

½ teaspoon garlic salt (optional)
3 ounces sherry cooking wine
½ teaspoon white pepper
32 ounces Velveeta cheese,
　　cut in small cubes

Peel and dice potatoes and onions. Place in large saucepan. Cover with water. Bring to slow boil and cook about 45 minutes. Mash potatoes with potato masher, about 6 times. Add butter, seasoning salt, garlic salt and wine. Add cheese. Mix until cheese melts. Adjust seasonings.

SOUPS

MUSHROOM SOUP

Preparation: 30 minutes   *Yield: 8 to 10 servings*
Cook: 25 minutes

2 tablespoons butter
2 tablespoons olive oil
2 medium onions, grated
1 clove garlic, split
2 pounds mushrooms, thinly
   sliced
6 tablespoons tomato paste
6 cups chicken stock

4 tablespoons sweet vermouth
1 tablespoon salt
Dash pepper
8 egg yolks
4 tablespoons chopped parsley
5 tablespoons grated Parmesan
   cheese

In a large heavy pan, melt butter and olive oil. Sauté grated onions with split garlic; let brown gently and discard garlic. Stir in mushrooms and sauté 5 to 6 minutes, add tomato paste and mix well. Stir in chicken stock, vermouth, salt and pepper. Simmer 10 to 12 minutes. Before serving, beat together egg yolks, parsley and Parmesan cheese. Slowly beat egg mixture into boiling soup and serve at once.

SOUP D'ONION

Preparation: 30 minutes   *Yield: 4 servings*
Cook: 2 ½ hours

4 to 6 medium yellow onions
¾ cup butter, melted
2 (10 ½ ounce) cans condensed
   beef bouillon broth
Salt to taste

4 slices Mozzarella cheese
4 bread slices, toasted
Parmesan cheese
4 teaspoons white wine
   (optional)

Thinly slice and separate onions and sauté in butter until tender and golden. While onions are sautéing, place the two cans of beef bouillon in large saucepan and add two cans of water. Heat to just boiling and remove from heat. Add sautéed onions and butter to broth and salt to taste. Cover and simmer for 1 ½ to 2 hours. About 30 minutes before serving, ladle the soup into individual oven bowls. Place a toasted bread slice and slice of Mozzarella cheese on top of soup. Cover and place on center rack in moderate oven, and bake for 15 to 20 minutes. Remove cover and sprinkle generously with Parmesan cheese. Place under broiler for 2 to 4 minutes. Remove from oven, lift toast carefully and add 1 teaspoon of wine to the soup.

IRISH POTATO SOUP

Preparation: 30 minutes   *Yield: 6 to 8 servings*
Cook: 45 minutes

½ cup butter or margarine
½ cup finely chopped onion
5 medium potatoes, peeled and
    quartered
1 ½ cups water
1 teaspoon salt

2 cups hot milk
½ cup cold milk
1 egg yolk
Few grains cayenne pepper
2 tablespoons chopped parsley

Melt butter or margarine in heavy pan over low heat. Add onions, stirring until tender. Add potatoes, water and salt. Cover pan and cook until potatoes are tender. Drain, reserving liquid. Press potatoes through sieve and add to liquid. Add hot milk and stir well. Combine cold milk and beaten egg yolk. Add slowly to warm soup, stirring constantly. Add cayenne pepper. Reheat soup slowly, but do not boil. Adjust seasonings. Add parsley just before serving.

HEARTY WINTER SOUP

Preparation: 20 minutes   *Yield: 8 to 10 servings*
Soak: Overnight
Cook: 2 hours

1 pound dry navy beans
3 cups diced ham
1 pound smoked sausage, cut
    in ½ inch slices
2 large onions, chopped
2 cups chopped celery with
    leaves

2 (1 pound) cans whole
    tomatoes (juice included)
3 quarts water
Salt to taste
1 (10 ounce) package frozen
    chopped spinach, thawed

Soak beans in water overnight. Sauté ham and smoked sausage. Combine beans, ham, sausage (drippings included), onions, celery, tomatoes (chopped slightly) with juice, water and salt. Simmer for two or more hours until beans are tender. Add spinach and cook for 10 minutes longer.

HINT: *Refrigerate soups and let grease harden on top. Remove the grease.*

49

SANDWICHES

BARBECUE BEEF SANDWICHES

Preparation: 20 minutes   *Can do ahead*   *Yield: 15 sandwiches*
Cook: 4 hours   *Can be frozen*

4 pound chuck roast
½ green pepper, chopped
1 rib celery, diced
1 large onion, chopped
1 (14 ounce) bottle ketchup
2 tablespoons barbecue sauce

1 tablespoon vinegar
¼ teaspoon hot sauce
1 tablespoon chili powder
1 tablespoon salt
½ teaspoon pepper
1 cup water

Cut meat in large pieces (trim before cooking) place in Dutch oven. Combine all other ingredients and pour over the meat. Heat to boiling. Cover and simmer 4 hours or until meat is tender. Shred meat with a fork. If sauce is too soupy, cook uncovered until the right consistency to spoon onto buns. If meat and sauce become too dry while cooking, add a little more water.

SHREDDED PORK BARBECUE

Preparation: 15 minutes   *Can do ahead*   *Yield: 10 to 12 servings*
Cook: 4 hours

3 pounds pork roast
Water
1 tablespoon salt
2 tablespoons shortening
1 cup chopped onions
2 teaspoons paprika
1 teaspoon pepper

1 teaspoon dry mustard
Dash cayenne pepper
½ teaspoon salt
1 tablespoon brown sugar
3 tablespoons Worcestershire
   sauce
1 clove garlic, minced
1 (6 ounce) can tomato paste

Cook meat until very tender in water to which salt has been added. While meat is cooking, make sauce: melt shortening and add onions; cook until tender, but not browned. Add remaining ingredients and cook over low heat for 20 minutes. When meat is done and cool, shred finely. Add meat to the sauce and mix well. Add cooking liquid to desired consistency. Cover and cook very slowly for 30 minutes. If necessary, add a little water if mixture becomes too thick. Serve on Corn Light Bread. (See Index)

Note: Beef may be substituted for pork.

CORNED BEEF BARBECUE

Preparation: 20 minutes   *Yield: 6 servings*

2 tablespoons shortening
1 medium onion, chopped
2 tablespoons chopped green
  pepper
1 (12 ounce) can corned beef
¼ cup water

1 cup ketchup
1 teaspoon Worcestershire
  sauce
¾ teaspoon celery seed
½ teaspoon salt
Hamburger buns

Brown corned beef, onion and green pepper in shortening. Stir in remaining ingredients. Cover. Bring mixture to a boil. Turn down to simmer and cook 10 minutes. Spoon mixture onto hamburger buns.

THE SUSTAINER

Preparation: 15 minutes   *Can do ahead*   *Yield: 10 to 12 servings*
Cook: 1 hour   *Can be frozen*

2 ½ cups ketchup
½ cup hickory smoked
  barbecue sauce
½ cup barbecue sauce
¼ cup brown sugar, tightly
  packed
2 tablespoons Worcestershire
  sauce

½ teaspoon salt
Dash of pepper
3 pounds flank steak, cooked
  and thinly sliced
½ cup beef broth
Buns <u>or</u> pita bread

Mix together ketchup, barbecue sauces, brown sugar, Worcestershire sauce, salt and pepper in a large saucepan. Let simmer for 20 to 30 minutes. Add the broth and the meat, simmer for 20 minutes more. Remove from heat for 15 minutes to let flavor develop. Reheat and serve on buns or in pita bread.

Note: 3 pounds pork, cooked and shredded may be substituted for the flank steak.

HINT: Desalt soups and stews by adding several chunks of raw potato to absorb excess salt. Remove the potato before serving.

SANDWICHES

HAMBURGERS DELUXE

Preparation: 10 minutes   *Yield: 4 servings*
Grill: 10 to 15 minutes

1 pound ground beef
3 tablespoons chili sauce
1 tablespoon minced onion
1 teaspoon prepared mustard

1 teaspoon prepared
  horseradish
1 tablespoon Worcestershire
  sauce
¼ to ½ cup bread crumbs
¼ cup red wine

Mix all ingredients together thoroughly. Shape into patties and grill.

HOT OPEN FACED SANDWICH

Preparation: 15 minutes   *Can do ahead*   *Yield: 4 servings*
Broil: few minutes   *Can be frozen*

1 cup grated <u>baby</u> Swiss
  cheese
¼ cup mayonnaise
8 ripe olives, finely
  chopped

4 slices bacon, cooked
  and crumbled
1 teaspoon prepared mustard
¼ teaspoon onion salt
  (optional)
Bread slices

Mix Swiss cheese, mayonnaise, olives, bacon and mustard in a large bowl. Trim crusts from bread. Toast. Cover with mixture and put under broiler until it bubbles. Sandwiches should be cut in halves or fourths.

OLD FASHIONED PIMENTO CHEESE

Preparation: 30 minutes   *Can do ahead*   *Yield: 3 to 4 cups*

1 egg, beaten slightly
½ cup vinegar
⅓ cup sugar

1 (2 ounce) jar pimentos
5 to 6 Kosher style dill pickles
1 ½ pounds Longhorn cheese

Combine egg, vinegar and sugar. Cook over low heat until thick, stirring frequently. Let cool. In grinder or food processor, combine pimentos, pickles and cheese. Mix cooled dressing in cheese mixture and refrigerate until ready to use.

HOT HAM SANDWICHES

Preparation: 15 minutes   *Can do ahead*   *Yield: 12 sandwiches*
Bake: 15 to 20 minutes   *Can be frozen*

2 pounds shaved boiled ham   **12 slices domestic Swiss**
12 buns   **cheese**

Mix together:

1 cup butter, softened   **1 teaspoon Worcestershire**
3 tablespoons prepared   **sauce**
mustard   **1 teaspoon poppy seed**
                1 small onion, grated

Spread <u>both</u> halves of buns with prepared mixture. Put ham and cheese inside each bun and wrap individually with foil. When ready to serve, put in 300° oven until cheese melts.

Note: May be used on biscuits or Slim Jim buns.

PIZZA SANDWICHES

Preparation: 15 minutes   *Can do ahead*   *Yield: 8 servings*
Broil: few minutes

4 slices bacon, fried crisp   **½ green pepper, finely chopped**
and crumbled   **2 hard boiled eggs, finely**
½ pound Cheddar cheese   **chopped**
(sharp or extra sharp), grated   **½ cup chili sauce**
1 small onion, grated   **English muffins or hamburger**
                buns

Mix together the bacon, cheese, onion, green pepper and hard boiled eggs. Add chili sauce. Spread on ½ English muffin or ½ bun and put under broiler until cheese bubbles.

HINT: To degrease soup, remove as much fat as possible from the top with spoon, then run a lettuce leaf across the top; discard lettuce before serving.

SANDWICHES

SLOPPY JOES

Preparation: 10 minutes   *Can do ahead*   *Yield: 6 servings*
Cook: 20 minutes   *Can be frozen*

1 pound ground beef
1 small onion, chopped
1 teaspoon sugar
⅛ teaspoon salt
⅛ teaspoon pepper

2 teaspoons Worcestershire
  sauce
3 tablespoons vinegar
1 cup ketchup
6 hamburger buns

Brown ground beef with chopped onion and drain off fat if necessary. Add
sugar, salt, pepper, Worcestershire sauce, vinegar and ketchup. Simmer 20
minutes. Serve on warm hamburger buns.

SORRY CHARLIE

Preparation: 15 minutes   *Yield: 4 to 6 servings*

2 (7 ounce) cans tuna,
  drained and flaked
1 cup celery, thinly sliced
2 tablespoons pimento,
  chopped
1 cup mayonnaise

1 tablespoon lemon juice
1 tablespoon prepared mustard
1 (3 ounce) can french fried
  onion rings
4 to 6 pita bread rounds

Combine tuna, celery, pimento, mayonnaise, lemon juice and mustard. Add
french fried onion rings just before serving. Warm pita bread - cut in half and
fill with tuna salad.

Salads & Salad Dressings

HUNTINGTON GALLERIES

SALADS

APPLE PEANUT SALAD

Preparation: 30 minutes   *Can do ahead*   *Yield: 6 servings*
Chill: 2 hours

4 ½ cups diced, unpeeled,
   cored apples
1 ½ cups chopped celery
1 ½ teaspoons lemon juice
4 teaspoons sugar

3 tablespoons mayonnaise
¾ cup plain yogurt
¾ cup coarsely chopped
   peanuts
Lettuce, optional

Combine apples and celery; sprinkle with lemon juice and toss well. Combine sugar, mayonnaise and yogurt; mix well and fold into apple mixture. Chill well. Add peanuts, tossing lightly. Serve on lettuce, if desired.

SANDY'S APRICOT MOLDED SALAD

Preparation: 20 minutes   *Can do ahead*   *Yield: 12 to 14 servings*
Chill: 3 hours

1 (16 ounce) can pears
1 (8 ounce) package cream
   cheese

1 (6 ounce) package apricot
   gelatin
1 (8 ounce) container frozen
   whipped topping, thawed

Drain pears and add water to reserved pear juice to equal 2 ¾ cups. Bring liquid to a boil and add gelatin. Mix pears and cream cheese in a blender until creamy; add to gelatin mixture. Refrigerate until partially set. Fold in whipped topping. Place in individual molds, ring mold or any desirable container. Chill until set.

Note: Any flavor of gelatin can be used.

HINT: *For more variety in green salads, combine crisp greens with tender ones, mild flavored greens with tangy greens and dark colored greens with lighter greens.*

BLUEBERRY SALAD

Preparation: 10 minutes *Can do ahead* *Yield: 10 to 12 servings*
Chill: 2 to 3 hours

1 large package raspberry
  gelatin
1 (21 ounce) can blueberry pie
  filling
1 (8 ounce) package cream
  cheese, softened

1 (8 ounce) carton commercial
  sour cream
½ cup sugar
½ cup chopped pecans

In a mixing bowl, combine gelatin dissolved in 1 cup hot water, pie filling and 2 cups of cold water; stir until well blended. Pour into an 11 ¾ x 7 ½ inch baking dish; chill until firm. Combine cream cheese, sour cream and sugar. Spread this mixture over the firm gelatin and sprinkle with pecans. Slice into squares and serve on a bed of lettuce.

CHERRY JUBILEE SALAD

Preparation: 20 minutes *Can do ahead* *Yield: 9 to 12 servings*
Chill: 2 to 3 hours

2 (3 ounce) package cherry
  gelatin
2 cups boiling water
1 (21 ounce) can cherry pie
  filling

1 cup crushed pineapple,
  drained
1 (8 ounce) package cream
  cheese
½ cup chopped pecans

Dissolve gelatin in boiling water; add cherry pie filling. Pour into a 9 x 13 inch pan and let stand until firm. Mix pineapple, cream cheese and nuts. Spread over firm gelatin.

HINT: *Creamy dressings are best on crisp greens such as iceberg or romaine lettuce; oil and vinegar dressings are good on tender greens such as Boston or bibb.*

SALADS

CRANBERRY RELISH COINTREAU

Preparation: 20 minutes   *Do 1 day ahead*   *Yield: 3 ½ cups*
                                     to blend flavors

1 pound fresh cranberries   **1 to 1 ½ cups sugar**
  (4 cups)   **3 tablespoons Cointreau,**
1 small navel orange, quartered   **Grand Marnier <u>or</u> bourbon**
  with peel left on

Using the metal blade of a food processor, add half the cranberries and half
the orange pieces to the beaker. Process, turning on and off rapidly, until
mixture is evenly chopped to desired texture. Transfer to a bowl. Repeat with
remaining cranberries and orange pieces. Return first batch to beaker. Add 1
cup sugar and liqueur and process to mix. Taste and add more sugar if
desired. Store in airtight container in refrigerator.

Note: Makes a wonderful accompaniment for a Thanksgiving turkey or
roast pork.

FESTIVE CRANBERRY CUPS

Preparation: 30 minutes   *Can do ahead*   *Yield: 8 servings*
Freeze: 8 hours

1 (3 ounce) package cream   **1 cup whipped cream**
  cheese   **1 (16 ounce) can jellied**
¼ cup powdered sugar   **cranberry sauce**
¼ cup mayonnaise   **3 tablespoons lemon juice**

Blend cream cheese, powdered sugar, mayonnaise and whipped cream. Set
aside. Combine cranberry sauce and lemon juice in a small bowl. If preparing
in paper cups, divide cranberry mixture into bottoms of 8 small paper cups.
Layer cream cheese mixture on top; freeze. If using a Pyrex dish, layer
cranberry sauce on bottom and cream cheese mixture on top; freeze. When
ready to serve, remove from paper cups, or cut into squares.

HINT: *Salad dressings adhere to greens better if the greens are dried before
tossing.*

HOLIDAY CRANBERRY-ORANGE MOLD

Preparation: 10 minutes   *Can do ahead*   *Yield: 8 servings*
Chill: 2 to 3 hours

1 cup cranberry juice cocktail
1 (3 ounce) package orange
  gelatin
½ cup orange juice
3 tablespoons lemon juice

1 (14 ounce) jar of cran-
  orange relish
½ cup chopped walnuts or
  pecans

Heat the cranberry juice to boiling in a medium saucepan. Remove from heat. Add the package of orange gelatin and stir until dissolved. Add orange and lemon juices. Refrigerate until the mixture has the consistency of unbeaten egg whites. Fold in the relish and walnuts. Pour into a lightly oiled one quart mold. Refrigerate until set.

FROZEN FRUIT SALAD

Preparation: 30 minutes   *Can do ahead*   *Yield: 12 servings*
Freeze: 8 hours

1 (3 ounce) package cream
  cheese
2 tablespoons cream
½ cup Hellmann's mayonnaise
2 tablespoons lemon juice
⅛ teaspoon salt

2 tablespoons sugar
1 cup diced canned pineapple
1 cup chopped orange sections
½ cup Royal Anne cherries,
  pitted and quartered
½ cup whipping cream, whipped

Blend cream cheese with cream. Add mayonnaise, lemon juice, salt and sugar. Combine with prepared fruits. Pour into 2 ½ inch foil cups or paper liners set in muffin tin and freeze until desired serving time. Top with the whipped cream to serve.

HINT: To remove the core from a head of iceberg lettuce easily, tap the core end of the head firmly on the counter or edge of the sink and then twist the core end. It should come out easily.

SALADS

GRAPEFRUIT SALAD

Preparation: 45 minutes   *Yield: 12 to 14 servings*
Chill: 2 to 3 hours

3 large grapefruit, peeled
  and sectioned
3 large oranges, peeled
  and sectioned
2 cucumbers, peeled and
  thinly sliced
1 medium onion, thinly sliced
  and separated into rings

1 apple, cored and diced
¾ cup sugar
1 cup orange juice
¾ cup red wine vinegar
1 ½ teaspoons salt
¼ teaspoon pepper
Lettuce leaves

Combine grapefruit, oranges, cucumbers, onion and apple; set aside. Combine sugar, orange juice, vinegar, salt and pepper; mix lightly with a wire whisk. Pour juice mixture over fruit, tossing gently. Cover; chill 2 to 3 hours. To serve, drain salad. Place in a lettuce-lined bowl. Serve at once.

MRS. BUSKIRK'S PINEAPPLE SALAD

Preparation: 30 minutes   *Can do ahead*   *Yield: 9 to 12 servings*
Cook: 5 minutes
Chill: Several hours

1 (16 ounce) can crushed
  pineapple with juice
1 cup sugar
Juice of 1 lemon
2 packages unflavored gelatin,
  dissolved in a small amount
  of cold water

1 cup shredded yellow cheese
  (Colby or Cheddar), firmly
  packed
1 pint whipping cream, whipped

Boil pineapple and sugar for 5 minutes. Remove from heat; add lemon juice and dissolved gelatin. Cool. Fold in cheese and whipped cream. Pour into a 9 x 9 inch pan and chill.

HINT: *The outer leaves of greens contain the best vitamins - consider this before discarding them.*

GRAPEFRUIT ASPIC

Preparation: 20 minutes   *Can do ahead*   *Yield: 8 to 10 servings*
Chill: 3 hours

1 ½ tablespoons unflavored
   gelatin
½ cup cold water
1 ½ cups boiling water
3 tablespoons lemon juice

¾ cup sugar
3 large grapefruits, sectioned,
   reserve juice
¾ cup chopped celery
½ cup slivered almonds

Soften gelatin in cold water. Add boiling water, stirring until dissolved. Add lemon juice and sugar. Stir well. Chill until almost set; add grapefruit, juice, celery and almonds. Pour into ring mold. Chill until firm.

FROZEN STRAWBERRY SALAD

Preparation: 45 minutes   *Can do ahead*   *Yield: 20 to 24 servings*
Freeze: Overnight

1 (3 ounce) package wild
   strawberry gelatin
1 cup boiling water (use juice
   from pineapple and add
   water to make 1 cup)
½ cup sugar
2 cups miniature marshmallows
1 (1 pound) package frozen
   sweetened strawberries,
   thawed

1 (3 ounce) package cream
   cheese, softened
1 (8 ounce) can crushed
   pineapple, drained
1 cup cottage cheese
2 bananas, mashed
½ pint whipping cream, whipped

Make gelatin with the cup of boiling juice and water. Add sugar and marsh-mallows. Stir until gelatin is dissolved. Add thawed strawberries. Blend together cream cheese and pineapple. Add to gelatin. Add cottage cheese and bananas. Stir well. Fold in whipped cream. Freeze.

HINT: *If a salad has mayonnaise in it, lightly grease the mold with mayonnaise to keep it from sticking.*

SALADS

LAYERED ANTIPASTO

Preparation: 15 to 20 minutes   *Can do ahead*   *Yield: 12 to 14 servings*
Stand: Overnight

½ head of shredded lettuce
4 medium tomatoes, thinly
  sliced
1 pound of sliced ham
½ pound of sliced salami
½ pound of sliced provolone
  cheese
½ pound of sliced pepperoni

1 (6 ounce) jar of black olives,
  drained
2 (6 ounce) jars marinated
  artichoke hearts, reserving
  liquid
2 (7 ounce) cans of tuna in oil,
  reserving liquid
2 (4 ounce) jars of roasted
  peppers, reserving liquid

In a 10 x 14 inch pan, layer lettuce, tomatoes, ham, salami, cheese, pepperoni, olives, artichoke hearts, tuna and peppers. Pour the liquid from the artichoke hearts, tuna and peppers over the top. Cover with plastic wrap and refrigerate. When ready to serve, cut into serving portions.

Note: Make this a day ahead in order to let all the oils soak through.

CELESTIAL SALAD

Preparation: 30 minutes   *Yield: 6 to 8 servings*

1 head lettuce
1 (11 ounce) can mandarin
  orange sections, drained,
  reserve liquid

1 cup green grapes, halved
½ cup chopped green onions
½ cup sliced toasted almonds,
  divided

Wash lettuce and tear into bite-size pieces. Combine lettuce, orange sections, grapes, onion and ¼ cup of almonds in a large salad bowl.

Dressing:

⅔ cup salad oil
Juice from mandarin oranges
¼ cup sugar
3 tablespoons vinegar

Salt to taste
Dash of dry mustard
1 teaspoon celery seed
2 tablespoons chopped parsley

Combine oil, orange juice, sugar, vinegar, salt, dry mustard and celery seed in a covered container. Shake well. Pour over salad and toss well. Sprinkle with parsley and remaining almonds.

HAIL CAESAR SALAD

Preparation: 45 minutes   *Can do ahead*   *Yield: 8 to 10 servings*
Chill: 2 to 3 hours

3 large heads romaine lettuce
Croutons, preferably made
   from French or Italian bread
4 to 8 tablespoons vegetable oil
1 egg, coddled then beaten
4 tablespoons lemon juice
¼ cup olive oil
½ teaspoon coarsely ground
   black pepper

1 teaspoon Worcestershire
   sauce
¼ to ⅜ teaspoon garlic powder
¼ to ½ teaspoon salt
½ cup grated Parmesan cheese
A few finely chopped anchovies,
   optional

Separate the romaine lettuce and wash the leaves under cold running water. Dry with paper towels. Break into bite sized pieces. Wrap lettuce in a dry kitchen towel and put in a large plastic bag. Refrigerate.

To prepare croutons, cut loaf of bread into ½ to ¾ inch slices, trim the crust and cut each slice into ½ to ¾ inch squares. In a skillet large enough to hold the croutons in a single layer, heat 4 tablespoons vegetable oil, adding a small amount of the garlic powder. Add croutons and brown them on all sides, turning with tongs, adding up to another 4 tablespoons of oil if necessary. Remove croutons to paper towels to drain, cool and crisp. Plunge the egg into boiling water for 10 seconds, remove and set aside. In a pint jar with a lid put the lemon juice, olive oil, pepper, egg, Worcestershire sauce, remaining garlic powder, salt, Parmesan cheese and anchovies, if desired. Put lid on the jar, shake the dressing, and refrigerate until ready to use. Shake again just before using. To serve, put romaine in a large bowl, add dressing, and toss. Add croutons and toss lightly again. Serve immediately.

Note: For quicker version, use packaged onion-garlic croutons, or toss plain croutons in garlic flavored oil just before using.

HINT: *When adding vinegar and oil separately to salad greens, add the oil first and mix before adding vinegar. The greens won't wilt as quickly.*

SALADS

DUMP SALAD

Preparation: 30 minutes   Yield: 12 to 15 servings
Chill: 2 to 3 hours

Salad:

10 to 12 crisp strips bacon,
  crumbled
1 (14 ounce) can artichoke
  hearts, drained and sliced
1 (6 ounce) can pitted ripe
  olives, drained and sliced
1 (14 ounce) can hearts of palm,
  drained and sliced

½ cup green Spanish olives,
  sliced
3 stalks celery, sliced
1 cucumber, chopped
½ cup slivered almonds, toasted
3 green onions, chopped
½ head iceberg lettuce, torn
2 tomatoes, optional

Mix salad ingredients and chill. Before serving, add dressing and toss.

Dressing:

¼ cup tarragon wine vinegar
¾ cup salad oil
1 teaspoon salt

¼ teaspoon oregano
¼ teaspoon parsley
⅛ teaspoon garlic powder

Mix dressing ingredients and shake well.

FRENCH GOURMET SALAD WITH VINAIGRETTE

Preparation: 30 minutes   Yield: Unlimited

Salad:

Boston, red leaf and/or
  romaine lettuce
Navel oranges, peeled and
  sectioned or 1 or 2 (11 ounce)
  cans mandarin oranges

Purple onions, thinly sliced
1 avocado, sliced in medium
  chunks
Toasted slivered almonds

Combine lettuces, oranges, onions, avocado and almonds. Toss with dressing just before serving.

Vinaigrette:

¼ cup white wine vinegar
  with tarragon
¾ cup salad oil

Pinch sugar
1 teaspoon salt
Freshly ground pepper

Combine all ingredients; whisk until blended.

64

SALAD WITH WALNUT OIL

Preparation: 20 minutes   *Yield: 4 servings*

Salad:

1 head lettuce <u>or</u> several
   heads Boston <u>or</u> Bibb
Salt and pepper
Walnut halves, coarsely
   chopped

2 hard cooked eggs, cut into
   quarters <u>or</u> sixths
Hearts of palm, optional

Croutes:

2 to 4 slices French <u>or</u>
   Italian bread

Butter
Garlic, optional

Cut bread into quarters; saute in butter; rub with garlic, if desired. Set aside.

Vinaigrette:

2 tablespoons cider <u>or</u>
   wine vinegar
Salt and pepper

2 teaspoons Dijon mustard,
   optional
6 tablespoons walnut oil

Combine all ingredients. Blend well; set aside. Put lettuce leaves and hearts of palm in a salad bowl. Add vinaigrette. Toss well and taste for seasoning. Sprinkle with walnuts, eggs and croutes. Serve at once.

Note: You may use prepared croutons instead of the croutes.

HINT: *Always tear greens for salad - never cut greens with a knife.*

HINT: *For crisping wilted celery - cover celery and a washed, unpeeled, cut potato with water and refrigerate for a few hours.*

SALADS

LAYERED SUMMER VEGETABLE SALAD

Preparation: 30 minutes   *Can do ahead*   *Yield: 10 servings*
Chill: 6 hours to overnight

Salad:

4 cups torn lettuce	1 cup shredded Swiss cheese
1 medium red onion, sliced	1 pint cherry tomatoes, halved
2 cups green pepper, sliced	4 cups zucchini, sliced

In a large deep bowl, layer lettuce, onion, green pepper and cheese. Add a ring of tomatoes; top with a ring of zucchini.

Dressing:

¾ cup mayonnaise	1 tablespoon Worcestershire
3 tablespoons prepared	sauce
horseradish	Dash of hot pepper sauce
2 tablespoons lemon juice	1 medium avocado, peeled
	and diced

In a medium bowl, stir together mayonnaise, horseradish, lemon juice, Worcestershire sauce and hot pepper sauce. Stir until smooth. Spoon over salad. Cover and refrigerate at least 6 hours. Just before serving, peel and dice avocado. Toss with lemon juice to prevent darkening. Sprinkle on top of salad.

SUPERB SALAD

Preparation: 45 minutes   *Can do ahead*   *Yield: 6 servings*

Salad:

1 (16 ounce) can mandarin	6 large fresh mushrooms or
oranges, drained	1 (4 ounce) can of
½ pound bacon, cooked crisp	mushrooms, sliced
1 (8 ½ ounce) can of artichoke	2 bunches of bibb, leaf or
hearts, drained and chopped	Boston lettuce
2 stalks celery, chopped	

SUPERB SALAD (Continued)

Combine oranges, artichoke hearts, celery and mushrooms with lettuce. Crumble bacon on top and mix.

Dressing:

¼ cup vinegar
1 teaspoon salt
¼ teaspoon pepper
¼ teaspoon oregano

Pinch each of bouquet garni, sweet basil, thyme and tarragon
¾ cup of oil

Combine vinegar, salt, pepper and herbs; add to oil; shake.

SPINACH SALAD

Preparation: 45 minutes   *Can do ahead*   *Yield: 6 to 8 servings*

Salad:

1 bag spinach, torn
1 cup water chestnuts
2 hard-cooked eggs

1 bunch fresh bean sprouts, optional
½ pound bacon, cooked and crumbled

Put spinach in large salad bowl. Slice water chestnuts and eggs on top of spinach. Add bean sprouts. Crumble crisp bacon over vegetables.

Dressing:

1 cup salad oil
½ cup vinegar
1 medium onion, diced
1 cup sugar

1 teaspoon Worcestershire sauce
2 teaspoons salt
⅓ cup ketchup

In blender, combine all ingredients; blend well. Pour over salad, toss and serve.

Note: This is enough dressing for two bags of spinach.

SALADS

SPINACH SALAD FROM EMPORIA

Preparation: 15 minutes   *Can do ahead*   *Yield:* 6 to 8 servings
Chill ahead

Salad:

2 (10 ounce) packages frozen
    chopped spinach
½ cup onion, chopped

½ cup celery, chopped
2 hard boiled eggs

Dressing:

1 ¼ cup mayonnaise
½ teaspoon salt
½ teaspoon hot pepper sauce
2 teaspoons prepared
    horseradish

1 teaspoon vinegar
1 cup grated sharp cheese
1 tablespoon bacon bits

Thaw and squeeze the spinach dry. Combine in mixing bowl with onion and eggs. In separate bowl, mix mayonnaise, salt, hot pepper sauce, horseradish and vinegar. Fold into spinach mixture. Refrigerate until serving time. Top with cheese and bacon bits.

HINT: Drop tomatoes in boiling water for just a minute for easy skinning.

HINT: To keep juice from tomato slices in the tomato instead of the salad, slice the tomato from stem to bottom instead of horizontally.

HINT: Always sprinkle gelatin on top of a cold liquid before bringing to a boil to dissolve.

TOMATO AND HEARTS OF PALM SALAD

Preparation: 30 minutes   *Yield: 6 servings*

Salad:

½ pound spinach, trimmed,
   washed and dried
2 large heads Bibb lettuce,
   separated into leaves,
   washed and dried

4 tomatoes, cored and cut
   into wedges
1 (14 ounce) can hearts of palm,
   drained and cut into 1 inch
   pieces
1 cup ripe olives

Line a large platter with spinach and lettuce, arrange the tomatoes and the hearts of palm in the center over the greens. Sprinkle the salad with the olives. Serve the salad with the Basil Vinaigrette.

Basil Vinaigrette:

3 tablespoons white wine
   vinegar
2 teaspoons Dijon-style
   mustard
½ cup salad oil

2 tablespoons minced fresh
   basil leaves <u>or</u> ½ teaspoon
   crushed dried basil
Salt and pepper to taste

In a bowl combine vinegar, mustard, salt and pepper to taste. Add the oil in a stream, beating until the dressing is emulsified.

HINT: Sprinkle lemon juice over fruit salad to prevent fruit from browning.

SALADS

ASPARAGUS MOLD

Preparation: 30 minutes   *Can do ahead*   *Yield: 8 servings*

Salad:

2 tablespoons unflavored
  gelatin
½ cup cold water
¾ cup sugar
½ cup vinegar
1 cup water
½ teaspoon salt
1 cup chopped celery

½ cup chopped pecans
1 (2 ounce) jar pimentos,
  chopped
1 (1 pound) can asparagus,
  chopped
Juice of ½ lemon
2 teaspoons grated onion
½ cup stuffed olives, chopped

Soften gelatin in ½ cup cold water. Boil sugar, vinegar and water 2 minutes. Add dissolved gelatin. Cool. Add salt, celery, pecans, pimentos, asparagus, onion and olives. Chill.

Dressing:

½ cup sour cream   ½ cup mayonnaise

Combine sour cream and mayonnaise and pour on just before serving.

ARTICHOKE RICE SALAD

Preparation: 40 minutes   *Can do ahead*   *Yield: 6 to 8 servings*
Chill: 30 minutes

1 (6 ounce) package chicken
  vermicelli rice mix
2 (6 ounce) jars marinated
  artichoke hearts
¼ to ⅓ cup mayonnaise

¾ teaspoon curry powder or
  less, according to taste
2 green onions, chopped
½ green pepper, chopped
12 stuffed olives, sliced

Cook rice as directed on package. Cool. Drain artichokes, reserving liquid from 1 jar and slice in halves. Combine liquid with mayonnaise and curry powder. Mix all ingredients. Chill.

SALAD OF ARTICHOKE BOTTOMS AND MUSHROOMS

Preparation: 30 minutes
Cook: 15 minutes
Stand: 2 hours

Salad:

4 large artichokes	1 ½ lemons, for preparing
¼ pound mushrooms, very	artichokes
thinly sliced	1 tablespoon chopped fresh
	chives or parsley

To cook artichoke bottoms, choose large artichokes to make a generous cup shape. Boil a large pot of water. Add salt and juice of ½ lemon. Add juice of another ½ lemon to a bowl of cold water. Break stem from artichoke; with a very sharp knife held close to side of artichoke, cut off all large bottom leaves, leaving a soft cone of central leaves. Trim cone level with top of artichoke base. Rub base well with another cut lemon to prevent discoloration. Cut off leaves under base and trim smooth, flattening the bottom. Rub again with cut lemon and keep in cold lemon water. Repeat. To cook, drain and put in boiling water and cover with a tea-towel or heatproof plate to keep them below water. Simmer 15 to 20 minutes or until tender. Drain and scoop out hairy choke with spoon. For salad, drain, plunge in cold water, then remove choke. Arrange on plates. Taste mushroom mixture for seasoning, then heap some in the middle of each artichoke bottom. Sprinkle with chopped chives or parsley just before serving.

Dressing:

1 teaspoon lemon juice	¼ cup heavy cream or crème
1 tablespoon wine vinegar	fraîche
Salt and pepper	1 clove garlic, minced

To make dressing, whisk together lemon juice, vinegar, salt and pepper. Gradually whisk in cream, then add the garlic. Pour over the mushrooms and mix well. Cover tightly and let marinate for at least 2 hours.

Note: Canned artichoke bottoms may be substituted if fresh ones are not available. To substitute simply drain, soak in cold water 10 minutes, then drain again. This also saves about 30 minutes preparation time.

BEET AND HORSERADISH RING WITH SEAFOOD AND RUSSIAN DRESSING

Preparation: 30 minutes   *Can do ahead*   *Yield: 6 to 8 servings*
Chill: 3 hours

Ring:

1 cup boiling water
1 (3 ounce) package lemon
  gelatin
Juice of 1 small lemon
1 (16 ounce) can whole beets,
  reserve liquid

3 tablespoons prepared
  horseradish
Lettuce for platter
1 or 2 avocados
¾ to 1 pound crab, shrimp, or
  lobster, or combination of
  seafood

Ring: In a bowl dissolve gelatin in one cup boiling water. Add beet juice, lemon juice and water, if needed, to make one cup. Mix and put into refrigerator until slightly set. Grate beets in another bowl, add horseradish and mix. Add to slightly set gelatin and mix well. Pour into oiled one quart ring mold. Return to refrigerator until firmly set. When ready to serve, unmold on platter with pieces of lettuce. Fill center with seafood slightly tossed in dressing. Garnish with peeled and sliced avocados. Serve additional dressing in bowl.

Dressing:

1 cup mayonnaise
½ cup ketchup
½ cup chili sauce
2 tablespoons lemon juice
1 tablespoon chives

1 tablespoon minced parsley
1 hard boiled egg, chopped
Dash salt and pepper
Paprika to taste

Dressing: Mix all ingredients well and chill.

Note: Can use one or two tablespoons of caviar to dressing for extra flavor.

JO'S BROCCOLI SALAD MOLD

Preparation: 45 minutes   *Can do ahead*   *Yield: 10 servings*
Chill: 3 hours

2 (10 ounce) packages frozen
  chopped broccoli
2 tablespoons unflavored
  gelatin
1 (10 ½ ounce) can chicken
  consommé
2 tablespoons lemon juice
1 teaspoon hot sauce

½ teaspoon salt
½ cup mayonnaise
3 hard boiled eggs, chopped
½ cup chopped celery
½ cup almonds or pecans,
  chopped
Salad greens
Salad dressing

Cook broccoli according to package directions. Soak gelatin in ½ cup consommé for 5 minutes. Heat remaining consommé and add to gelatin mixture. Stir until dissolved. Drain broccoli. Combine all ingredients with broccoli. Add consommé and gelatin mixture. Pour into mold and chill. Slice and serve on salad greens. Serve with salad dressings (French, Thousand Island or Blue Cheese).

COLE SLAW

Preparation: 1 hour   *Can do ahead*   *Yield: 8 servings*
Chill: 2 hours

3 pounds shredded cabbage
1 medium onion, chopped

1 green pepper, chopped
2 cups sugar

Toss cabbage, onion, green pepper in a large bowl and pour the sugar over the mixture.

Sauce:

1 cup salad oil
1 cup vinegar

1 teaspoon celery seeds
1 teaspoon salt

In a medium saucepan, blend oil, vinegar, celery seeds and salt well; bring to a boil. Pour over cabbage mixture and toss. Put in refrigerator and chill well before serving.

SALADS

VEGETABLE SALAD

Preparation: 30 minutes   *Can do ahead*   *Yield: 12 to 15 servings*
Chill: 24 hours

2 bunches broccoli, chopped
½ head cauliflower, chopped
⅔ cup sliced pitted black
  olives
⅔ cup sliced green olives

⅔ cup mayonnaise
1 small onion, chopped fine
1 tablespoon lemon juice
3 hard boiled eggs, chopped
Salt and pepper

Mix all together and let stand overnight.

CAULIFLOWER SALAD

Preparation: 30 minutes   *Can do ahead*   *Yield: 6 to 8 servings*
Marinate: 6 hours

1 package frozen peas
1 medium head of cauliflower
3 stalks celery, sliced
1 small onion, chopped

1 cup Hellmann's mayonnaise
½ teaspoon seasoned salt
3 to 4 tablespoons milk

Cook peas according to package directions. Drain. While peas cool, break apart cauliflower and slice thin. Combine cauliflower and peas; add sliced celery and chopped onion. Mix together mayonnaise, salt and milk. Mix with the cauliflower mixture. Marinate in refrigerator.

SUPERB SOUR CREAM CUCUMBERS

Preparation: 20 minutes   *Can do ahead*   *Yield: 4 servings*
Chill: 30 to 40 minutes

⅓ cup sour cream
1 teaspoon finely minced onion
1 teaspoon cider vinegar

2 medium cucumbers, very
  thinly sliced
Salt, optional
Lettuce
Tomato wedges

Place sour cream, onion and vinegar in a bowl and mix thoroughly. Season cucumbers with salt, if desired; add to sour cream mixture. Toss until cucumbers are coated. Chill thoroughly. Serve on lettuce with tomato wedges as garnish when using as a salad; or serve as a side vegetable for a meal.

FRESH CORN SALAD

Preparation: 1 hour   *Can do ahead*   *Yield: 6 to 8 servings*
Chill: 3 hours

8 ears fresh corn
½ cup salad oil
¼ cup cider vinegar
1 tablespoon fresh lemon juice
3 tablespoons chopped fresh
  parsley
2 teaspoons salt
1 teaspoon sugar
1 tablespoon chopped fresh
  basil or ½ teaspoon dried leaf
  basil

¼ teaspoon cayenne
2 large tomatoes, peeled
  and chopped
½ cup chopped fresh bell
  pepper, red, if possible
½ cup steamed fresh green
  peas or thawed frozen peas
3 scallions, chopped
Salad greens

Husk corn, remove silks and put in large kettle half-full of boiling water. Return to boil. Remove from heat and let stand 5 minutes. Drain and cool. In large bowl, mix oil, vinegar, lemon juice, parsley, salt, sugar, basil and cayenne. Cut corn off cobs and add to dressing with tomatoes, bell pepper, peas and scallions. Mix well. Cover and chill several hours. Serve in bowl lined with salad greens.

CUCUMBER SALAD RING

Preparation: 30 minutes   *Can do ahead*   *Yield: 10 to 12 servings*
Chill: 12 hours

1 (3 ounce) package lemon
  gelatin
1 cup boiling water
1 cup mayonnaise
1 pint large curd cottage
  cheese
1 large cucumber, peeled
  and diced

½ cup finely chopped celery
1 small onion, grated
1 teaspoon salt
1 tablespoon vinegar
1 tablespoon prepared
  horseradish
½ cup blanched almonds

Dissolve gelatin in boiling water. Let cool to room temperature. Add remaining ingredients. Stir gently until well blended. Pour into 9 cup ring mold. Refrigerate. Fill center with chicken salad or tuna salad if desired.

SALADS

THE GARDENER'S SALAD

Preparation: 30 minutes   Can do ahead   *Yield: 8 servings*
Marinate: 2 hours

8 small to medium size
  zucchini, chopped
2 tomatoes, peeled, seeded
  and chopped
1 green pepper, chopped
1 small onion, finely chopped
1 teaspoon sugar

1 teaspoon salt
½ teaspoon ground black
  pepper
Oregano to taste
¼ teaspoon paprika
2 to 4 tablespoons mayonnaise
  <u>or</u> salad dressing

Put chopped vegetables in a large bowl. Add all other ingredients except salad dressing and mix well. Cover and marinate in refrigerator. Just before serving, drain the vegetables well and add salad dressing.

Note: Low calorie version is to serve salad without dressing. Medium cucumbers may be substituted for zucchini.

MARINATED SALAD

Preparation: 30 minutes   Can do ahead   *Yield: 12 to 15 servings*
Chill: overnight

1 cup vinegar
1 cup sugar
½ cup salad oil
1 (16 ounce) can French-style
  green beans, drained
1 (8 ounce) can peas, drained
2 carrots, thinly sliced

1 green pepper, finely chopped
1 red onion, thinly sliced
1 (2 ounce) jar chopped
  pimento, drained
1 cucumber, thinly sliced
3 stalks celery, chopped

Bring vinegar to a boil in a small saucepan; stir in sugar and oil. Cool slightly. Combine remaining ingredients; add vinegar mixture. Cover and refrigerate.

GAZPACHO MOLD WITH AVOCADO SAUCE

Preparation: 25 minutes　　　*Can do ahead*　　　*Yield: 8 to 10 servings*
Chill: 3 hours

Salad:

2 envelopes unflavored gelatin
3 cups tomato juice
⅓ cup red wine vinegar
1 teaspoon salt
Dash Tabasco

2 small tomatoes, peeled and
　diced
½ medium bell pepper, diced
¼ cup onion, chopped
¼ cup celery, chopped
1 tablespoon chives, chopped

Sprinkle gelatin over tomato juice and stir over low heat until dissolved. Remove from heat and add vinegar, salt and Tabasco. Stir. Chill until partially set. Add vegetables and stir. Pour into 1 ½ quart mold or pan. Refrigerate until ready to serve.

Dressing:

1 ripe avocado
1 tablespoon lemon juice
½ cup light cream
½ cup commercial sour cream

1 clove garlic, minced
⅛ teaspoon sugar
½ teaspoon salt
1 tablespoon grated onion
Dash cayenne pepper

Peel and mash avocado with lemon juice. Stir light cream into sour cream and blend. Add seasonings. Stir the avocado in and chill.

MARINATED ZUCCHINI SALAD

Preparation: 20 minutes　　　*Can do ahead*　　　*Yield: 6 to 8 servings*
Chill: 1 hour plus

4 medium zucchini, sliced
2 green onions, with tops,
　chopped
1 small green pepper, seeded,
　chopped

1 stalk celery, chopped
⅓ cup sugar
⅓ cup white vinegar
3 tablespoons salad oil
½ teaspoon salt

Combine zucchini, onions, green pepper and celery in bowl. Blend or process sugar, vinegar, oil and salt well. Pour over vegetables and mix. Cover and chill.

SALADS

MARINATED MUSHROOMS

Preparation: 20 minutes *Can do ahead* *Yield: 6 servings*
Chill: overnight

1 pound fresh mushrooms
¼ cup Hellmann's mayonnaise

1 clove garlic, minced
Juice of ½ fresh lemon

Clean and slice mushrooms; add garlic, mayonnaise and lemon juice. Cover and refrigerate.

SNOW PEA SALAD WITH SESAME DRESSING

Preparation: 30 minutes *Can do ahead* *Yield: 4 to 6 servings*
Chill: 4 hours
Bake: 5 to 8 minutes

Salad:

1 (7 ounce) package frozen
  Chinese snow peas
½ head cauliflower, separated
  into bite size clusters

1 (5 ounce) can water chestnuts,
  drained and sliced
1 tablespoon chopped pimento

Cook peas in small amount of boiling salted water until barely tender, about 1 minute after water boils again. Drain. Cook cauliflower clusters in boiling salted water until tender but still crisp, about 3 minutes after water returns to boil; drain. Combine peas and cauliflower with water chestnuts and pimento; chill covered.

Sesame Seed Dressing:

2 tablespoons sesame seed
⅓ cup salad oil
1 tablespoon lemon juice
1 tablespoon vinegar

1 tablespoon sugar
½ clove garlic, minced
½ teaspoon salt

Preheat oven at 350°. Place sesame seed in shallow pan and bake until golden brown. Cool. In jar, combine salad oil, lemon juice, vinegar, sugar, garlic, salt and toasted sesame seed. Cover and chill.

Just before serving, mix vegetables with about 3 tablespoons dressing.

FRENCH POTATO SALAD

Preparation: 2 hours　　　*Can do ahead*　　　*Yield: 6 cups*

8 to 10 medium boiling
　potatoes
¼ cup dry white wine
2 tablespoons wine vinegar
1 teaspoon prepared mustard

¼ teaspoon salt
6 tablespoons good olive oil
1 to 2 tablespoons minced green
　onions or shallots
2 to 3 tablespoons chopped
　mixed herbs or parsley

Scrub potatoes. Drop potatoes in boiling salted water to cover and boil until potatoes are just tender when pierced with a knife. Drain. As soon as they are cool enough to handle, peel and cut into slices ⅛ inch thick. Place potatoes in a 3 quart mixing bowl. Pour wine over the warm potato slices and toss gently. Set aside for a few minutes until the potatoes have absorbed the liquids. Beat the vinegar, mustard and salt in a small bowl with a wire whip until the salt has dissolved. Beat in oil by drops. Season to taste and stir in green onions or shallots. Pour dressing over the potatoes and toss gently to blend. Serve them while warm or chill. Decorate with chopped herbs before serving.

TOMATO RELISH SALAD

Preparation: 30 minutes　　*Can do ahead*　　*Yield: 6 to 8 servings*
Chill: 4 hours

3 tomatoes, sliced
1 medium cucumber, thinly
　sliced
1 medium onion, thinly sliced
　and separated into rings
½ cup sliced carrots
½ cup sliced celery

½ cup tarragon vinegar
½ cup water
¼ cup sugar
1 teaspoon salt
1 teaspoon paprika
Dash of pepper

Combine tomatoes, cucumber, onions, carrots and celery, and toss gently. Combine remaining ingredients, mix well, and pour over vegetables. Cover salad and chill.

SALAD DRESSINGS

BLUE CHEESE DRESSING

Preparation: 30 minutes   *Can do ahead*   *Yield: 1 ½ quarts*
Chill: 24 hours

1 (8 ounce) package blue
  cheese, hand crumbled
½ teaspoon salt, optional
1 quart mayonnaise
1 cup buttermilk
1 ounce orange juice

2 teaspoons Worcestershire
  sauce
1 clove garlic, optional
1 teaspoon garlic powder or salt
1 teaspoon Tabasco
1 teaspoon steak sauce

Combine in bowl. Pour into jars and chill 24 hours.

Note: May also be used as dip.

SWEET FRENCH DRESSING

Preparation: 10 minutes   *Can do ahead*   *Yield: 5 cups*

2 cups salad oil
1 cup sugar
1 cup chili sauce

1 cup vinegar
¾ teaspoon salt
1 medium onion, grated

Pour oil in a bowl, add sugar, chili sauce, vinegar, salt and beat well. Add grated onion and stir again. Refrigerate. Shake well before serving.

POPPY SEED DRESSING

Preparation: 10 minutes   *Can do ahead*   *Yield: 2 cups*

¾ cup cider vinegar
1 tablespoon lemon juice
⅓ cup honey
1 cup salad oil
⅔ cup sugar

1 teaspoon dry mustard
1 teaspoon paprika
1 teaspoon poppy seeds
  or celery seed
½ teaspoon salt

Blend vinegar, lemon juice and honey. Add oil, by drops. When oil is thoroughly blended and the mix is the consistency of heavy cream, fold in the sugar, mustard, paprika, poppy seeds and salt. Refrigerate.

RED ROQUEFORT SALAD DRESSING

Preparation: 10 minutes　　　*Can do ahead*　　　*Yield: 2 ½ cups*

1 cup vegetable oil
¼ cup wine vinegar
¼ cup sugar
1 teaspoon soy sauce

⅓ cup ketchup
¼ cup finely minced onion
½ cup crumbled Roquefort
　cheese <u>or</u> Bleu cheese

Combine all ingredients except cheese in a large jar. Stir until sugar is dissolved. Add cheese. Cover jar and shake until cheese is mixed with other ingredients. Refrigerate until ready to use.

ROQUEFORT SALAD DRESSING

Preparation: 10 minutes　　　*Can do ahead*　　　*Yield: 3 ½ cups*

1 pint Hellmann's mayonnaise
1 cup buttermilk
1 tablespoon Worcestershire
　sauce

1 teaspoon garlic salt <u>or</u>
1 clove garlic
3 ounces Roquefort cheese

Mix all ingredients.

EDNA S. CALDWELL'S RUSSIAN DRESSING

Preparation: 30 minutes　　　*Can do ahead*　　　*Yield: 2 quarts*

½ pint heavy cream, stiffly
　whipped
1 quart salad dressing
6 green onions, thinly sliced
4 hard boiled eggs, chopped

6 Kosher baby dill pickles,
　finely chopped
3 celery hearts, finely chopped
2 tablespoons chili sauce
1 (2 ounce) jar black caviar

Fold together whipped cream and salad dressing. Fold in onions, eggs, pickles, celery and chili sauce. Gently fold in caviar. Chill before serving on salad greens.

Note: One pound of picked crab meat added to half the recipe may be used as a spread for crackers <u>or</u> as a filling for halved avocados.

SALAD DRESSINGS

SWISS SALAD DRESSING

Preparation: 10 minutes   Can do ahead   *Yield: 2 cups*
Chill: Overnight

¾ cup oil
⅓ cup vinegar
1 teaspoon salt
¼ teaspoon paprika

½ teaspoon sugar
½ teaspoon celery seed
1 clove garlic, minced
1 cup grated Swiss cheese

Mix thoroughly and chill.

Breads

WHEELING
DOWNS

BREADS

MOM'S ALABAMA BISCUITS

Preparation: 20 minutes
Stand: 2 hours
Cook: 15 to 20 minutes

2 ½ cups flour
½ teaspoon salt
½ teaspoon baking soda
4 tablespoons sugar
½ package yeast

¼ cup warm water
6 tablespoons shortening
1 cup buttermilk
Melted butter

Sift dry ingredients together; dissolve yeast in water. Add yeast, shortening and buttermilk to dry ingredients; mix well by hand. Place dough on floured surface; knead 20 times. Roll out ¼ inch thick and cut with a biscuit cutter. Roll biscuits in melted butter and stack one on top of the other in twos. Let rise 2 hours. Preheat oven to 400°. Bake 15 to 20 minutes.

GOURMET CREAM BISCUITS

Preparation: 15 minutes
Cook: 15 to 20 minutes

Yield: 15 biscuits

1 ¼ cups flour
1 tablespoon baking powder
½ teaspoon salt

¼ cup well chilled unsalted butter
1 cup (plus 2 tablespoons if needed) whipping cream

Preheat oven to 425°. Sift flour, baking powder and salt together. Cut butter into small pieces and add to sifted ingredients. Using a pastry blender or 2 knives, cut in butter until mixture looks like coarse meal. Add 1 cup of cream and blend. Dough should be soft. If necessary, add more cream. Turn dough out onto a lightly floured board and roll to ¾ inch thickness. Cut into 1 ½ inch squares. Put biscuits on an ungreased baking sheet, about ½ inch apart. Bake for 15 to 20 minutes, or until biscuits are golden. Serve immediately.

ANGEL BISCUITS

Preparation: 15 minutes   *Can do ahead*   *Yield: 36 miniature muffins*

2 cups self-rising flour
1 cup butter

8 ounces commercial sour
cream

Preheat oven to 400°. Cut in butter by hand or with food processor. Mix in sour cream. Spoon into greased small (miniature) muffin tins. Bake 18 to 20 minutes.

CORN MUFFINS

Preparation: 10 minutes   *Yield: 12 muffins*
Bake: 25 minutes

⅓ cup shortening
⅓ cup sugar
1 beaten egg
1 ¼ cups milk

1 cup flour
½ teaspoon salt
4 teaspoons baking powder
1 cup yellow corn meal

Preheat oven to 425°. Grease muffin cups. Cream shortening and sugar. Add egg and milk; add flour sifted with salt and baking powder. Add corn meal, stirring only enough to mix. Fill muffin cups ⅔ full. Bake for 25 minutes.

WHEAT BRAN MUFFINS

Preparation: 20 minutes   *Can do ahead*   *Yield: 2 dozen*
Bake: 20 minutes

1 cup bran cereal
1 cup crushed shredded wheat
¼ cup boiling water
½ cup shortening
1 ½ cups sugar
2 eggs, slightly beaten

2 ½ cups flour
2 ¼ teaspoons baking soda
½ teaspoon salt
¼ teaspoon baking powder
2 cups buttermilk
½ cup raisins (optional)

Combine cereals and boiling water and set aside. Cream together shortening and sugar; add eggs and then cereal mix. In a large bowl sift together flour, soda, salt and baking powder. Add buttermilk to cereal mixture. Stir in raisins. Add mixture to flour and mix. Store in a tightly covered container in refrigerator up to 2 weeks or more. Preheat oven to 400°. Use as much dough as desired returning the rest to refrigerator. Fill greased muffin pans ⅔ full. Bake 20 minutes.

BREADS

FRENCH BREAKFAST PUFFS

Preparation: 10 minutes   *Yield: 12 puffs*
Bake: 20 to 25 minutes

⅓ cup shortening
½ cup sugar
1 egg
1 ½ cups sifted flour

1 ½ teaspoons baking powder
½ teaspoon salt
¼ teaspoon cinnamon
½ cup milk

Coating:

6 tablespoons butter, melted
½ cup sugar

1 teaspoon cinnamon

Preheat oven to 350°. Grease muffin cups. Mix shortening, ½ cup sugar and egg. Sift together flour, baking powder, salt and ¼ teaspoon cinnamon. Alternating dry ingredients and milk, stir them into the shortening mix. Fill muffin cups ⅔ full. Bake for 20 to 25 minutes until golden brown. Remove from pan and immediately roll in melted butter and then in the mix of cinnamon and ½ cup of sugar.

ORANGE FRUIT MUFFINS

Preparation: 30 minutes   *Can do ahead*   *Yield: 18 muffins*
Bake: 25 minutes   *Can be frozen*

½ cup butter, softened
2 cups sugar, divided
2 eggs
¾ cup buttermilk
¾ teaspoon baking soda
2 cups flour

Pinch of salt
½ cup chopped nuts
1 (8 ounce) package chopped
   dates
2 ½ tablespoons grated orange
   rind, divided
½ cup orange juice

Preheat oven to 350°. Cream butter, 1 cup sugar and eggs; beat well. Combine buttermilk and soda. Combine flour and salt. Add to creamed mixture alternately with buttermilk mixture. Mix well after each addition. Stir in dates, nuts and 1 ½ tablespoons orange rind. Pour batter into greased muffin tins and bake for 25 minutes. Combine 1 cup sugar, orange juice and 1 tablespoon orange rind in small saucepan. Stir over low heat until sugar is dissolved and glaze is hot. Prick muffins with fork while hot and spoon glaze over top.

DAD'S WHOLE WHEAT ZUCCHINI MUFFINS

Preparation: 15 minutes   *Yield: 24 muffins*
Bake: 15 to 20 minutes

3 eggs	1 teaspoon salt
1 cup oil	3 teaspoons cinnamon
¾ cup sugar	3 cups presifted whole wheat
2 cups grated zucchini	flour
2 teaspoons vanilla	1 teaspoon baking soda
¼ teaspoon baking powder	½ cup chopped nuts, optional

Preheat oven to 350°. Beat eggs. Add oil, sugar, grated zucchini and vanilla. Add all dry ingredients. Mix well. Put in well greased or paper lined muffin tins. Bake 15 to 20 minutes.

CINNAMON ROLL-UPS

Preparation: 30 minutes   *Freeze ahead*   *Yield: 48 roll-ups*
Bake: 15 minutes

48 slices fresh white bread,	2 egg yolks
trim crusts	½ cup sugar
1 cup butter	¼ cup butter, melted
16 ounces cream cheese,	Cinnamon and sugar
softened	

Make a light brown mixture of cinnamon and sugar. Cream together butter, cream cheese, egg yolks and sugar. Spread cream mixture on bread and roll-up. Brush with butter and roll in cinnamon and sugar mixture. FREEZE! Bake for 15 minutes in 400° preheated oven. Do not thaw before baking. Serve warm.

HINT: In the summer, let dough rise in your car, parked in the sun, since the house is usually cool from the air conditioner.

BREADS

REFRIGERATOR RISE BUTTER HORNS

Preparation: 30 minutes   *Can do ahead*   *Yield: 36 rolls*
Rise: 2 to 24 hours
Bake: 20 minutes

2 packages active dry yeast	**⅓ cup butter, softened**
⅔ cup warm water	**2 eggs**
½ cup evaporated milk, diluted	**6 cups unsifted flour**
with ½ cup water	**Softened butter or margarine**
⅓ cup sugar	**Melted butter or margarine**
1 ¾ teaspoons salt	

Sprinkle yeast into warm water in large, warm bowl; stir until dissolved. Add milk, sugar, salt, ⅓ cup butter, eggs and half of flour. Beat with wooden spoon about 1 minute until smooth; then beat vigorously 150 strokes, scraping sides of bowl occasionally. Gradually stir in remaining flour. Turn out on floured surface; round into ball. Knead 5 to 10 minutes or until dough is light, elastic, smooth and no longer sticky. Cover; let rise 20 minutes. Punch down. Divide dough into 3 equal portions. Roll each portion into a circle about 12 inches in diameter; spread with softened butter. Cut each into 12 pie-shaped wedges. Start rolling at wide end and roll toward point to make horn. Place on greased baking sheets with points down. Brush with melted butter. Cover. Let rise in refrigerator for 2 to 24 hours. When ready to bake, uncover and allow to stand at room temperature while oven preheats to 375°. Puncture any surface bubbles; bake for about 20 minutes or until lightly browned. Serve warm.

Note: If you want to make brown and serve rolls, underbake by about 5 minutes, then finish baking at serving time.

HINT: *Thaw frozen bread by removing plastic wrapper and placing dough in a brown bag in a 325° oven for 5 minutes.*

HINT: *Line your bread basket with foil and then cover with a napkin to keep breads warmer.*

REFRIGERATOR RISE ROLLS (BASIC RECIPE)

Preparation: 40 minutes   *Can do ahead*
Rise: 2 to 24 hours
Bake: 20 to 25 minutes

5 to 6 cups flour
2 packages active dry yeast
½ cup sugar
1 ½ teaspoons salt

½ cup softened butter <u>or</u>
  margarine
1 ½ cups hot tap water
2 eggs at room temperature
Cooking oil

Combine 2 cups flour, undissolved yeast, sugar and salt in large bowl. Stir well to blend. Add butter. Add hot tap water. Beat with electric mixer at medium speed for 2 minutes. Scrape bowl occasionally. Add eggs and 1 cup more flour. Beat with electric mixer at high speed for 1 minute or until thick and elastic. Gradually stir in just enough of remaining flour with wooden spoon to make a soft dough which leaves sides of bowl. Turn out onto floured surface. Knead 5 to 10 minutes or until dough is smooth and elastic. At this point it may be placed in a greased bowl, turning to coat all sides. Cover and refrigerate overnight. Punch down, shape as desired and let rise three hours before baking. Or you may cover with a towel. Let rest 20 minutes on board. Punch down. Divide and shape into one inch balls and place three in each greased muffin cup, or twelve in a greased 8 x 8 inch pan, or 18 in greased 9 x 13 inch pan. Brush surface of dough with cooking oil. Cover pans loosely with plastic wrap. Refrigerate 2 to 24 hours. When ready to bake, remove from refrigerator and uncover. Let stand for 10 minutes while preheating oven to 375°. Puncture bubbles on surface with oiled toothpick just before baking. Bake for 20 to 25 minutes or until done on lower oven rack. Remove from pans at once and cool on wire racks. Brush with butter or frost as desired.

HINT: To keep cornbread from sticking, heat oil to very hot and add a little cornmeal in the bottom of the pan or skillet before pouring batter.

BREADS

RICH CHRISTMAS ROLLS

Preparation: 40 minutes   *Yield: 3 dozen*
Rise: 2 to 24 hours
Bake: 20 to 25 minutes

1 recipe Refrigerator Rise   **2 teaspoons grated orange rind**
  Rolls*   **1 cup powdered sugar**
1 cup raisins   **1 to 2 tablespoons orange juice**

*Prepare recipe for Refrigerator Rise Rolls <u>except</u> use three eggs instead of two. Stir raisins and orange rind into dough after the second beating step, before kneading. When ready to shape, divide dough in half. Divide each half into 18 equal pieces. Shape each piece to look like an egg and flatten slightly. Place in greased 9 x 13 inch pans. Brush tops of rolls with oil and cover pans loosely with plastic wrap. Refrigerate as directed in basic recipe. Bake in preheated 375° oven for 25 to 30 minutes or until done. Bake on lower oven rack. Combine orange juice and powdered sugar while rolls are baking. Add juice to make frosting of spreading consistency. Remove baked rolls from pans, place on wire racks and frost while warm.

MELT-IN-YOUR-MOUTH BRAN ROLLS

Preparation: 20 minutes   *Can be frozen*   *Yield: 4 dozen rolls*
Rise: 3 ½ hours
Bake: 15 minutes

2 packages yeast   **1 cup boiling water**
1 cup water   **1 cup shortening**
⅔ cup sugar <u>or</u> ⅓ cup honey   **1 cup Miller's bran**
1 ½ teaspoons salt   **2 eggs**
6 cups flour

Dissolve yeast in warm water. Pour boiling water over shortening in mixing bowl. Stir in sugar, bran and salt until lukewarm. Beat eggs well, mix into shredded bran. Add yeast mixture and mix well. Mix in flour, let rise 2 ½ hours. Punch down and shape. Place in greased muffin pans. Let rise 1 hour. Bake for 15 minutes in preheated 375° oven.

SPECIAL YEAST ROLLS

Preparation: 30 minutes   Can be frozen   *Yield: 3 dozen*
Rise: 2 to 2 ½ hours
Bake: 15 to 20 minutes

2 cups milk, scalded
4 tablespoons shortening
1 teaspoon salt

¾ cup sugar
1 cake yeast
6 to 7 cups flour

Scald milk. Pour into large bowl. While hot, add shortening, salt and sugar. Stir. Allow to cool to lukewarm, <u>then</u> add yeast. Make sure yeast is dissolved. Add flour to make sticky dough. Cover and let rise until double in bulk, about 60 minutes. Punch down and make into Parkerhouse or Cloverleaf rolls. (Can be frozen at this point.) Let rise 1 ½ hours (for frozen) or until doubled. Bake for 15 to 20 minutes in preheated 400° oven.

OVERNIGHT COFFEE CAKE

Preparation: 20 minutes   Do ahead   *Yield: 1 cake*
Chill: Overnight
Bake: 35 to 40 minutes

¾ cup butter <u>or</u> margarine, softened
1 cup sugar
2 eggs
1 (8 ounce) carton commercial sour cream
2 cups flour
1 teaspoon baking powder

1 teaspoon baking soda
½ teaspoon salt
1 teaspoon ground nutmeg
¾ cup firmly packed brown sugar
½ cup chopped pecans <u>or</u> walnuts
1 teaspoon ground cinnamon

Combine butter and sugar; cream until light and fluffy. Add eggs and sour cream, mixing well. Combine flour, baking powder, soda, salt and nutmeg; add to batter and mix well. Pour batter into a greased and floured 9 x 13 inch baking pan. Combine brown sugar, nuts and cinnamon; mix well and sprinkle evenly over batter. Cover and chill overnight. Uncover and bake in preheated 350° oven for 35 to 40 minutes or until cake tests done.

BREADS

SHARON'S STRUDEL

Preparation 2 ½ hours
Chill: Overnight

Yield: 8 strudels

Pastry:

4 cups flour
1 pound margarine

1 pint vanilla ice cream

Filling:

1 (1 pound) box raisins
1 (16 ounce) jar apricot jam
1 (6 ounce) jar maraschino
   cherries, chopped

1 (7 ounce) can coconut
2 cups chopped nuts

Let margarine and ice cream stand at room temperature for 10 minutes. Cream together, add flour, work into a dough. Divide into 8 equal parts (balls) and refrigerate wrapped in waxed paper overnight. Next day on well-floured board, roll each ball very thin, working with one at a time. Preheat oven to 350°. Spread with jam, then other ingredients and roll up into log. Bake seam side down for 35 minutes. Sprinkle with powdered sugar, cut in one-inch slices while warm.

Note: You can change filling ingredients to suit your taste.

HINT: Brush a mixture of 1 teaspoon vinegar and 1 egg white onto the top of homemade bread during the last few minutes of baking to create a nice glossy top.

HINT: Do not overmix muffins - they will become tough and have a flat or peaked top. Stir batter only until it is barely moistened.

SOUTHERN COFFEE CAKE

Preparation: 15 minutes   *Yield: 1 cake*
Bake: 40 to 45 minutes

½ cup pecans, chopped
¼ cup sugar
½ teaspoon cinnamon
½ cup margarine
1 cup sugar
2 eggs
1 cup bananas, mashed

1 teaspoon vanilla
½ cup commercial sour cream
2 cups flour
1 teaspoon baking powder
1 teaspoon baking soda
¼ teaspoon salt

Preheat oven to 350°. Mix together pecans, sugar and cinnamon. Set aside. Combine margarine, sugar, eggs, bananas, vanilla and sour cream. Combine dry ingredients and blend with creamed mixture. Place half of mixture in a well greased bundt pan. Pour half of cinnamon mixture, pour rest of cake mixture and end with cinnamon mixture on top. Bake 40 to 45 minutes. Cool 5 minutes on wire rack before removing from pan.

CORN CHILI BREAD

Preparation: 15 minutes   *Yield: 9 to 12 servings*
Bake: 1 hour

3 ears of fresh, uncooked corn
1 cup yellow cornmeal
2 teaspoons salt
3 teaspoons baking powder
1 cup commercial sour cream

¾ cup melted butter
2 eggs, well beaten
¼ pound Monterey Jack or
   Gruyere cheese, finely diced
1 (4 ounce) can peeled green
   chilies, finely chopped

Preheat oven to 350°. Scrape kernels from corn cobs and combine with the remaining ingredients. Pour into a well-buttered 9-inch square baking dish or 2 ½ quart soufflé dish. Bake for 1 hour.

Note: Frozen corn may be substituted for fresh corn.

BREADS

CORN LIGHT BREAD

Preparation: 15 minutes   *Yield: 1 loaf*
Bake: 50 to 60 minutes

2 cups yellow corn meal   ½ teaspoon salt
½ cup sugar   ⅓ cup oil
½ cup flour   1 egg
½ teaspoon baking soda   2 cups buttermilk

Preheat oven to 350° to 375°. Combine dry ingredients. Add liquid ingredients. Pour into a loaf pan. Bake 50 to 60 minutes. Cool and slice.

OLD VIRGINIA SPOON BREAD

Preparation: 15 minutes   *Yield: 6 to 8 servings*
Bake: 30 minutes

1 cup white corn meal   2 cups boiling water
½ teaspoon salt   1 cup cream (or undiluted
1 teaspoon sugar   canned milk)
                                 2 eggs

Preheat oven to 400°. Put meal, salt and sugar in saucepan. Add boiling water and cook, stirring constantly, until thick. Remove from heat, add cream. Fold in eggs which have been beaten until thick (eggs may be separated and beaten and folded in separately, which produces a soufflé-like result). Pour into well-buttered 1 ½ quart baking dish. Bake until browned thoroughly, about 30 minutes.

HINT: *For lighter bread, use two packages of yeast instead of one.*

HINT: *It is easier to knead dough if you have rubbed your hands with oil.*

BRIOCHE LOAF

Preparation: 15 minutes   *Yield: 1 loaf*
Rise: 3 hours
Bake: 35 to 40 minutes

1 package active dry yeast   **1 teaspoon salt**
¼ cup warm milk   **½ cup butter**
1 tablespoon sugar   **2 eggs, lightly beaten**
2 cups flour

Dissolve yeast in warm milk with sugar. Combine flour and salt. Cut butter
into flour mixture. Add yeast mixture and eggs and combine. Turn out onto
lightly floured board and knead until smooth. Place in a greased bowl, turning
to coat all sides. Cover and let rise in warm place until doubled in bulk, about
1 ½ to 2 hours. Punch down, knead several times, shape into a loaf and place
in a buttered loaf pan. Cover and let rise until doubled, about 1 hour. Bake for
35 to 40 minutes in a preheated 350° oven.

CARROT LEMON BREAD

Preparation: 30 minutes   *Yield: 1 loaf*
Bake: 1 hour

3 eggs   **3 cups flour**
1 cup vegetable oil   **1 teaspoon salt**
1 ¾ cups sugar   **1 teaspoon baking soda**
2 cups shredded carrots   **½ teaspoon baking powder**
½ medium lemon

Preheat oven to 350°. Grind lemon half (pulp and peel) with blender or food
processor. Beat eggs in mixing bowl. Add oil and sugar. Mix well. Add carrots
and lemon and blend. Sift together dry ingredients, add to liquid ingredients
and mix, just to blend. Pour into a greased loaf pan and bake about 1 hour.

HINT: *Protect the muffin tin by filling the unused cups with water to prevent
scorching.*

BREADS

CHEESE BRAIDS

Preparation: 20 minutes   *Yield: 4 loaves*
Rise: Overnight
Bake: 15 to 20 minutes

Dough:

1 (8 ounce) carton commercial
   sour cream, scalded
½ cup sugar
½ cup butter or margarine,
   melted
2 packages dry yeast

1 teaspoon salt
½ cup warm water
2 eggs, beaten
4 cups flour
Filling
Glaze

Combine scalded sour cream, sugar, butter and salt. Mix well. Cool to lukewarm. Dissolve yeast in warm water in large mixing bowl, stir in sour cream mixture and eggs. Gradually stir in flour (dough will be soft). Cover tightly. Refrigerate overnight. Divide dough into 4 equal portions. Turn each portion onto heavily floured surface and knead 4 to 5 times. Roll each to 12 x 8 inch rectangle. Spread ¼ of the filling over each rectangle leaving a ½ inch margin all around. Carefully roll up jellyroll fashion beginning at long side. Firmly pinch edge and ends to seal. Carefully place on greased baking sheets, seam side down. Make 6 equally spaced x-shaped cuts across top of each loaf. Cover and let rise in warm place, free from drafts, for 1 hour or until doubled in bulk. Bake in preheated 375° oven for 15 to 20 minutes. Spread with glaze while loaves are hot.

Filling:

2 (8 ounce) packages cream
   cheese, softened
1 egg, beaten

¾ cup sugar
⅛ teaspoon salt
2 teaspoons vanilla

Combine cream cheese, egg, sugar, salt and vanilla. Process in food processor or with mixer until smooth and well blended. Makes 2 cups.

Glaze:

2 cups sifted powdered sugar
¼ cup milk

2 teaspoons vanilla

Combine sugar, milk and vanilla and mix well. Yield: 1 cup.

CRANBERRY BREAD

Preparation: 30 minutes   *Yield: 1 loaf*
Bake: 1 hour

1 cup sugar
2 cups flour
½ teaspoon baking powder
½ teaspoon baking soda
½ teaspoon salt
1 egg

2 tablespoons hot water
½ cup orange juice
1 cup fresh cranberries,
   chopped
½ cup chopped walnuts
2 tablespoons melted
   shortening or oil

Preheat oven to 350°. Sift together sugar, flour, baking powder, soda and salt. Then add egg, hot water, oil and orange juice. Blend well and then add cranberries and walnuts. Bake in greased loaf pan for 1 hour. Remove from pan after cooling slightly and put on wire rack to finish cooling.

DILLY CASSEROLE BREAD

Preparation: 20 minutes   *Yield: 1 loaf*
Rise: 2 ½ hours
Bake: 40 to 50 minutes

1 package yeast
¼ cup warm water
1 cup creamed cottage cheese,
   heated to lukewarm
2 tablespoons sugar
1 tablespoon instant minced
   onion

1 tablespoon butter
2 teaspoons dill seed
1 teaspoon salt
¼ teaspoon baking soda
1 unbeaten egg
2 ¼ to 2 ½ cups flour

Soften yeast in ¼ cup warm water. Combine cottage cheese, sugar, onion, butter, dill seed, salt, soda and egg. When yeast is dissolved and bubbly, add it to the combined mixture. Add flour until it forms a stiff dough, beating well after each addition. Knead five minutes until smooth and elastic. Cover and let rise until double in size, about 1 ½ hours. Stir down dough and turn into a greased round 8 inch casserole. Let rise until light. Bake in a preheated 350° oven for 40 to 50 minutes. Brush with butter and sprinkle with salt.

BREADS

ENGLISH MUFFIN BREAD

Preparation: 30 minutes   *Yield: 1 loaf*
Stand: 2 hours
Bake: 40 to 45 minutes

2 ½ to 3 cups flour, divided	¾ teaspoon salt
1 package active dry yeast	1 ¼ cups water
1 tablespoon sugar	Cornmeal

In large mixer bowl, combine 1 cup flour and the yeast. In saucepan, heat the sugar, salt, and water till warm, stirring to dissolve sugar. Add to the dry mixture in bowl. Beat at low speed with electric mixer for 30 seconds, scraping bowl. Beat 3 minutes at high speed. By hand, stir in enough flour to make a soft dough. Shape into ball. Place in a lightly greased bowl; turn once to grease surface. Cover; let rise until double (about 1 hour). Punch down. Cover; let rest 10 minutes. Grease a 1 quart casserole or a 9 x 5 x 3 inch loaf pan; sprinkle with cornmeal. Place dough into casserole or pan; sprinkle with cornmeal. Cover, let rise till double (45 to 60 minutes). Bake in preheated 400° oven for 40 to 45 minutes. Cover loosely with foil if top browns too quickly. Remove from pan and cool.

SWEET POPPY SEED BREAD

Preparation: 15 minutes   *Yield: 2 loaves*
Bake: 45 minutes

3 eggs	2 ¼ cups sifted flour
⅔ cup oil	1 ½ cups sugar
1 ¼ cups evaporated milk	¾ cup poppy seeds (about 4
1 teaspoon vanilla	ounces)
	4 ½ teaspoons baking powder

Preheat oven to 350°. Grease and flour two 9 x 5 inch loaf pans. Lightly beat eggs in a large mixing bowl. Add oil, milk and vanilla. Beat well. Add dry ingredients and mix until smooth. Divide batter evenly between the two pans and bake until toothpick inserted in center comes out clean, approximately 45 to 50 minutes.

Note: Decrease oven heat to 325°, if using glass loaf pans.

QUICK OATMEAL RAISIN BREAD

Preparation: 20 minutes   *Yield: 1 loaf*
Bake: 70 minutes

2 ¼ cups flour
¾ cup quick-cooking oats,
  uncooked
¼ cup whole bran cereal
¾ cup packed brown sugar
4 teaspoons baking powder
1 teaspoon salt
1 ½ teaspoons cinnamon
½ teaspoon ground cloves

2 eggs, beaten
1 ½ cups milk
½ cup vegetable oil
1 cup raisins
⅓ cup quick-cooking oats,
  uncooked
¼ cup packed brown sugar
2 tablespoons butter, melted

Combine flour, ¾ cup oats, bran cereal, brown sugar, baking powder, salt, cinnamon and cloves in a large bowl. In a separate small bowl, combine eggs, milk and oil. Make a well in center of dry ingredients; add liquid ingredients and stir just until moistened. Stir in raisins. Pour into a lightly greased and floured 9 x 5 inch loaf pan. Combine remaining ingredients; sprinkle over batter, and press gently with a fork. Bake at 325° for 70 minutes or until it tests done. Cook in pan 10 minutes; remove to cooling rack. Cool completely before slicing.

PUMPKIN BREAD

Preparation: 20 minutes   *Yield: 3 loaves*
Bake: 1 hour

3 ½ cups flour, sifted
2 teaspoons baking soda
1 ½ teaspoons salt
2 teaspoons cinnamon
1 ½ teaspoons nutmeg
3 cups sugar

4 eggs, beaten
⅔ cups water
1 cup salad oil
1 (16 ounce) can pumpkin
1 cup chopped pecans (optional)

Preheat oven to 350°. In large bowl, combine flour, soda, salt, cinnamon, nutmeg and sugar. Add the remaining ingredients and mix well. Pour mixture into 3 loaf pans until ½ full. Bake at 350° for 1 hour.

BREADS

WHOLE WHEAT BREAD

Preparation: 30 minutes   *Yield: 2 loaves*
Rise: 3 hours
Bake: 50 minutes

1 package active dry yeast
2 cups warm water
2 tablespoons sugar
2 teaspoons salt
4 cups sifted flour

½ cup hot water
½ cup brown sugar
3 tablespoons shortening
4 cups whole wheat flour

Soften yeast in warm water. Add the 2 tablespoons sugar, salt and flour. Mix until smooth. Keep in warm place until light and bubbly. Combine hot water, brown sugar and shortening. Stir and cool until lukewarm (shortening does not need to melt). Add to the flour/yeast mixture and mix slightly. Add the whole wheat flour. Mix until smooth. Turn onto floured surface and knead until smooth, about 10 minutes. Place in greased bowl. Turn over so greased side is up. Cover and let rise til double. Punch dough down. Cut in half with a sharp knife. Shape each half into a ball. Cover and let rest 10 minutes. Roll into a 10 x 14 inch rectangle. Break surface bubbles. Roll up like a jelly roll beginning with narrow end. Seal ends. Place loaves in lightly greased loaf pan. Cover, let rise until double in bulk. Bake in preheated 375° oven for 50 minutes.

ZUCCHINI BREAD

Preparation: 30 minutes   *Yield: 2 loaves*
Bake: 1 hour

3 eggs
1 cup vegetable oil
2 cups sugar
2 cups grated unpared zucchini
2 teaspoons vanilla extract
3 cups sifted flour
1 teaspoon salt

1 teaspoon baking soda
1 teaspoon baking powder
1 tablespoon cinnamon
½ teaspoon ground cloves
1 ½ teaspoons allspice
1 cup golden raisins
¾ to 1 cup chopped walnuts

Preheat oven to 350°. Beat eggs until light and foamy. Add oil and sugar; beat well. Stir in zucchini and vanilla. Mix lightly but well. Sift together sifted flour, salt, baking soda, baking powder and spices. Add to zucchini mixture and blend thoroughly. Stir in raisins and nuts. Pour batter into 2 greased and floured 9 x 5 inch loaf pans. Bake for about 1 hour.

Eggs, Cheese, Rice and Pasta

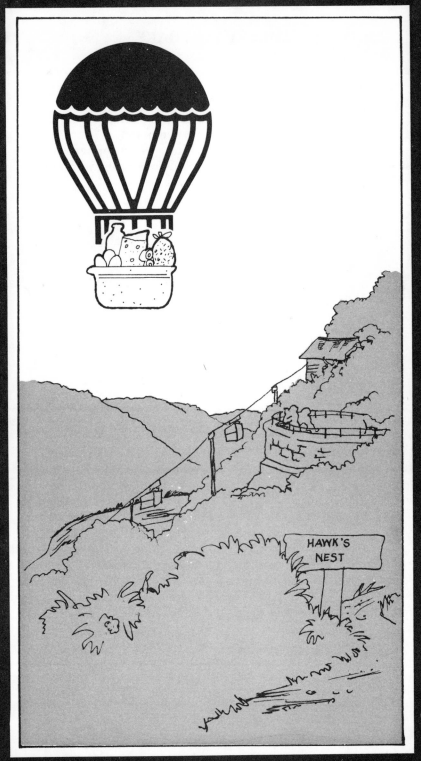

EGGS, CHEESE, RICE AND PASTA

CHEESY EGG BAKE

Preparation: 15 minutes
Bake: 15 minutes

Yield: 2 to 4 servings

1 (8 ounce) package grated
   Gruyere cheese, divided
4 eggs
2 strips bacon, fried and
   crumbled

1 teaspoon chopped chives <u>or</u>
   green onion
Ground white pepper
¼ cup fine dry bread crumbs

Preheat oven to 300°. Butter baking dish or pan. Spread half of the cheese over the bottom of the baking dish. Break the eggs and space them over the cheese. Sprinkle the bacon and chives over the eggs. Cover with the remaining cheese. Season with ground pepper to taste. Sprinkle the bread crumbs over the top. Bake in oven for 15 minutes or until mixture is set. Slightly brown the top under the broiler and serve at once.

CHEESY HAM AND EGG CUPS

Preparation: 20 minutes
Bake: 15 minutes

Yield: 12 cups

12 slices bread
3 tablespoons butter <u>or</u>
   margarine
8 eggs, beaten

¼ pound Velveeta cheese,
   cubed
1 cup finely chopped ham
2 tablespoons onion, chopped
1 teaspoon parsley flakes

Preheat oven to 350°. Trim crust from bread, butter each slice. Place each slice in the cup of a medium size muffin pan. Bake 15 minutes. Melt butter in a large skillet over low heat. Combine eggs, cheese, ham, onions and parsley. Pour into skillet. Cook slowly, stirring occasionally until eggs are cooked. Spoon into toast cups and serve.

Note: Cooked sausage or bacon may be used instead of ham.

HINT: *To keep sour cream, yogurt and cottage cheese fresher longer, store upside down in the refrigerator.*

EGGS, CHEESE, RICE AND PASTA

DUTCH BABIES

Preparation: 20 minutes   *Yield: Varies*
Bake: 20 to 25 minutes

Pan Size	Butter	Eggs	Milk and Flour
8 x 8 inch	¼ cup	3	¾ cup each
2 to 3 quart	¼ cup	3	¾ cup each
3 to 4 quart	⅓ cup	4	1 cup each
4 to 4 ½ quart	½ cup	5	1 ¼ cup each
4 ½ to 5 quart	½ cup	6	1 ½ cup each

Pinch of nutmeg

Toppings:

Classic: powdered sugar and lemon
Fruits: strawberries, peaches, etc. (sweetened)
Syrups: honey, maple, fruit
Hot fruit: apple, pear, banana, (sauté in butter, offer with cinnamon sugar,
    sour cream or yogurt)
Canned pie fillings: add lemon juice and serve with sour cream

Put butter into pan and place in 425° oven. Blend eggs at high speed for 1
minute. While blending, gradually add milk then slowly add flour. Continue
blending for 30 seconds. Remove pan from oven and pour batter into hot
melted butter. Return to oven and bake until puffy and well browned, 20 to 25
minutes depending on pan. Dust with ground nutmeg at once and serve with
any of the mentioned toppings.

Note: Pan should be fairly shallow. For example, iron frying pans or Corning
Ware

*HINT: Yogurt and sour cream are interchangeable although the flavor will
differ slightly. Yogurt is lower in calories.*

EGGS, CHEESE, RICE AND PASTA

EASY BRUNCH CASSEROLE

Preparation: 20 minutes　　　　　　　　　　*Yield: 10 servings*
Bake: 40 minutes

4 cups toasted bread cubes
1 (8 ounce) package shredded
　Cheddar cheese
8 slightly beaten eggs
4 cups milk

1 teaspoon salt
1 teaspoon prepared mustard
⅛ teaspoon pepper
10 slices bacon, crisply cooked

Preheat oven to 325°. Spread toasted bread cubes in bottom of greased baking dish. Sprinkle cheese over bread. Blend eggs, milk, salt, mustard and pepper. Pour over bread and cheese mixture. Bake until set, 30 to 35 minutes. Remove from oven and crumble bacon on top. Return to oven and continue baking 10 minutes.

FANCY EGG SCRAMBLE

Preparation: 45 minutes　　　*Can do ahead*　　　*Yield: 8 servings*
Bake: 30 minutes

9 tablespoons margarine,
　divided
2 tablespoons flour
½ teaspoon pepper
2 cups milk
1 cup shredded processed
　American cheese
1 cup diced Canadian bacon

½ cup chopped green onion
12 beaten eggs
1 (3 ounce) can sliced
　mushrooms or 4 ounces fresh
2 ½ cups soft bread crumbs
⅛ teaspoon paprika
Salt and pepper to taste

Melt 2 tablespoons margarine. Blend in 2 tablespoons flour, ½ teaspoon pepper. Add 2 cups milk. Cook and stir until bubbly. Stir in 1 cup cheese until melted. Set aside. Sauté bacon and onion in 3 tablespoons of margarine until tender but not brown. Add eggs and scramble until set. Fold mushrooms and cooked eggs into cheese sauce. Put into 12 x 7 inch baking dish. Combine remaining margarine (4 tablespoons), crumbs and paprika. Sprinkle over eggs. Cover, chill until serving time. Bake uncovered in 350° oven for 30 minutes.

Note: Pork chops can be used instead of Canadian bacon. You may also add chopped green pepper.

EGGS, CHEESE, RICE AND PASTA

HAM AND CHEESE QUICHE

Preparation: 20 minutes *Yield: 6 servings*
Bake: 40 to 45 minutes

Pastry for a 9 inch pie or
   quiche pan
½ cup milk
½ cup mayonnaise
2 eggs, slightly beaten
1 tablespoon cornstarch

1 ½ cups diced cooked ham or
   1 pound cooked and crumbled
   sausage
1 ½ cups cubed Swiss cheese
⅓ cup chopped green pepper
⅓ cup sliced green onion
Dash of pepper

Preheat oven to 350°. Line 9 inch pie or quiche pan with pastry. Bake until golden. Combine milk, mayonnaise, eggs and cornstarch. Mix until smooth. Stir in ham, cheese, green pepper, green onion and pepper. Pour into shell. Bake for 40 to 45 minutes or until knife inserted in middle is clean.

HEARTY HAM AND EGGS BAKE

Preparation: 20 minutes *Yield: 6 servings*
Bake: 30 to 40 minutes

4 eggs
½ clove garlic, crushed
2 tablespoons chopped parsley
⅔ cup grated Swiss cheese
4 tablespoons milk
Salt and pepper to taste

1 medium onion, chopped
2 tablespoons oil, divided
¼ cup diced ham
3 medium potatoes, peeled and
   coarsely grated
2 tablespoons butter

Preheat oven to 375°. Beat eggs. Add garlic, parsley, cheese, milk, salt and pepper. Sauté onion in 1 tablespoon oil until transparent, but not browned. Add sautéed onion and ham to egg mixture. Squeeze any liquid from the grated potatoes and then add them to the egg mixture. Heat remaining 1 tablespoon oil and butter in baking dish. Pour egg mixture into dish and bake 30 to 40 minutes.

HINT: *Cheese can be cut thinner with a heated knife.*

EGGS, CHEESE, RICE AND PASTA

HERBED MUSHROOM CRESCENT PIE

Preparation: 20 minutes   *Yield: 1 (9 inch) pie*
Bake: 45 minutes

1 can refrigerated crescent
  rolls
1 tablespoon butter, melted
1 pound fresh mushrooms,
  sliced
1 medium green pepper,
  chopped
3 small green onions, chopped

1 teaspoon basil
2 teaspoons parsley flakes
½ teaspoon marjoram
1 teaspoon chives
3 eggs, beaten
3 ounces Monterey Jack
  cheese, shredded
⅓ cup dry vermouth

Preheat oven to 350°. Spread dough triangles smoothly together in a 9 inch pie plate. Sauté mushrooms, green pepper and onions in the butter. Add basil, parsley, marjoram and chives. Mix well. Mix the eggs, cheese and vermouth together in a bowl. Place mushroom mixture in the pie plate. Add egg mixture. Bake for 45 minutes. Cool and slice.

SWISS EGGS

Preparation: 15 minutes   *Yield: 4 servings*
Bake: 10 minutes

3 tablespoons butter, divided
8 eggs
½ cup milk
½ teaspoon salt
⅛ teaspoon pepper

¼ teaspoon seasoned salt
¼ teaspoon oregano
1 cup grated Swiss cheese
1 tablespoon dry bread crumbs

Preheat oven to 400°. Melt 2 tablespoons butter in a heavy skillet. Beat eggs with milk, salt and pepper. Pour into skillet and cook, stirring until eggs are set but still soft. Pour into buttered, medium-sized baking dish. Sprinkle the top with seasoned salt, oregano and Swiss cheese. Dot the top with 1 tablespoon butter and sprinkle with bread crumbs. Bake for 10 minutes.

EGGS, CHEESE, RICE AND PASTA

CHEESE FONDUE

Preparation: 45 minutes   *Yield: 4 servings*

1 loaf French or Italian bread,
   cubed
1 pound Swiss cheese or
   ½ pound Gruyere cheese or
   ½ pound Ementhaler cheese
3 tablespoons flour

1 clove garlic
2 cups dry white wine
1 tablespoon lemon juice
3 tablespoons Kirsch or brandy
Nutmeg (optional)

Cut bread into cubes. Dredge cheese lightly with flour. Rub cooking pot with garlic; pour in wine. Set over moderate heat. When wine is hot, but not boiling, add lemon juice. By the handful, add cheese, stirring constantly with wooden spoon until cheese is melted. Bring to bubble stage briefly. Add Kirsch, stirring until blended. A pinch of nutmeg may be added, if desired. With fondue fork dip bread cube into cheese.

CHEESY PINEAPPLE BAKE

Preparation: 15 minutes   *Can do ahead*   *Yield: 10 to 12 servings*
Bake: 45 minutes

2 cups sugar
1 cup flour
1 teaspoon cinnamon
60 ounces pineapple chunks,
   drained

1 ½ cups grated Cheddar
   cheese, divided
½ cup butter, melted
3 dozen buttery flavored
   crackers, crushed

Preheat oven to 375°. Mix sugar, flour and cinnamon. Add pineapple and ¾ cup of cheese mixing well until coated. Pour into a buttered 9 x 13 inch pan. Pour the remaining cheese on top of casserole. Melt the butter slowly and add crackers. Cover the top of the casserole with cracker crumbs. Bake 45 minutes.

HINT: Add a tablespoon of oil to cooking water to keep spaghetti and other pasta from boiling over or sticking together.

EGGS, CHEESE, RICE AND PASTA

CHEESE STRATA

Preparation: 15 minutes　　　　*Do ahead*　　　　*Yield: 12 servings*
Stand: Overnight
Bake: 30 to 35 minutes

18 slices bread, crusts removed　　**½ teaspoon salt**
12 slices Old English cheese　　　**8 eggs**
2 cups milk　　　　　　　　　　　**½ cup grated Cheddar cheese**

Layer 6 slices of bread in the bottom of greased pan. Top with 6 slices of cheese. Repeat layers and end with a layer of bread. Mix milk, salt and eggs. Pour evenly over cheese and bread layers. Refrigerate overnight. Preheat oven to 350°. Before baking, flip over each of the six sections and top with grated cheese. Bake 30 to 35 minutes.

FRIED CHEESE—ITALIAN STYLE

Preparation: 20 minutes　　　　　　　　　　*Yield: 4 servings*
Refrigerate: 1 hour
Cook: 45 minutes

1 (16 ounce) package unsliced　　**⅔ cup seasoned fine dry bread**
**　Mozzarella cheese**　　　　　　　**　crumbs**
3 eggs, beaten　　　　　　　　　　**¼ cup cooking oil**
¼ cup flour

Cut cheese into 2 ½ x 2 ½ inch pieces. Dip in egg, then into flour, then into egg again, and finally in the bread crumbs. Place on waxed paper lined baking sheet and refrigerate one hour.

Sauce:

1 small clove garlic, minced　　　**1 teaspoon dried oregano,**
1 tablespoon cooking oil　　　　　**　crushed**
1 (28 ounce) can tomatoes,　　　　**½ teaspoon sugar**
**　cut up**　　　　　　　　　　　　　**¼ teaspoon dried basil, crushed**
¼ teaspoon salt

In heavy 2 quart saucepan, cook garlic in 1 tablespoon oil. Add tomatoes, salt, sugar, oregano and basil. Mix well. Simmer, uncovered for 45 minutes or until thick. In skillet, fry cheese in ¼ cup hot oil until browned, turning once. (Entire cooking takes 2 to 2 ½ minutes). Drain on paper towels and serve with sauce.

EGGS, CHEESE, RICE AND PASTA

GOLDEN BUCK

Preparation: 20 minutes   *Can do ahead*   *Yield: 6 servings*

1 tablespoon butter
1 small onion, minced
1 pound New York sharp
  cheese, shredded
1 egg, beaten
½ cup beer

Dash of salt
Dash of cayenne pepper
⅛ teaspoon Worcestershire
  sauce
1 (8 ounce) can tomato soup,
  undiluted

Sauté onion in butter. In top of double boiler, place onion and cheese. Stir in egg, beer, seasonings and soup. Heat thoroughly.

Note: Pour hot cheese mixture over toast or English muffin topped with soft poached egg.

NEVER FAIL CHEESE SOUFFLE

Preparation: 45 minutes   *Yield: 4 servings*
Bake: 40 minutes

3 tablespoons butter
3 tablespoons flour
1 cup milk

Salt to taste
3 eggs, separated
1 cup sharp cheese, grated

Melt butter, add flour, cook until blended and add milk. Stir until sauce thickens, add salt to taste. Remove from heat and carefully add 3 egg yolks. Return to heat and add cheese. This may be done ahead to this point. Preheat oven to 350°. Butter soufflé dish. Beat egg whites until stiff and fold in cheese sauce. Bake for 30 to 40 minutes.

HINT: *If refrigerated, cooked rice will keep up to one week. To reheat, add 2 tablespoons of liquid to each cup of rice and simmer 4 to 5 minutes over low heat.*

STRAWBERRY BLINTZ BRUNCH CASSEROLE

Preparation: 15 minutes   *Yield: 12 servings*
Bake: 1 ½ hours

Batter:

1 cup margarine, melted   3 teaspoons baking powder
½ cup sugar   ⅛ teaspoon salt
2 eggs   ¼ cup milk
1 cup flour, sifted   1 teaspoon vanilla

Filling:

2 pounds ricotta cheese   ¼ cup lemon juice
2 eggs   1 (8 ounce) package cream
¼ cup sugar   cheese, softened
⅛ teaspoon salt

Topping:

1 (8 ounce) carton commercial   1 (10 ounce) package frozen
  sour cream   sweetened strawberries,
                                   thawed <u>or</u> fresh strawberries

Preheat oven to 300°. Mix batter ingredients by hand and spoon ½ of batter into a greased 9 x 13 inch pan. Combine filling ingredients. Spread filling on batter carefully with a spatula. <u>DO NOT MIX</u>. Spread remaining batter over filling. Bake for 1 ½ hours. Serve topped with dollops of sour cream and fresh or frozen strawberries.

HINT: *To reheat pasta, place it in a pot of boiling water and cook just enough to heat it through.*

BRAZILIAN RICE

Preparation: 30 minutes   *Yield: 8 to 10 servings*
Bake: 30 to 35 minutes

¼ cup butter
4 eggs, separated
1 pound sharp Cheddar cheese,
  grated
1 cup milk
1 tablespoon chopped onion
1 tablespoon Worcestershire
  sauce

2 teaspoons salt
1 teaspoon marjoram, crushed
1 teaspoon thyme, crushed
1 teaspoon rosemary, crushed
1 (10 ounce) package frozen,
  chopped spinach, cooked and
  well drained
3 cups cooked rice

Preheat oven to 350°. Melt butter. Add beaten egg yolks, grated cheese, milk, onion and seasonings. Stir over medium heat until sauce is thickened and cheese is melted. Add the drained, cooked spinach. Combine mixture with rice. Beat egg whites until stiff, but not dry, and fold into cheese-rice mixture. Pour into greased 2 quart baking dish. Set baking dish in a pan of warm water. Bake for 30 to 35 minutes.

RICE CASSEROLE

Preparation: 15 minutes   *Yield: 8 servings*
Bake: 30 to 40 minutes

2 cups rice, uncooked
3 cups commercial sour cream
2 (4 ounce) cans chopped green
  chilies, drained
1 (4 ounce) jar pimentos

1 ¼ teaspoons salt
1 ½ teaspoons pepper
1 (12 ounce) package Monterey
  Jack cheese, sliced thin
2 teaspoons paprika

Preheat oven to 350°. Cook rice according to package directions. Mix sour cream, green chilies, pimentos, salt and pepper with rice. Layer: rice, cheese, rice. Garnish with paprika. Bake 30 to 40 minutes.

EGGS, CHEESE, RICE AND PASTA

RICE MOLNAR

Preparation: 20 minutes   *Can do ahead*   *Yield: 4 to 6 servings*
Bake: 1 ½ hours

4 to 6 strips bacon	**1 cup long grain rice**
1 onion, chopped	**1 (10 ½ ounce) can beef broth**
4 tablespoons butter	**1 can water**

Cook bacon until crisp. Drain fat. Cook onion in butter for 3 to 5 minutes; add rice and cook a few minutes. Stir in beef broth and water and add crumbled crisp bacon. Pour into 1 ½ quart baking dish. Bake at 350°for 1 ½ hours or until liquid is absorbed.

Note: This is a wonderful fix-ahead dish. Assemble it and hold until ready to pop in the oven. For variations, add sautéed fresh mushrooms, sliced celery or slivered almonds. Can substitute chicken broth. This is delicious with beef, ham and chicken.

SPICY SPANISH RICE

Preparation: 25 minutes   *Yield: 4 servings*
Cook: 30 minutes
Bake: 30 minutes

½ pound bacon	**2 tablespoons Worcestershire**
1 tablespoon bacon grease	**sauce**
½ cup chopped onion	**¼ to ½ teaspoon hot sauce**
Salt	**3 cups cooked white rice**
¼ teaspoon ground black	**1 ½ to 2 cups canned tomatoes**
pepper	**and juice**

Preheat oven to 350°. Fry bacon until crisp. Remove bacon and drain off all bacon grease except about 1 tablespoon. Sauté onion in bacon grease until golden. Crumble cooked bacon and add to onion. Add very little salt, pepper, Worcestershire sauce and hot sauce; mix well. Add rice and cut up canned tomatoes and juice. Mix well. Pour into buttered casserole and bake for about 30 minutes.

EGGS, CHEESE, RICE AND PASTA

RICE PILAF

Preparation: 10 minutes   *Yield: 6 to 8 servings*
Bake: 45 minutes

3 tablespoons olive oil   1 minced garlic clove
1 ½ cups converted rice   2 cups hot chicken broth
½ cup chopped onion   1 cup dry white wine
½ cup chopped celery   Salt and pepper to taste
¼ cup chopped fresh parsley   Pinch of dried oregano, thyme
                                  and rosemary

Preheat oven to 375°. Heat olive oil in fireproof 2 quart casserole. Add rice, onion, celery, parsley and garlic and cook for about 5 minutes, stirring frequently. Add chicken broth, wine and seasonings. Bring to a boil, then cover and bake for 30 minutes. Uncover, stir gently with a fork, cover again and continue baking about 10 additional minutes.

WILD RICE RISOTTO

Preparation: 15 to 20 minutes   *Can do ahead*   *Yield: 6 to 8 servings*
Bake: 30 to 35 minutes

1 ½ cups wild rice   3 tablespoons finely minced
3 quarts boiling water   celery
1 ½ tablespoons salt   4 tablespoons butter
3 tablespoons finely minced   1 ½ cups brown stock or
   carrots   canned beef bouillon
3 tablespoons finely minced   1 bay leaf
   onions   ¼ teaspoon thyme
                                  Salt and pepper to taste

Preheat oven to 350°. Drop the rice in boiling salted water. Boil uncovered for 5 minutes, then drain thoroughly. While the rice is boiling, cook the minced vegetables slowly in the butter in a 2 ½ quart baking casserole for 5 to 6 minutes until tender but not browned. Add the drained rice and stir over moderate heat for 2 minutes to let butter flavor permeate it. Add the stock or bouillon, bay leaf, thyme and seasonings to taste. Bring to a boil. Cover casserole and place in lower third of oven for 30 to 35 minutes or until rice is tender and has absorbed all the liquid. Add a few drops more liquid if all has been absorbed before the rice is tender. The rice grains should be separate and lightly filmed with butter. Discard bay leaf. Fluff rice with a fork and correct seasoning.

EGGS, CHEESE, RICE AND PASTA

DUMPLINGS ITALIAN STYLE

Preparation: 45 minutes   *Can do ahead*   *Yield: 4 to 6 servings*
                               Can be frozen

2 ½ cups boiled potatoes,   2 ¼ cups flour
   mashed   4 quarts boiling water with
2 eggs, lightly beaten   2 tablespoons salt
½ teaspoon salt   1 cup Parmesan cheese

Place potatoes, eggs and salt in mixing bowl and mix thoroughly. Add 1 ½ cups flour. Place dough on floured board and add rest of flour. Knead dough 3 or 4 minutes. If too sticky, add more flour. Divide dough into 6 pieces and roll into long strips. Cut into pieces ⅔ inch long. Sprinkle with flour. Place ⅓ of dumplings in boiling water and remove with strainer when they rise to the top. Place in hot serving dish and repeat, until all dumplings are cooked (keep water boiling). Add Basic Tomato Sauce <u>or</u> Chicken Cacciatori sauce and ⅔ of the cheese. Mix well. Sprinkle rest of the cheese on top.

Note: See index for sauces.

EASY SPAGHETTI BAKE

Preparation: 45 minutes   *Yield: 6 servings*
Bake: 45 minutes

2 slices bacon, cut up   1 teaspoon chili powder
2 medium onions, chopped   2 (8 ounce) cans tomato sauce
1 clove garlic, minced   3 cups water
½ pound ground beef   ½ pound spaghetti, uncooked
1 ½ teaspoons salt   1 cup shredded Cheddar cheese
¼ teaspoon pepper

In skillet fry bacon for two minutes. Stir in onions and garlic, cook until tender. Add meat and brown lightly. Stir in salt, pepper, chili powder, tomato sauce and water. Cover and simmer about 25 minutes. Preheat oven to 350°. Break half of the spaghetti into greased 2 quart casserole. Cover with half the sauce, then top with half the cheese. Repeat the layers. Cover. Bake for 30 minutes. Uncover and bake 15 minutes longer until browned and bubbly.

EGGS, CHEESE, RICE AND PASTA

FETTUCCINI ALFREDO
from
Rocco's Ristorante

Preparation: 45 minutes   *Yield: 1 serving*

¼ pound fettuccini noodles
2 tablespoons butter
  (not margarine)
⅔ cup heavy cream

⅔ cup imported Parmesan
  cheese
White pepper
Nutmeg
Parsley, chopped

Cook fettuccini according to package directions. Drain. Melt butter with cream very slowly in skillet or double boiler. Add cheese and stir. Bring this mixture to the boiling point, being careful not to burn or scorch. Add fettuccini to sauce, cook another 30 to 60 seconds to desired consistency. Top with white pepper, dash of nutmeg and chopped parsley.

HAM AND FETTUCCINI

Preparation: 30 minutes   *Yield: 4 servings*
Cook: 30 minutes

1 (12 ounce) package fettuccini,
  cooked and hot
½ cup butter
2 cups sliced cooked ham,
  cut in strips
6 to 10 mushrooms, sliced
1 medium onion, chopped
1 large tomato, seeded and
  chopped

½ cup fresh peas, if available
  (optional)
½ cup cream
2 egg yolks
¼ cup chopped fresh parsley
½ to ¾ cup grated Parmesan
  cheese, freshly grated if
  possible

Cook fettuccini according to package directions. While it is cooking sauté ham, mushrooms, onion and tomato in butter until onion is tender. Add peas. Blend cream, egg yolks, parsley, cheese and add to ham mixture. Toss with fettuccini. If sauce is too thick, a little more cream may be needed. Serve immediately.

Note: This is excellent with chicken or shrimp instead of ham.

EGGS, CHEESE, RICE AND PASTA

CLAIRE'S MACARONI RING

Preparation: 30 minutes　　　　　　　　　　　　　*Yield: 8 servings*
Bake: 1 hour

1 ½ cups cooked macaroni
1 cup diced Velveeta cheese
1 cup soft bread crumbs
1 tablespoon minced parsley
3 tablespoons minced pimento

3 tablespoons butter
1 tablespoon minced onion
1 cup scalded milk
1 egg, beaten
Salt and pepper to taste

Preheat oven to 375°. Mix together all ingredients. Bake for 1 hour in greased ring on rack over pan of hot water.

Note: Place peas or creamed meat in center, if desired.

KRAUT NOODLES

Preparation: 30 minutes　　　　*Can do ahead*　　　　*Yield: 4 servings*
Stand: 30 minutes

1 (2 pound) head green cabbage
2 tablespoons salt
4 tablespoons butter or
　margarine

2 cups chopped onions
1 (8 ounce) package broad
　noodles
Freshly ground black pepper

Chop cabbage very fine discarding core. Put in mixing bowl, add salt and let stand 30 minutes. Drain well and squeeze to remove as much moisture as possible. Heat butter in skillet and cook onions, stirring frequently, until golden brown. Add cabbage, stirring over low heat until cabbage is cooked. Cook noodles according to package directions and drain. Mix with cabbage and sprinkle on black pepper.

HINT: Place a small hole in the large end of an egg and place the egg in cold water in order to prevent the egg from cracking while it cooks.

EGGS, CHEESE, RICE AND PASTA

MAC N' CHEESE PIE

Preparation: 45 minutes   *Yield: 8 servings*
Bake: 50 minutes

Pastry:

1 cup flour
½ teaspoon salt
⅓ cup shortening

½ cup shredded Cheddar
    cheese
4 or 5 tablespoons iced water

Preheat oven to 425°. In medium bowl combine flour and salt. With pastry blender or two knives used scissor fashion, cut in shortening until mixture resembles coarse crumbs; stir in cheese. Gradually add water and stir with fork until flour is moistened and pastry almost cleans side of bowl. Shape pastry into a ball. On lightly floured surface roll pastry into an 11 inch circle. Line 9 inch pie plate with pastry; flute edges. Prick bottom and sides with fork. Bake for 15 minutes; set aside.

Sauce:

¼ cup butter or margarine
¼ cup flour
2 cups milk
2 tablespoons chopped parsley
1 teaspoon salt

⅛ teaspoon cayenne pepper
1 (3 ounce) package cream
    cheese
2 cups shredded Cheddar
    cheese
1 ½ cups cooked and drained
    elbow macaroni

Melt butter in saucepan over low heat, add flour and stir until smooth and bubbly. Gradually add milk, stirring constantly. Cook until sauce is thick; add parsley, salt and pepper. Remove sauce from heat. Add cream cheese and 1 ¼ cups Cheddar cheese (reserve remaining Cheddar for topping) and stir until cheeses have melted. Add macaroni to sauce and stir. Pour mixture into partially baked pie shell. Reduce oven temperature to 350° and bake for 20 minutes. Sprinkle remaining Cheddar on top and bake 10 to 15 more minutes.

HINT: *To freeze egg yolk - add $\frac{1}{16}$ teaspoon salt to each yolk. To freeze egg whites - just place them in a small container and freeze.*

EGGS, CHEESE, RICE AND PASTA

SHELLS ALLA SALSA DI COMODORI

Preparation: 1 hour
Simmer: 3 hours
Bake: 35 minutes

Yield: 8 to 10 servings

Sauce:

1 pound ground pork
1 pound ground beef
2 cloves garlic
1 teaspoon salt
¼ teaspoon pepper

1 teaspoon oregano
1 green pepper, chopped
1 (12 ounce) can tomato paste
2 to 3 cans of water

Brown beef and pork. Drain. Add garlic, salt, pepper, oregano, green pepper, tomato paste and water. Simmer 3 hours in covered pan until thick. Thin with water if necessary. Remove garlic cloves.

1 (12 ounce) box <u>large</u>
pasta shells
1 pound cottage cheese,
drained
1 egg, beaten lightly
½ cup Mozzarella cheese,
shredded
½ cup Parmesan cheese, grated

½ cup Cheddar cheese,
shredded
½ onion, chopped
1 stalk celery, chopped
1 tablespoon butter
1 (10 ounce) box chopped
frozen spinach, drained

Mixture:

Cook shells according to package directions. In large bowl mix cottage cheese, egg and cheeses. Sauté onion and celery in butter and add to bowl. Squeeze spinach, add and mix. Preheat oven to 350°. Stuff shells with cheese mixture and place in large baking dish. Pour sauce over top and bake 35 minutes.

Note: Sauce may be prepared one week ahead.

HINT: Do not freeze dishes containing hard boiled egg whites as they will toughen.

MACARONI AND CHEESE SOUFFLÉ

Preparation: 45 minutes   *Yield: 6 to 8 servings*
Bake: 50 minutes

½ cup dried macaroni
3 tablespoons butter or
   margarine
1 cup soft bread cubes
1 ½ cups milk

2 cups shredded Cheddar
   cheese
1 tablespoon grated onion
½ teaspoon salt
3 eggs, separated
¼ teaspoon cream of tartar

Cook macaroni in salted water and drain. Preheat oven to 350°. Add margarine or butter to macaroni. Set aside. Heat milk and add bread cubes. Add shredded cheese. Let stand until soft and melted. Add grated onion and salt. Combine macaroni, milk, bread and shredded cheese. Beat 3 egg yolks and add to above mixture. Beat 3 egg whites stiffly with cream of tartar. Fold gently into above mixture. Pour into ungreased soufflé dish. Bake for 50 minutes.

SPAGHETTI PIZZA

Preparation: 30 minutes   *Can do ahead*   *Yield: 2 (9 x 13) pans or*
                          Can be frozen   *4 (9 x 9) pans*

1 (1 pound) box of spaghetti
2 eggs, beaten
½ cup milk

Garlic powder (generous dash)
3 cups shredded Mozzarella
   cheese

Break spaghetti into 3 pieces and cook according to package directions. Drain. Combine eggs, milk, garlic powder and cheese. Toss with spaghetti. Spread into greased pans. Bake at 350° for 15 minutes.

Sauce:

2 pounds ground beef
2 (48 ounce) jars spaghetti
   sauce
½ teaspoon oregano

½ teaspoon basil
Pepperoni slices
Shredded Mozzarella cheese

Brown ground beef in large skillet or Dutch oven. Drain. Add spaghetti sauce, oregano and basil. Simmer 10 minutes. Spread over baked spaghetti. (At this point the casserole may be frozen). Return to room temperature before continuing. Top with pepperoni slices and lots of Mozzarella cheese. Bake at 350° for 30 minutes. Let stand five minutes before cutting into squares.

SPINACH EGG PASTA
from
Rocco's Ristorante

Preparation: 1 hour or longer　　　　　　　　*Yield: 4 servings*
Stand: 20 minutes

4 cups flour
4 eggs
4 tablespoons olive oil
Pinch of salt

1 (10 ounce) package frozen, chopped spinach; thawed and drained to make ½ cup liquid

In bowl, put 4 cups flour and make a "well" in the middle. Put eggs, olive oil, salt and spinach in blender or food processor, until puréed. Place mixture in "well". With fork, start mixing until dough becomes firm. If too wet, add a little flour. If too dry, add a little olive oil. Let set 20 minutes to rest, covered. Divide into 4 pieces. Roll out each piece at a time until very thin. Cut noodles to desired width. Boil in salted water 2 to 3 minutes only until done.

VEGETABLE LASAGNA

Preparation: 30 minutes　　*Can do ahead*　　*Yield: 8 to 12 servings*
Bake: 40 to 60 minutes　　*Can be frozen*

1 large onion, chopped
1 to 2 garlic cloves, minced
4 tablespoons oil
½ pound mushrooms, sliced
1 (15 ounce) can tomato sauce
1 (6 ounce) can tomato paste
1 (1 pound) can stewed
　tomatoes, drained
1 teaspoon sugar
1 teaspoon salt
Dash of pepper

½ teaspoon basil
½ teaspoon oregano
2 (10 ounce) packages frozen
　chopped spinach, cooked
12 lasagna noodles, cooked
1 (1 ½ pound) carton cottage
　cheese or ricotta cheese
2 eggs
½ pound Mozzarella cheese,
　shredded
¾ cup grated Parmesan or
　Romano cheese

Preheat oven to 375°. Sauté onion and garlic in 2 tablespoons oil. Add mushrooms, cook until tender. Stir in tomato sauce, tomato paste, stewed tomatoes and seasonings. Simmer 5 minutes. Stir in spinach. Put 6 lasagna noodles in greased 9 x 13 inch baking dish. Spoon on half the tomato-spinach mixture. Mix the ricotta cheese with eggs and Mozzarella. Spoon cheese mixture on top of tomato mixture. Sprinkle with ½ the Parmesan. Repeat layers. Lasagna may be covered and refrigerated at this point. Bake uncovered for 40 minutes.

Vegetables

VEGETABLES

ARTICHOKE PIQUANT

Preparation: 20 minutes　　　*Can do ahead*　　　*Yield: 5 to 6 servings*

2 (9 ounce) packages frozen
　artichoke hearts
¾ cup mayonnaise
¼ cup milk
2 tablespoons chopped parsley

2 tablespoons lemon juice
1 tablespoon grated onion
¼ teaspoon Worcestershire
　sauce
2 hard-boiled eggs, chopped
　(optional)

Cook frozen artichoke hearts as directed. Drain. In a saucepan, slowly heat mayonnaise, milk, parsley, lemon juice, onion and Worcestershire sauce. DO NOT BOIL. Arrange artichokes in oblong casserole. Pour sauce over artichokes. Can be done ahead and reheated slowly. Sprinkle chopped eggs on top if desired.

Note: 2 (14 ½ ounce) cans of artichoke hearts, drained, may be substituted for frozen artichoke hearts.

ASPARAGUS-ALMOND CASSEROLE

Preparation: 30 minutes　　　*Can do ahead*　　　*Yield: 6 to 8 servings*
Cook: 35 to 40 minutes

1 ½ cups round buttery
　cracker crumbs
½ cup finely chopped almonds
6 tablespoons butter
1 (10 ¾ ounce) can mushroom
　soup, undiluted

¾ cup liquid from asparagus
1 ½ cups grated Cheddar
　cheese
1 to 2 teaspoons Worcester-
　shire sauce
2 (10 ½ ounce) cans asparagus
　tips

Preheat oven to 350°. Combine cracker crumbs and almonds, set aside. Combine butter, soup, liquid, cheese and Worcestershire sauce in saucepan. Heat until blended and smooth. Alternate layers of asparagus, sauce and cracker crumbs making two layers of each. Bake 35 to 40 minutes.

MRS. BURTON'S BAKED BEANS

Preparation: 15 minutes   *Can do ahead*   *Yield: 8 to 10 servings*
Cook: 1 hour

1 pound lean hamburger
1 medium onion, chopped
1 (46 ounce) can pork and
   beans
½ teaspoon salt

½ teaspoon pepper
2 tablespoons sugar
2 tablespoons vinegar
½ cup ketchup
2 teaspoons chili powder

Preheat oven to 300°. Brown meat and onions, add other ingredients. Bake in uncovered casserole for approximately one hour. This can be cooked at 350° for less time if necessary. Should not be runny but have a nice consistency to the sauce when ready to serve.

LUMBERJACK BEANS

Preparation: 10 minutes   *Can do ahead*   *Yield: 10 to 12 servings*
Cook: 1 hour

6 to 8 slices of bacon,
   browned and crumbled
¾ cup brown sugar
¼ cup cider vinegar
1 teaspoon mustard
1 teaspoon ginger
1 teaspoon salt
1 small onion, chopped

1 (16 ounce) can butter beans,
   drained
1 (16 ounce) can lima beans,
   drained
1 (16 ounce) can kidney beans,
   drained
1 (16 ounce) can pork and beans

Combine brown sugar, vinegar, dry mustard, ginger, salt and chopped onion in saucepan and simmer for 30 minutes. Preheat oven to 350°. Mix bacon, vinegar mixture and beans together. Put in casserole and bake for 1 hour. This can be put in a crockpot, turn on low and heat for 4 hours.

HINT: In addition to seasonings, add a leaf of lettuce to canned peas for better flavor.

VEGETABLES

TART GREEN BEANS WITH BACON

Preparation: 30 minutes   *Yield: 4 servings*
Cook: 20 minutes

1 pound half-runner green
   beans (frozen <u>or</u> canned
   green beans may be
   substituted for fresh)
4 slices bacon cut in ½ inch
   pieces, cooked crisp
⅓ cup finely chopped onion

2 tablespoons vinegar
2 tablespoons water
2 tablespoons sugar
¼ teaspoon salt
¼ teaspoon monosodium
   glutamate
Dash of pepper

Wash, cut off ends and cut green beans into cross-wise pieces. Cook 15 to 20 minutes in water until tender. Meanwhile, fry bacon until crisp. Add onion, vinegar, water, sugar, salt, monosodium glutamate and pepper to bacon and drippings in skillet. Bring to a boil. Drain cooked beans. Pour bacon mixture over beans and toss lightly together.

CHEESE AND ONION GREEN BEANS

Preparation: 15 minutes   *Yield: 4 servings*
Cook: 15 minutes

1 pound fresh green beans,
   cut into bite size pieces
1 (1 ⅜ ounce) envelope dry
   onion soup mix
1 cup water

2 to 3 tablespoons butter <u>or</u>
   margarine
¼ cup slivered almonds
3 tablespoons grated Parmesan
   cheese
Paprika

Combine green beans, onion soup mix, and water in a medium saucepan. Cook over low heat until the beans are tender, approximately 10 to 15 minutes. Drain. Cut butter into small pieces. Stir in the butter, almonds and cheese. Put the beans in a serving dish and sprinkle with paprika.

Note: Frozen green beans may be substituted for fresh beans.

THREE VEGETABLE CASSEROLE

Preparation: 30 minutes   *Can do ahead*   *Yield: 6 servings*
Cook: 20 minutes

1 (9 ounce) package frozen
cut green beans
1 (10 ounce) package frozen
Fordhook lima beans
1 (10 ounce) package frozen
peas

½ cup commercial sour cream
½ cup mayonnaise
⅓ cup grated Parmesan cheese
⅛ teaspoon paprika

Preheat oven to 325°. Cook green beans, lima beans and peas separately as directed on labels; drain. Combine sour cream and mayonnaise and mix with vegetables. Put in shallow 2 quart baking dish and sprinkle with cheese and paprika. Bake 20 minutes.

BURGUNDY BEANS

Preparation: 30 minutes   *Can do ahead*   *Yield: 6 to 8 servings*
Cook: 45 minutes

4 slices bacon, cut in
½ inch pieces
1 large onion, chopped
½ green pepper, chopped
1 clove garlic, minced
1 teaspoon dry mustard

1 tablespoon dark brown sugar
1 cup good Burgundy wine
1 (8 ounce) can tomato sauce
2 (28 ounce) cans kidney beans,
drained
Salt and pepper

Preheat oven to 350°. Fry bacon until crisp. Remove bacon from pan. Add onion, green pepper and garlic to bacon drippings in pan. Cook over low heat until tender without browning. Stir in bacon, mustard, brown sugar, Burgundy wine, tomato sauce and beans in a 2 quart bean pot or casserole. Season to taste with salt and pepper. Bake for about 45 minutes.

HINT: *When cooking okra, add lemon juice or vinegar to the water to eliminate a slimy texture.*

VEGETABLES

LIMA BEANS AND SOUR CREAM

Preparation: 20 minutes *Yield: 6 to 8 servings*
Cook: 20 minutes

2 (10 ounce) packages frozen
   lima beans
½ pint commercial sour cream
1 small onion, chopped

1 (2 ounce) can pimentos
½ cup margarine
1 teaspoon sugar

Cook beans according to package directions, drain. Sauté onion in margarine. Add pimentos, sour cream and sugar. Heat through. Pour over beans and mix. Serve immediately.

BEETS A L'ORANGE

Preparation: 10 minutes *Yield: 4 to 6 servings*
Cook: 10 minutes

4 tablespoons orange peel
   cut in tiny slivers
2 tablespoons butter
2 tablespoons flour
1 tablespoon honey

2 tablespoons light brown sugar
1 cup orange juice
2 teaspoons lemon juice
½ teaspoon salt
3 cups shoestring style beets

Boil slivered orange peel in salted water for two minutes and drain. Set aside. Melt butter and stir in flour. Add honey, brown sugar, orange juice, lemon juice and salt. Cook until thick stirring constantly. Add orange peel and the shoestring beets.

PICKLED BEETS

Preparation: 10 minutes *Can do ahead* *Yield: 4 servings*
Cook: 5 minutes

1 (16 ounce) can sliced beets
   and liquid
¼ cup brown sugar

8 to 10 whole cloves
¼ cup vinegar
1 small piece of bay leaf

Add sugar, cloves, vinegar and bay leaf to the sliced beets and liquid in a small saucepan. Bring to a boil, and boil gently 5 minutes. Remove cloves and bay leaf. Can be served hot or refrigerated covered in the liquid. To serve hot or cold drain the liquid off the beets and serve.

BACON BROCCOLI

Preparation: 20 minutes   *Yield: 4 servings*
Cook: 5 minutes

6 strips of bacon, fried until   **3 stalks fresh broccoli, cleaned**
crisp, reserve drippings   **and cut into flowerets**
                                          ¼ to ½ cup water

Fry bacon in large skillet until crisp. Remove bacon and add fresh broccoli to bacon drippings. Stir fry adding water. Cook 5 minutes or until desired doneness. Remove from pan and crumble bacon over broccoli. Toss lightly.

BROCCOLI CASSEROLE SUPREME

Preparation: 20 minutes   *Can do ahead*   *Yield: 8 servings*
Cook: 20 to 25 minutes

4 cups broccoli cut into 1 inch   **¾ cup commercial sour cream**
pieces (trim and peel stalks)   **1 cup sliced (on bias) celery**
1 (10 ¾ ounce) can cream of   **½ teaspoon pepper**
mushroom soup, undiluted   **1 teaspoon salt**
1 cup sliced fresh mushrooms   **1 cup grated Cheddar cheese**
1 (2 ounce) jar chopped
pimentos

Preheat oven to 350°. Cook broccoli. Drain. Add mushroom soup, fresh mushrooms, pimentos, sour cream, celery, pepper and salt. Put in greased casserole. Top with Cheddar cheese. Bake 20 to 25 minutes.

ITALIAN BROCCOLI CASSEROLE

Preparation: 10 minutes   *Can do ahead*   *Yield: 6 to 8 servings*
Cook: 30 minutes

2 (10 ounce) packages frozen   **½ teaspoon dried oregano**
cut broccoli   **1 (8 ounce) can stewed**
2 beaten eggs   **tomatoes, cut up**
1 (11 ounce) can condensed   **3 tablespoons grated Parmesan**
Cheddar cheese soup   **cheese**

Preheat oven to 350°. Cook broccoli in unsalted boiling water 5 to 7 minutes; drain well. Combine eggs, Cheddar cheese soup and oregano. Stir in stewed tomatoes and cooked broccoli. Put the vegetable-cheese mixture into a 10 x 6 x 2 inch baking dish. Sprinkle with Parmesan cheese. Bake uncovered for 30 minutes.

VEGETABLES

BROCCOLI WITH SESAME SEEDS

Preparation: 30 minutes　　　　　　　　　　　　*Yield: 6 servings*
Cook: 10 minutes

1 bunch fresh broccoli
2 tablespoons sesame seeds
3 tablespoons vegetable oil
2 teaspoons minced onions
1 (8 ounce) can sliced water
　chestnuts

3 tablespoons white wine
3 tablespoons soy sauce
½ teaspoon sugar
¼ teaspoon garlic salt

Clean and trim broccoli into bite size pieces. Discard tough ends and lower stalks. Set aside clean broccoli. Toast sesame seeds in wok or skillet; remove and set aside. Pour oil into wok or skillet. Add broccoli, stir fry 2 minutes. Add onion, water chestnuts, wine, soy sauce, sugar and garlic salt. Mix well. Cover and cook until desired doneness. Sprinkle sesame seeds over top.

NUTTY BRUSSELS SPROUTS WITH CHEESE

Preparation: 10 minutes　　　　　　　　　　　　*Yield: 8 servings*
Cook: 30 minutes

2 pounds small tight
　Brussels sprouts
12 tablespoons butter

Salt
Pepper
2 cups grated Parmesan cheese

Wash the sprouts and discard any shrivelled outer leaves. Without drying, place sprouts in hot, melted butter in a saucepan. Sprinkle with salt and a dash of black pepper; cover, turn heat very low and let sprouts cook in their own steam for at least 30 minutes. Sprouts should be nutty and not at all soggy. Place in heated bowl and sprinkle with cheese.

HINT: *Dried beans cooked in salted water may become tough and the skins will come off; add salt when beans are tender.*

COLCANNON (IRISH CABBAGE)

Preparation: 25 minutes 　　*Can do ahead* 　　*Yield: 4 servings*
Cook: 20 minutes

1 large onion, coarsely chopped
¼ cup butter <u>or</u> margarine
　(divided)
1 cup mashed potatoes
1 cup chopped cooked cabbage

Salt
Pepper
½ cup dry bread crumbs
½ cup grated sharp Cheddar
　cheese

Preheat oven to 350°. Sauté onion in 1 tablespoon butter until translucent. Add potatoes, cabbage and 1 tablespoon butter to the onions. Cook about 5 minutes until heated through; stirring frequently. Add salt and pepper to taste. Spread the vegetable mixture in a shallow greased baking dish. Sprinkle with crumbs; dot with remaining 2 tablespoons of butter; sprinkle with cheese. Bake for 20 minutes or until brown.

GERMAN RED CABBAGE

Preparation: 15 to 20 minutes 　　　　*Yield: 10 to 12 servings*
Cook: 45 minutes

1 small head of red cabbage
5 McIntosh apples
2 tablespoons sugar
1 cup red wine

Pinch of ground cloves
2 tablespoons vinegar
2 tablespoons red currant jelly
Flour

Wash cabbage; drain and cut as for cole slaw. Wash, core and peel apples. Cut into small pieces. Combine cabbage, apples, sugar, wine and cloves in a saucepan. Cover and simmer for about 45 minutes or until tender. At the end of the cooking time add vinegar and jelly. Mix well. Just before serving, sprinkle a little flour on top to absorb liquid.

HINT: Fresh mushrooms should be wiped with a damp paper towel; they absorb water easily.

VEGETABLES

SCALLOPED CABBAGE

Preparation: 1 hour　　　*Can do ahead*　　　*Yield: 8 to 10 servings*
Cook: 30 to 45 minutes

1 to 1 ½ heads cabbage	3 cups grated Cheddar cheese
1 small onion, chopped	½ cup margarine
Seasoning salt to taste	½ cup flour
Seasoning pepper to taste	3 cups milk
¼ teaspoon monosodium	Bread crumbs
glutamate	¼ cup margarine

Cut up cabbage and cook in boiling salted water. Drain. Place cabbage in greased 9 x 13 inch casserole. Place chopped onion on top of cabbage. Sprinkle with salt, pepper and monosodium glutamate. Add grated cheese; set aside. Preheat oven to 350°. Melt ½ cup margarine and add flour. Slowly add milk, stirring constantly until thick. Pour over cabbage mixture. Top with bread crumbs that have been tossed in ¼ cup melted margarine. Bake for 30 to 45 minutes or until bubbly.

CARROT BAKE

Preparation: 25 minutes　　　*Can do ahead*　　　*Yield: 8 servings*
Cook: 20 to 25 minutes

3 pounds carrots	Buttered bread crumbs
2 cups mayonnaise	Paprika
2 tablespoons minced onions	Chopped parsley
2 tablespoons prepared	
horseradish	

Preheat oven to 375°. Peel, slice lengthwise and cook the carrots until tender. Drain, saving ½ cup of the liquid. Mix mayonnaise, minced onions, horseradish and the cooled carrot liquid. Place carrots in a 9 x 13 inch buttered baking dish. Spread the mixture over the carrots. Toss buttered bread crumbs with parsley and paprika and sprinkle over top. Bake for 20 to 25 minutes.

HINT: Marjoram adds a nice flavor to cooked carrots.

CARROT CASSEROLE

Preparation: 30 minutes   *Can do ahead*   *Yield: 8 servings*
Cook: 1 hour

2 cups mashed cooked carrots (about 2 pounds fresh)	1 cup soft butter
1 cup cracker crumbs	¼ cup grated onion
1 cup milk	1 teaspoon salt
¾ cup grated sharp Cheddar cheese	¼ teaspoon pepper
	⅛ teaspoon cayenne pepper
	3 eggs

Preheat oven to 350°. Combine carrots, crumbs, milk, cheese, butter, onion and seasonings. Beat eggs until slightly puffy. Fold into carrot mixture. Pour into well-greased 1 ½ quart casserole. Bake for 1 hour.

Note: This recipe may be baked in a well-greased ring mold, decreasing baking time to 45 to 50 minutes.

GLAZED CARROTS

Preparation: 25 minutes   *Can do ahead*   *Yield: 6 servings*
Cook: 40 minutes

1 ½ pounds carrots, peeled, quartered and cut into 2 inch lengths (about 5 ½ cups)	2 tablespoons sugar
	Pinch of pepper
1 ½ cups good brown stock <u>or</u> canned beef bouillon	6 tablespoons butter
	Salt and pepper
	2 tablespoons finely minced parlsey

Boil the carrots slowly in a covered 3 quart saucepan (enameled, heavy-bottomed) with the stock or bouillon, sugar, pepper and butter for 30 to 40 minutes or until the carrots are tender and the liquid has reduced to a syrupy glaze. Correct seasoning. When ready to serve, reheat and roll the carrots gently in the pan to coat them with syrup. Transfer to a hot vegetable dish or arrange around meat, and sprinkle with parsley.

HINT: *Use warm milk when making mashed potatoes to prevent lumps.*

VEGETABLES

CARROT SOUFFLÉ

Preparation: 30 to 45 minutes *Yield: 6 servings*
Cook: 45 minutes

1 pound carrots, peeled
  and sliced
½ cup melted butter
3 tablespoons flour

1 teaspoon baking powder
3 eggs
1 cup sugar
3 tablespoons vanilla

Preheat oven to 350°. In a covered pan, cook peeled and sliced carrots until tender in boiling salted water. Drain and combine carrots and butter in blender (or food processor) until smooth. Add flour, baking powder, eggs, sugar and vanilla and blend well. Spoon mixture into greased 1 quart casserole dish. Bake for 45 minutes until firm.

SCALLOPED CARROTS AND CELERY

Preparation: 30 minutes *Can do ahead* *Yield: 6 servings*
Cook: 30 minutes

3 cups diced carrots
1 ½ cups diced celery
4 tablespoons butter or
  margarine
4 tablespoons flour
½ teaspoon salt

Dash of white pepper
2 cups milk
½ cup grated cheese
½ cup bread crumbs
Parmesan cheese

Cook carrots and celery together in water in saucepan until tender. Drain. Set aside. Preheat oven to 375°. Make white sauce by melting butter in saucepan over low heat. Blend in flour, salt and dash of white pepper. Add milk all at once, stirring constantly. Cook quickly, stirring constantly until mixture thickens and bubbles. Add cheese and bread crumbs to sauce mixture. Fill a well greased 9 x 13 inch baking dish or a 2 quart casserole with alternate layers of vegetables and white sauce. Sprinkle with Parmesan cheese. Cover and bake for 30 minutes.

HINT: *Use hard-boiled egg slicer to slice fresh mushrooms.*

CORN FRITTERS

Preparation: 20 minutes   *Yield: 4 servings*

1 cup corn (not creamed)   ¼ teaspoon pepper
1 egg yolk   1 egg white, beaten to form
3 tablespoons flour   stiff peaks
½ teaspoon salt   ½ cup oil

Combine corn, egg yolk, flour, salt and pepper. Gently fold in egg white. Heat oil in heavy skillet. Drop 1 tablespoon of batter per fritter into hot oil. Cook and turn. Watch for burning. Add more oil to pan as needed. Drain on paper towel.

DELICIOUS CORN PUDDING

Preparation: 15 minutes   *Can do ahead*   *Yield: 10 to 12 servings*
Cook: 1 hour

2 (16 ounce) cans cream   1 (4 ounce) can pimentos,
  style corn   chopped
2 tablespoons sugar   2 tablespoons flour
2 tablespoons melted butter   2 eggs, beaten
                                 ½ pound grated Cheddar cheese

Preheat oven to 350°. Mix together corn, sugar, butter, pimentos, flour and eggs. Put half of the corn mixture in greased baking dish. Sprinkle half the cheese on corn. Add remaining corn mixture and top with remaining cheese. Bake one hour.

GRANNY'S CORN PUDDING

Preparation: 15 minutes   *Can do ahead*   *Yield: 4 servings*
Cook: 50 to 60 minutes

2 eggs   1 (17 ounce) can whole kernel
⅓ cup sugar   corn, drained
3 tablespoons flour   ¼ cup melted butter or
Pinch of salt   margarine
1 cup milk

Preheat oven to 350°. Beat eggs slightly, add sugar. Mix well. Stir in flour and salt. Mix well. Add milk, corn and butter, mixing well after each addition. Pour into 1 quart casserole. Bake 50 to 60 minutes depending on depth of casserole.

VEGETABLES

GOURMET CORN ON THE COB

Preparation: 15 minutes   *Yield: 6 servings*
Cook: 15 to 20 minutes

6 ears of corn   **½ teaspoon salt**
½ cup butter, softened   **Dash of pepper**
1 tablespoon prepared mustard   **Snipped parsley**
1 teaspoon prepared
** horseradish**

Combine butter, mustard, horseradish, salt, pepper and parsley. Cream until light and fluffy. Spread mixture over corn. Wrap aluminum foil securely around each ear. Don't seal seam, rather fold or twist around ears (that way corn will roast instead of steam). Cook about 15 to 20 minutes on grill or about 1 hour at 350° in oven.

EGGPLANT CASSEROLE

Preparation: 30 minutes   *Can do ahead*   *Yield: 6 to 8 servings*
Cook: 30 minutes

1 medium eggplant, peeled   **1 medium onion, chopped**
** and diced**   **¾ cup grated Cheddar cheese**
1 cup milk   **Salt and pepper to taste**
2 eggs   **Buttered cracker crumbs**
2 slices white bread broken
** into small pieces**

Cook peeled and diced eggplant in boiling salted water for 15 minutes. Drain well. Preheat oven to 375°. Beat eggs and add milk. Soak broken bread in egg and milk mixture. Add onion, cheese, salt and pepper. Stir to mix. Add drained eggplant to egg and milk mixture. Mix well. Place in a greased 1 quart casserole. Cover mixture with buttered cracker crumbs. Bake for approximately 30 minutes.

EGGPLANT CRUNCH CASSEROLE

Preparation: 15 minutes   *Can do ahead*   *Yield: 6 to 8 servings*
Cook: 25 to 30 minutes

1 pound eggplant, pared and
  cubed (6 cups)
1 cup chopped celery
½ cup chopped green pepper
4 tablespoons butter

1 (8 ounce) can tomato sauce
4 ounces sharp cheese
1 ½ cups coarsely crushed
  corn chips

In a large skillet or saucepan, cook eggplant, celery, onion and green pepper in butter until tender (about 15 minutes). Preheat oven to 350°. Stir in tomato sauce, cheese and 1 cup of the crushed corn chips. Turn into 1 ½ quart casserole. Bake covered for 25 to 30 minutes until heated through. Before serving, top with remaining ½ cup corn chips.

ITALIAN VEGETABLE PIE

Preparation: 30 minutes   *Can do ahead*   *Yield: 8 to 10 servings*
Cook: 40 to 45 minutes

1 eggplant, peeled and cubed
2 medium zucchini, cubed
1 large onion, chopped
¼ cup oil
4 tomatoes, peeled and
  chopped
½ pound sliced mushrooms
3 eggs

¾ cup Parmesan cheese divided
  into 3 portions
1 tablespoon parsley
¼ teaspoon basil
½ teaspoon oregano
Salt and pepper to taste
¼ pound Mozzarella cheese

Sauté eggplant, zucchini and onion in oil until soft. Add tomatoes and mushrooms. Cover, simmer for 20 minutes. Preheat oven to 350°. Beat eggs with ¼ cup Parmesan cheese, parsley, basil and oregano. Add to vegetables. Pour half the mixture into a greased 9 inch pie plate. Top with ¼ cup Parmesan cheese. Layer with remaining vegetables and ¼ cup Parmesan cheese. Top with Mozzarella cheese. Bake uncovered 40 to 45 minutes or until set and brown on top.

VEGETABLES

MUSHROOM CHEESE PIE

Preparation: 30 minutes   *Can do ahead*   *Yield: 6 servings*
Cook: 45 minutes
Stand: 15 minutes

Pastry for 1 crust pie
1 tablespoon chopped onion
1 cup grated Cheddar cheese
1 pound fresh mushrooms
  sliced, sautéed and drained
  (or 2 (6 ounce) cans sliced
  mushrooms, drained)

½ cup milk
1 cup light cream
3 eggs, beaten
½ teaspoon Worcestershire
  sauce
½ teaspoon salt
Dash pepper

Preheat oven to 375°. Line 9 inch pie pan with crust pastry. Spread onion, cheese and mushrooms in pie shell. In a small saucepan, heat milk and cream until film forms on surface. Slowly pour hot milk into beaten eggs, stirring constantly. Season with Worcestershire sauce, salt and pepper. Pour into pie shell. Bake for 45 to 50 minutes or until center seems firm. Let stand 15 minutes.

SOUR CREAM MUSHROOMS

Preparation: 15 to 20 minutes   *Yield: 4 servings*
Cook: 10 minutes plus broil

1 pound fresh mushrooms
3 tablespoons butter
3 tablespoons minced onion
½ teaspoon salt
¼ teaspoon pepper

8 ounces commercial sour
  cream blended with 1
  teaspoon flour
Grated Parmesan cheese
Bread crumbs for topping

Wash and clean mushrooms. Simmer with butter, onion, salt and pepper in a tightly covered pan until transparent (about 10 minutes). Pour into a medium sized baking dish and cover with the sour cream. Sprinkle with the Parmesan cheese and bread crumbs for topping. Brown under broiler or in a very hot oven for a few minutes.

STUFFED MUSHROOMS

Preparation: 45 minutes   *Can do ahead*   *Yield: 4 servings*
Cook: 15 minutes

8 whole mushrooms	2 teaspoons chopped parsley
¼ pound butter, divided	2 teaspoons flour
2 shallots, chopped	½ cup milk
2 ounces chopped mushrooms	2 ounces Gruyere or
2 ounces cooked and diced	Swiss cheese, grated
ham	Salt and pepper to taste

Preheat oven to 350°. Sauté whole mushrooms in 4 tablespoons butter, about 2 minutes on each side. Remove and place in shallow baking dish. Sauté the shallots, mushrooms and ham. Add the parsley and stir in flour. Cook over low heat, continuing to stir for about 2 minutes. Remove from heat and add milk. Return pan to heat and cook the mixture, stirring until it is thickened and smooth. Fill each mushroom cap with about 1 tablespoon of the mixture. Sprinkle with grated cheese and dot with butter. Season with salt and pepper. Bake for 10 to 15 minutes or until cheese is melted and lightly brown. This mixture is also delicious as a filling for artichoke bottoms.

BAKED VIDALIA ONIONS

Preparation: 15 minutes   *Yield: 6 to 8 servings*
Cook: 1 hour

6 to 8 Vidalia onions (seasonal)	Salt
6 to 8 teaspoons butter or	Pepper
margarine	6 to 8 ice cubes
6 to 8 beef bouillon cubes	

Preheat oven to 350°. Core the top center of each onion (½ inch). Place a teaspoon of butter in each onion. Add beef bouillon cube to each onion. Sprinkle salt and pepper over all. Top each onion with an ice cube and wrap individually in foil. Twist top of foil. Bake for approximately 60 minutes.

VEGETABLES

ENGLISH PEAS

Preparation: 30 minutes   *Can do ahead*   *Yield: 10 to 12 servings*
Cook: 20 minutes

¼ pound margarine
1 cup chopped onion
1 cup chopped bell pepper
½ cup chopped celery
2 (16 ounce) cans small early
  peas
1 (10 ¾ ounce) can cream of
  mushroom soup, undiluted

1 (2 ounce) jar pimentos,
  chopped
1 (8 ounce) can water
  chestnuts, sliced
1 cup bread crumbs
1 tablespoon melted margarine

Preheat oven to 350°. Melt margarine in skillet and sauté onions, bell pepper and celery. Set aside. Mix together peas, mushrooms soup, pimentos and water chestnuts. Add sautéed mixture to peas. Put in greased 2 quart casserole. Toss bread crumbs in melted margarine and top casserole. Bake for approximately 20 minutes or until bubbly.

FRENCH PEAS

Preparation: 15 minutes   *Yield: 4 servings*
Cook: To heat

4 slices of bacon
2 tablespoons bacon grease
1 small onion, chopped
2 tablespoons flour

Salt
Pepper
1 (17 ounce) can sweet peas
  and liquid

Fry bacon until crisp and crumble. Set aside. Using 2 tablespoons of the hot bacon grease, just barely brown the onion. Blend in flour and salt and pepper to taste. Drain the liquid from the peas and add the liquid to the onion mixture. Blend and cook until smooth and thick. Add the drained peas, and cook gently until warm. Add the crumbled bacon, serve immediately.

DELMONICO POTATOES

Preparation: 60 minutes   *Can do ahead*   *Yield: 12 servings*
Cook: 25 minutes

9 medium potatoes
1 teaspoon salt
⅓ cup butter <u>or</u> margarine
⅓ cup flour
2 ¼ cups milk

⅛ teaspoon pepper
1 cup shredded Cheddar cheese
3 tablespoons buttered bread
   crumbs

In a large, covered saucepan over medium heat, cook potatoes in their jackets in one inch boiling salted water, until tender. Drain and cool. When cool, remove jackets and dice. Preheat oven to 375°. Melt butter and stir in flour until well blended and smooth. Gradually add milk and cook, stirring constantly until mixture is thick and bubbly. Stir in salt and pepper, then add to the potatoes. Pour potato mixture evenly in well greased 9 x 13 inch baking dish. Sprinkle with cheese, then bread crumbs. Bake about 25 minutes until cheese is melted and mixture is bubbly.

GRATIN DAUPHINOIS

Preparation: 15 minutes   *Can do ahead*   *Yield: 8 servings*
Cook: 1 hour, 10 minutes

6 large potatoes, peeled and
   thinly sliced (about 10 cups)
2 cloves garlic, peeled

½ cup plus 2 tablespoons butter
⅛ teaspoon nutmeg
3 cups heavy cream

Preheat oven to 450°. Dry potato slices in a cloth. Rub the garlic around the inside of a large baking dish. Butter the dish well, using a third of the butter. Arrange the potato slices in layers. Season the layers with salt, sprinkle the top lightly with nutmeg and pour the cream over all. Dot the remaining butter on the surface. Bake in preheated oven 10 minutes, then reduce heat to 350° and cook 1 hour longer.

VEGETABLES

POTATOES STUFFED WITH SPINACH

Preparation: 2 hours　　　*Can do ahead*　　　*Yield: 8 servings*
Cook: 25 to 30 minutes

8 large Idaho baking potatoes
1 (11 ounce) bag fresh spinach,
　washed and trimmed
½ cup water
½ cup butter
2 medium onions, minced
　very fine
1 ½ teaspoons salt
2 teaspoons pepper

8 ounces commercial sour
　cream
8 ounces cream cheese
2 cups shredded sharp
　Cheddar cheese
½ cup milk (approximately)
　start with ¼ cup and continue
　to add if necessary

Preheat oven to 400°. Bake potatoes about 1 to 1 ½ hours until soft. Wash spinach several times in clean cold water. Drain. Place in saucepan with ½ cup water. Cook covered until spinach is tender. Drain spinach. Press to eliminate excess water. Chop spinach fine. When cool enough to handle, slice a lengthwise cap (about ½ inch thick) off the top of each potato. Remove insides of potatoes carefully with a tablespoon keeping shells intact. A thin layer of potato should be left in each shell to keep skins from tearing. Sauté onion in butter, only until onion is barely tender. To the potatoes, add sautéed onions, salt, pepper, spinach, sour cream, cream cheese, milk and 1 cup of shredded cheese. Combine with the mixer until smooth. Stuff potato mixture back into shells. Sprinkle remaining 1 cup of Cheddar cheese on top. Reduce oven to 375°. Bake covered 25 to 30 minutes.

SESAME POTATO STICKS

Preparation: 15 to 20 minutes　　*Can do ahead*　　*Yield: 8 servings*
Cook: 35 to 40 minutes　　　　　*Can be frozen*

6 to 8 medium baking potatoes,
　peeled
¾ cup sesame seeds

½ cup Parmesan cheese
½ cup melted butter
Seasoning salt

Preheat oven to 400°. Cut potatoes into sticks 1 inch thick. Sprinkle sesame seeds in a thin layer on waxed paper. Dip potato sticks in butter; coat on one side of stick with sesame seeds. Place sticks on a well greased baking sheet. Sprinkle with Parmesan cheese and seasoning salt. Bake 35 to 40 minutes or until done.

BIG MAMA HAMMOND'S SWEET POTATO SOUFFLE

Preparation: 45 minutes   *Can do ahead*   *Yield: 8 servings*
Cook: 25 minutes

6 medium sweet potatoes,   ¼ pound butter
  boiled   1 cup white sugar
¼ cup liquid from potatoes   ½ cup brown sugar
3 eggs, beaten   ½ teaspoon nutmeg

Topping:

2 cups crumbled flake cereal   ½ cup butter, melted
1 cup chopped pecans

Boil sweet potatoes until tender. Preheat oven to 300°. Skin and cream potatoes with liquid and add eggs, butter, sugars and nutmeg. Bake for 10 minutes before adding the topping. Add cereal and nuts to melted butter. Mix well and sprinkle on top of potatoes. Bake an additional 15 minutes.

ORANGE SWEET POTATOES

Preparation: 40 minutes   *Can do ahead*   *Yield: 6 to 8 servings*
Cook: 30 minutes

6 medium sweet potatoes   Salt to taste

Orange Sauce:

1 cup orange juice   2 tablespoons margarine
½ cup sugar   Dash cinnamon
1 tablespoon cornstarch

Boil sweet potatoes until tender. Cool, skin and slice in ½ inch slices. Place in flat pan and sprinkle with salt. Preheat oven to 350°. Combine orange juice, sugar, cornstarch and margarine and pour over potatoes. Sprinkle with cinnamon. Bake about 30 minutes until sauce is clear.

VEGETABLES

CREAM CHEESE SPINACH

Preparation: 20 minutes   *Can do ahead*   *Yield: 6 to 8 servings*
Cook: 20 to 30 minutes

2 (10 ounce) packages frozen
  chopped spinach
1 (8 ounce) package cream
  cheese, softened
½ cup margarine, softened

¼ pound bacon, cooked
  and crumbled
¼ cup shredded Cheddar
  cheese
1 medium tomato

Cook spinach according to package directions. Drain thoroughly. Preheat oven to 350°. While spinach is still warm, mix in cream cheese and margarine. Pour this mixture into a 1 quart baking dish. Sprinkle with cooked bacon and shredded Cheddar cheese. Cut tomato into wedges. Place wedges around the sides of the casserole. Bake 20 to 30 minutes.

SPINACH PIE

Preparation: 25 minutes   *Can do ahead*   *Yield: 6 to 8 servings*
Cook: 45 to 55 minutes

3 ounces cream cheese,
  softened
5 eggs
½ teaspoon salt
¼ cup green onion
2 tablespoons chopped parsley
¾ cup shredded Colby or
  Longhorn cheese

¾ cup shredded Monterey Jack
  cheese
1 (10 ounce) package frozen
  chopped spinach, thawed
1 (9 inch) unbaked pastry crust
Tomato slices
Grated Parmesan cheese

Preheat oven to 350°. Add eggs, one at a time, to softened cream cheese. Beat well. Add salt, onion and parsley. Fold in cheeses and spinach. Pour mixture into pastry crust and top with tomato slices. Sprinkle pie with grated Parmesan and bake for 45 to 55 minutes.

SPINACH SOUFFLÉ

Preparation: 10 minutes   *Can do ahead*   *Yield: 6 servings*
Cook: 45 minutes

½ cup margarine
3 tablespoons flour
Seasoned salt to taste
1 (10 ounce) package frozen
  chopped spinach, thawed
  and drained

1 (8 ounce) carton cottage
  cheese
4 eggs, well beaten
4 ounces shredded Mozzarella
  cheese
¼ cup Parmesan cheese

Preheat oven to 350°. Melt margarine and sprinkle in flour while over heat. Add salt. Set aside. Mix spinach, cottage cheese, eggs, Mozzarella and Parmesan cheese. Add the margarine, flour and salt mixture to spinach. Bake in ungreased 2 quart casserole for 45 minutes.

SQUASH-CARROT CASSEROLE

Preparation: 30 minutes   *Can do ahead*   *Yield: 10 to 12 servings*
Cook: 30 to 40 minutes

2 dozen round buttery crackers
1 (8 ounce) package cream
  cheese, softened
2 (10 ¾ ounce) cans cream of
  chicken soup, undiluted
2 eggs, beaten
½ cup margarine, melted

8 cups (about 2 ½ pounds)
  sliced yellow cooked squash
6 small carrots, grated
1 cup finely chopped onion
1 cup herb-seasoned stuffing
  mix

Preheat oven to 350°. Place crackers in greased 9 x 13 inch baking dish. Set aside. Combine cream cheese, soup, eggs and margarine. Beat well. Stir in squash, carrots and onion. Spoon into baking dish and sprinkle stuffing mix over top. Bake 30 to 40 minutes.

VEGETABLES

CRUSTY BAKED TOMATOES

Preparation: 15 minutes   *Yield: 8 servings*
Cook: 30 minutes

4 medium tomatoes | 6 tablespoons melted butter
Seasoning salt | ½ cup herb dressing mix
Dijon style mustard | ½ cup grated Parmesan cheese
½ cup sliced fresh mushrooms

Preheat oven to 350°. Cut tomatoes in half. Sprinkle cut side with seasoning salt; spread with mustard. Combine butter, dressing mix and cheese. Top tomatoes with mushrooms and crumb mixture. Bake until crumbs are brown and tomatoes are tender about 30 minutes.

PARTY TOMATOES

Preparation: 10 minutes   *Yield: 4 to 6 servings*
Cook: 2 to 3 minutes

2 large tomatoes cut in ½ inch | 4 tablespoons Parmesan cheese
  slices or 4 small tomatoes | 4 tablespoons chopped onion
  halved | 2 tablespoons minced parsley
4 tablespoons mayonnaise | or chopped chives

Mix mayonnaise, Parmesan cheese, onion and parsley together. Spread on sliced tomatoes. Broil 2 to 3 minutes.

Note: If it is winter and the tomatoes seem tough, bake the tomatoes 5 to 10 minutes at 350° and then broil until the top is bubbly (approximately 1 minute).

HINT: *To preserve the color of fresh vegetables, add a small pinch of baking soda to water or leave the top off the pan for the first few minutes of cooking.*

STUFFED TOMATOES SUPREME

Preparation: 45 minutes *Can do ahead* *Yield: 12 servings*
Cook: 25 minutes

12 small whole fresh tomatoes
1 pound bacon
2 tablespoons bacon drippings
½ cup chopped onion

2 (10 ounce) packages frozen
    chopped spinach
1 cup commercial sour cream
Shredded sharp Cheddar
    cheese

Remove centers of tomatoes leaving only shells. Drain. Salt shells well. While hulling tomatoes, fry bacon until crisp, drain, reserving 2 tablespoons drippings. Cook onion in bacon drippings until done. Cook spinach according to package directions, drain. Add spinach to onion and drippings mixing well. Remove from heat and add sour cream and crumbled bacon. Salt and pepper to taste. Fill tomato shells with spinach mixture. Bake at 375° for 20 to 25 minutes. Top each tomato with shredded Cheddar cheese and return to oven for 3 minutes.

TOMATO PUDDING

Preparation: 15 minutes *Can do ahead* *Yield: 4 servings*
Cook: 30 minutes

1 (10 ounce) can tomato purée
¼ cup boiling water
¼ teaspoon sweet basil
¼ teaspoon salt

6 tablespoons brown sugar
1 cup bread cubes
¼ cup melted butter

Preheat oven to 375°. Place the tomato purée in a saucepan. Rinse can with ¼ cup boiling water and add to purée. Heat to the boiling point and add basil, salt and brown sugar. Set aside. Place bread cubes in greased 1 quart casserole. Pour melted butter over bread cubes. Pour the tomato mixture over the buttered bread cubes and cover tightly. Bake for 30 minutes. Do not remove cover until ready to serve.

VEGETABLES

BECKY'S VEGETABLE MÉLANGE

Preparation: 15 minutes   *Can do ahead*   *Yield: 6 to 8 servings*

¼ head of cabbage, chopped
2 medium zucchini, sliced
2 medium yellow squash, sliced
1 small onion, sliced
3 tomatoes, cut in wedges

1 green pepper, chopped
1 (4 ounce) package shredded
  Cheddar cheese
½ teaspoon oregano
½ teaspoon salt

Mix cabbage, zucchini, yellow squash, onion, tomatoes and green pepper in Dutch oven or large pan. Cook over low heat until vegetables are tender (it will make its own liquid). Stir in Cheddar cheese, oregano and salt. Serve immediately or keep until necessary.

Note: Other fresh vegetables can be added as desired.

STIR-FRIED VEGETABLES

Preparation: 15 minutes   *Yield: 6 to 8 servings*
Cook: 5 minutes

2 tablespoons peanut oil
2 garlic cloves, minced
1 small Chinese cabbage
  cut into 2 inch pieces
3 stalks fresh broccoli, sliced
  into 1 inch pieces
1 cup frozen peas
1 small summer squash,
  thinly sliced

1 medium leek <u>or</u> 3 green
  onions cut into ½ inch pieces
1 tablespoon pale dry sherry
1 teaspoon salt
½ teaspoon sugar
½ cup peanuts
2 tablespoons oyster sauce <u>or</u>
  soy sauce

Prepare the vegetables. Heat the oil in a wok. Brown garlic; add Chinese cabbage, broccoli, peas, squash and leek and stir fry until heated (do not over cook). Make a well in the center and add the sherry, sugar and salt. Stir fry 1 minute. Add peanuts and oyster sauce. Mix and serve.

Note: Bok choy or romaine lettuce may be substituted for Chinese cabbage.

VEGETABLE CASSEROLE

Preparation: 10 minutes   *Can do ahead*   *Yield: 8 servings*
Cook: 45 minutes

1 (16 ounce) can white shoe
   peg corn, drained
1 (16 ounce) can French style
   green beans, drained
½ cup chopped onion
½ cup chopped celery
¼ cup chopped green pepper

½ cup Parmesan cheese
½ cup commercial sour cream
1 (10 ¾ ounce) can cream of
   celery soup, undiluted
Herb-seasoned stuffing mix
Butter or margarine

Preheat oven to 350°. Mix together shoe peg corn, green beans, onion, celery, green pepper, Parmesan cheese, sour cream and celery soup. Place in 2 ½ to 3 quart casserole. Top with stuffing mix and dot with butter or margarine. Bake 45 minutes.

MARGARET ANN'S ZUCCHINI CASSEROLE

Preparation: 50 minutes   *Can do ahead*   *Yield: 8 servings*
Cook: 30 minutes

2 medium yellow squash, sliced
2 medium zucchini, sliced
2 tablespoons butter
1 green pepper, sliced
½ red pepper, sliced
2 stalks celery, sliced
1 small onion, diced
1 ½ tomatoes, diced
5 rings of mild red or
   chili peppers

¼ teaspoon thyme
¾ teaspoon dried parsley
¼ cup Parmesan cheese
1 to 2 cloves garlic
½ teaspoon salt
¼ teaspoon pepper
¾ teaspoon sugar
1 (4 ounce) package shredded
   sharp Cheddar cheese

Precook squash in salted water. Sauté pepper, celery and onion in butter until tender. Drain squash and add to sautéed mixture and fry several minutes until blended. Add tomatoes, pepper rings, thyme, parsley, Parmesan cheese, garlic, salt, pepper and sugar. Simmer 10 to 15 minutes. Preheat oven to 350°. Drain liquid. Pour in greased casserole (2 or 3 quart size) layering vegetables alternately with cheese. Bake for 20 minutes or until heated through completely.

VEGETABLES

ZUCCHINI-CHEESE PUFF

Preparation: 25 minutes *Can do ahead* *Yield: 4 servings*
Chill: 1 hour
Cook: 40 to 45 minutes

1 pound zucchini, sliced
  (3 cups)
4 slices cracked wheat bread
1 (8 ounce) package shredded
  sharp cheese
2 tablespoons margarine,
  softened

3 eggs, beaten
¼ cup minced onion
½ teaspoon salt
½ teaspoon dry mustard
Dash cayenne pepper
1 ½ cups milk

Cook zucchini in boiling water (about 5 minutes). Drain and pat dry. Line a greased 9 inch baking pan with bread slices. Combine zucchini with cheese and margarine. Spread over bread. Beat eggs, onion, salt, mustard, pepper and milk. Pour over zucchini mix. Refrigerate for 1 hour. Bake at 350° until puffed, set and browned, about 40 to 50 minutes.

ZUCCHINI SAUTÉ

Preparation: 30 minutes *Yield: 4 servings*
Cook: 3 to 5 minutes
Stand: 20 minutes

1 ½ pounds small zucchini
  squash
2 tablespoons salt
¼ cup butter
2 tablespoons olive oil
Freshly ground black pepper

Freshly grated nutmeg
2 to 3 tablespoons commercial
  sour cream
2 tablespoons minced fresh
  herbs (parsley, chervil, basil)

Cut zucchini in half lengthwise and slice. Transfer slices to a large mixing bowl and sprinkle with salt. Let stand 20 minutes, then drain thoroughly. Remove additional water by squeezing zucchini, a handful at a time, in the corner of a kitchen towel. Heat butter and oil in a saucepan. Add zucchini and sauté until soft, about 3 to 5 minutes. Season highly with pepper and nutmeg. Add sour cream and serve sprinkled with fresh herbs.

Seafood

SEAFOOD

BAKED SALMON STEAKS IN SOUR CREAM

Preparation: 30 minutes   *Yield: 6 servings*
Bake: 25 to 40 minutes

6 frozen or fresh salmon steaks
  1 inch thick (about 1 pound
  each steak)
Oil
¼ teaspoon of salt to sprinkle
  on steaks
2 cups commercial sour
  cream

1 teaspoon salt
1 small onion, finely chopped
  (about ½ cup)
1 teaspoon dried tarragon or
  1 tablespoon fresh chopped
  dill
1 tablespoon lemon juice
Chopped parsley

Preheat oven to 450°. Place steaks in a lightly greased 12 x 8 inch pan. Brush lightly with oil. Sprinkle with salt. Bake for 25 minutes for frozen steaks, or 10 minutes for fresh steaks. Add 1 teaspoon salt to remaining ingredients except parsley; mix well and spoon over steaks. Continue baking until fish flakes easily, about 15 minutes. Sprinkle with parsley just before serving.

BROILED FISH

Preparation: 10 minutes   *Yield: 4 to 6 servings*
Broil: 7 to 10 minutes

½ cup butter
¼ cup lemon juice
1 to 2 teaspoons Worcestershire sauce

¼ teaspoon onion salt
2 pounds fish (flounder, sole,
  scrod or any white fish)
Paprika

Melt butter in pan. Add lemon juice, Worcestershire sauce and onion salt. Brush both sides of fish with butter mixture. Broil 2 inches from heat, basting occasionally for 7 to 8 minutes or until fish flakes easily with a fork. Do not turn. Sprinkle with paprika if desired.

Note: This may be done on the grill, cooking about 10 minutes.

150

FILET OF SOLE A LA LINDOR
from
Guyan Golf and Country Club

Preparation: 25 minutes   *Yield: 6 servings*
Bake: 20 minutes

Sauce:

½ pound mushrooms, sliced
3 tablespoons butter or
  margarine
3 tablespoons flour
1 cup heavy cream
1 cup half and half or milk
1 (2 ounce) jar pimentos,
  chopped

15 Spanish olives, sliced
3 tablespoons chopped fresh dill
  or 2 teaspoons dried
1 clove garlic, minced
1 teaspoon salt
Dash white pepper
⅛ to ¼ teaspoon each celery
  salt, thyme and tarragon

Sauté mushrooms in butter or margarine. When juice has formed, remove from heat; stir in flour until blended. Gradually stir in cream and half and half. Cook, stirring constantly, until sauce thickens; boil 1 minute. Add pimentos, olives, dill, garlic and seasonings. Set aside.

6 filets of sole (about
  2 ½ pounds)
1 to 2 eggs, slightly beaten

1 cup dry bread crumbs
Salt
4 tablespoons melted butter
Fresh dill

Preheat oven to 350°. Rinse filets under cold water; pat dry with paper towels. Roll up and dip first in beaten egg, then in salted crumbs. Arrange filets in ovenproof baking dish, drizzle with butter. Bake for about 20 minutes, basting occasionally with butter. When filets are done, pour off butter. Pour hot sauce around them and garnish with fresh dill.

HINT: *Cooking fish - (does not apply to shellfish). Baked, braised, broiled, fried, poached, sautéed, or steamed, the cooking time is always the same-10 minutes/per inch of thickness. Measure thickness of rolled filets after they have been rolled. Bake fish in 450° oven. Start timing on poached fish when water starts to simmer. When cooking fish that is started from a frozen state, double the time.*

CHEESY FLOUNDER BAKE

Preparation: 10 minutes   *Yield: 4 servings*
Bake: 20 to 25 minutes

¼ cup fine dry bread crumbs   1 pound flounder fillets
¼ cup grated Parmesan cheese   ¼ cup mayonnaise

Preheat oven to 375°. Combine bread crumbs and cheese in a shallow dish. Brush all sides of fillets with mayonnaise, then coat with crumb mixture. Arrange fish in a single layer in a shallow baking pan. Bake 20 to 25 minutes or until golden and fish flakes easily with a fork.

FLOUNDER ROLL-UPS

Preparation: 20 minutes   *Yield: 8 servings*
Bake: 40 minutes

2 (10 ounce) packages frozen   1 (10 ¾ ounce) can cream of
  broccoli spears, cooked   celery soup, undiluted
  and drained   ¼ cup mayonnaise
8 flounder fillets (2 pounds),   1 tablespoon lemon juice
  completely thawed

Preheat oven to 350°. Divide the broccoli among the fillets and roll it up inside them. Secure with toothpicks. Arrange in baking dish. Bake for 20 minutes. Meanwhile, combine the remaining ingredients. Pour sauce over fish, stirring in liquid around sides. Bake 15 to 20 minutes more or until done. Arrange roll-ups on platter. Stir sauce; pour over roll-ups. Garnish with lemon if desired.

GOURMET FISH FILLETS

Preparation: 10 minutes   *Yield: 4 servings*
Bake: 30 minutes

1 pound fillet of sole <u>or</u>   1 teaspoon dill weed
  flounder   ½ cup Chablis
Seasoned salt   ½ cup butter
1 teaspoon dried parsley flakes   Lemon slices for garnish

Preheat oven to 350°. Place fish in a buttered baking dish. Sprinkle fish with seasonings; dot with butter and add Chablis. Bake for about 30 minutes.

SANDY'S STUFFED SOLE

Preparation: 20 minutes   *Can do ahead*   *Yield: 4 to 6 servings*
Bake: 25 minutes

Filling:

1 pound filet of sole
1 tablespoon sherry
1 tablespoon grated Cheddar
  cheese

1 ½ slices bread, torn
½ cup frozen crabmeat,
  thawed and drained
Dash of salt

Combine sherry, Cheddar cheese, torn bread, crabmeat and salt. Spoon on filets and roll up. Place seam side down in lightly greased baking dish.

Sauce:

½ cup frozen crabmeat,
  thawed and drained
1 tablespoon butter
1 tablespoon flour

½ cup whipping cream
  and 1 ½ cups milk
1 tablespoon sherry
½ teaspoon salt

Preheat oven to 350°. Sauté crabmeat for 5 minutes. In saucepan melt butter, add flour and cook 2 to 3 minutes. Add cream, milk and sherry and cook until thick. Add crabmeat and heat through. Pour sauce over filets and bake for 25 minutes.

HINT: *Thaw frozen fish in milk to give it a fresh caught flavor. Drain before cooking. Always use bread crumbs for frying fish. Cracker crumbs absorb grease.*

SEAFOOD

SNAPPER ROLLS ELEGANTE

Preparation: 30 minutes
Bake: 35 minutes

Yield: 8 servings

¼ cup chopped onion
4 tablespoons butter or
   margarine
½ cup chopped mushrooms
1 (7 ½ ounce) can crabmeat,
   drained and cartilage
   removed

12 saltine crackers, coarsely
   crushed
2 tablespoons snipped parsley
Dash pepper
2 pounds red snapper fillets,
   skinned (8 fillets)

In a skillet, cook onion in the butter or margarine until tender but not brown. Stir mushrooms into skillet with crabmeat, cracker crumbs, parsley and pepper. Spread mixture over snapper fillets. Roll up each fillet, securing with wooden picks if necessary. Place seam side down in a greased 11 ¾ x 7 ½ inch baking dish. Pour Wine and Cheese Sauce over all.

Wine and Cheese Sauce:

3 tablespoons butter or
   margarine
3 tablespoons flour
1 ½ cups milk

⅓ cup dry white wine
1 cup shredded processed Swiss
   cheese
½ teaspoon paprika

Preheat oven to 400°. In saucepan, melt the butter and blend in flour. Add milk and wine to saucepan. Cook and stir until mixture thickens and bubbles; pour over fillets. Bake for 25 minutes. Sprinkle with cheese and paprika; return to oven and bake 10 more minutes.

SOLE WITH ASPARAGUS AND TOMATOES

Preparation: 30 minutes
Bake: 30 minutes

Yield: 4 servings

1 pound sole fillets or any
   white fish fillets
½ cup dry white wine
1 cup (½ of 10 ounce package)
   frozen cut asparagus,
   cooked and drained

½ cup halved cherry tomatoes
½ cup sliced mushrooms
2 tablespoons butter or
   margarine
2 tablespoons flour
½ teaspoon salt

SOLE WITH ASPARAGUS AND TOMATOES
(Continued)

Dash white pepper
1 ¼ cups milk
1 slightly beaten egg yolk
¼ cup dry white wine

1 cup soft bread crumbs
(1 ½ slices bread)
¼ cup grated Parmesan cheese

In a covered skillet, poach sole fillets in the ½ cup wine for 2 or 3 minutes or until fish flakes easily with a fork. Drain and arrange in a 10 x 6 inch baking dish; season with a little salt. On top of fillets, put asparagus, cherry tomatoes and mushrooms. Preheat oven to 350°. In small saucepan, melt butter or margarine. Stir in flour, salt and pepper. Stir in milk; cook, stirring constantly, until mixture thickens. Stir small amount of the hot mixture into egg yolk. Return egg yolk mixture to saucepan; cook and stir until mixture bubbles. Remove from heat and stir in remaining wine. Pour evenly over fish and vegetables in the baking dish. Combine the bread crumbs and Parmesan cheese. Sprinkle evenly over all. Bake uncovered for 30 minutes.

BAKED CRAB

Preparation: 10 minutes   *Yield: 8 servings*
Bake: 30 to 45 minutes

1 pound white crabmeat
1 raw egg, beaten
2 chopped hard boiled eggs
1 tablespoon grated onion
½ cup chopped celery
1 tablespoon mayonnaise
1 tablespoon ketchup
1 teaspoon prepared mustard
1 teaspoon Worcestershire
  sauce

1 teaspoon prepared
  horseradish
1 tablespoon lemon juice
2 tablespoons bacon grease
1 (10 ½ ounce) can cream of
  mushroom soup, undiluted
1 cup dry stuffing mix
Salt and pepper to taste
Dash garlic powder
Dash Tabasco

Preheat oven to 350°. Combine all ingredients, tossing lightly, and put in greased 1 ½ quart casserole. Bake 30 to 45 minutes.

Note: Stuffing, drizzled with butter may be sprinkled on top rather than mixing into the casserole.

SEAFOOD

CHEESY VERSATILE CRAB

Preparation: 15 minutes   *Can do ahead*   *Yield: 4 servings*
Bake: 40 minutes

6 ounces cream cheese, softened	2 hard boiled eggs, minced
1 (8 ounce) jar mayonnaise	¼ teaspoon dry mustard
2 cups grated sharp Cheddar cheese	½ teaspoon paprika
1 (6 ½ ounce) can crabmeat	1 tablespoon parsley flakes (optional)
1 onion, minced	Ground white pepper
	Cooked rice or noodles

Reserve 2 tablespoons mayonnaise. Mix the softened cream cheese and remaining mayonnaise until smooth. Rinse crabmeat in cold water and drain. Remove cartilage. Add the rest of the ingredients and mix well. More mayonnaise may be added, if desired. Refrigerate until ready to use. Combine the crab mixture with cooked noodles or rice, put in a buttered casserole and bake in preheated 350° oven for 40 minutes.

Or: Heat the crab mixture in the top of a double boiler until cheese is melted and mixture is hot. Serve over cooked rice or noodles for an entrée.

Or: Serve the heated crab mixture in a chafing dish with crackers or fresh vegetables as an appetizer.

Or: Add one or more of the following to the unheated mixture to make crab salad: chopped celery, tomatoes or green pepper.

Or: Add more mayonnaise to the cold mixture and spread on bread for tea sandwiches or cold appetizers.

HINT: Before using canned shrimp in recipe, soak in ice water for ½ hour to refresh. It takes away canned salty taste.

SPINACH AND CRAB QUICHE

Preparation: 20 minutes   *Yield: 8 servings*
Bake: 45 minutes

9 inch pastry shell, partially
  baked
2 tablespoons minced green
  onion
2 tablespoons butter
1 (10 ounce) package frozen
  chopped spinach, thawed
  and well drained
½ teaspoon salt
⅛ teaspoon pepper
Dash nutmeg
¾ to 1 cup cooked fresh
  crabmeat

2 tablespoons dry white
  Vermouth
¼ teaspoon salt
Dash pepper
3 tablespoons butter
2 tablespoons minced green
  onion
3 eggs
1 to 1 ½ cups whipping cream
  or half and half
⅛ teaspoon pepper
¼ to ½ cup grated imported
  Swiss cheese (Gruyere
  preferred)

Cook 2 tablespoons green onion in 2 tablespoons butter. Add spinach, from which all liquid has been removed, and stir over medium heat to evaporate all water. Stir in ½ teaspoon salt, ⅛ teaspoon pepper and a dash of nutmeg. Taste for seasoning. Cook 2 tablespoons green onion in 3 tablespoons butter for 1 to 2 minutes over moderate heat. Stir in crab, which has been checked for shells. Stir gently a few minutes and sprinkle with ¼ teaspoon salt and a dash of pepper. Add Vermouth, raise heat and boil 1 minute. Let cool slightly. Preheat oven to 375°. Beat eggs with cream. Stir in spinach mixture and shellfish mixture. Pour into partially baked pastry shell. Sprinkle with grated Swiss cheese. Bake for 25 to 30 minutes or until knife inserted halfway between edge and center comes out clean. Cool on wire rack briefly and serve warm.

Note: This is a colorful, elegant entrée for a luncheon or brunch. Serve with wedges of melon, fresh pineapple or frosted grapes. Another accompaniment is glazed baby carrots sprinkled with fresh minced parsley. This is delightful served with a light, dry white wine such as a Moselle or a French Columbard.

HINT: *Milk cartons make great freezing containers for fish, shrimp or other food that must be frozen in water.*

SEAFOOD

VERMICELLI CRAB

Preparation: 30 minutes   *Yield: 4 servings*
Cook: 15 to 20 minutes
Stand: 10 minutes

1 to 2 cups stone <u>or</u> snow crab
¼ pound butter
1 teaspoon minced garlic
1 teaspoon coarse black
   pepper

½ teaspoon seasoned salt
½ cup grated Parmesan cheese
1 (8 ounce) package vermicelli
Juice of 1 lemon

In large heavy skillet melt butter, add seasonings and lemon juice. Sauté crab chunks in hot butter for 2 to 3 minutes. Meanwhile, cook vermicelli al denté. Drain the vermicelli immediately and stir into skillet. Blend in grated Parmesan cheese. Sauté entire mixture gently for 2 to 3 minutes. Cover and let stand 10 minutes to blend flavors. Reheat and serve.

SCALLOPS IN WHITE WINE

Preparation: 10 minutes   *Yield: 2 to 3 servings*
Cook: 10 minutes

2 tablespoons butter
2 shallots, peeled and chopped
2 tablespoons minced fresh
   parsley

16 scallops, each sliced into
   2 or 3 pieces
¼ cup dry white wine,
   preferably Muscadet <u>or</u>
   Chablis

Melt the butter in a skillet and sauté the shallots and parsley for a few moments. Add the scallops and cook over high heat for 5 minutes, turning the pieces until they are golden. Season with salt and plenty of freshly ground pepper. Remove the skillet from the heat and spoon the scallops into individual shells or a warm serving dish. Pour the wine in the skillet and bring quickly to a boil. Pour over scallops and serve.

Note: Serves 6 as an appetizer.

SEAFOOD CASSEROLE

Preparation: 15 minutes   *Can do ahead*   *Yield: 8 servings*
Bake: 30 to 35 minutes   *Can be frozen*

1 cup chopped onion
1 cup chopped celery
1 green pepper, chopped
2 tablespoons butter
½ cup wild rice
½ cup white rice
1 pound cooked shrimp

1 (6 ounce) package crabmeat
1 ½ cups condensed mushroom
   soup
1 (4 ounce) can mushrooms
¼ cup sliced almonds
1 (2 ounce) jar pimentos
Buttered bread crumbs

Preheat oven to 350°. Sauté onion, celery and green pepper in butter. Cook the rice according to package directions. Assemble all ingredients into greased 2 quart casserole and top with buttered bread crumbs. Bake for 30 to 35 minutes or until brown and bubbly. If mixture seems too dry after ingredients are combined, more mushroom soup may be added.

SHRIMP AND BROCCOLI CASSEROLE

Preparation: 20 minutes   *Can do ahead*   *Yield: 8 servings*
Bake: 30 minutes

1 (12 ounce) bag frozen,
   peeled deveined shrimp
2 (10 ounce) packages frozen
   chopped broccoli
2 cups shredded sharp
   Cheddar cheese
¾ cup butter

4 tablespoons chopped onion
4 tablespoons flour
¼ teaspoon curry powder
1 teaspoon salt
2 cups milk or half and half
2 tablespoons lemon juice
1 ½ cups soft bread crumbs

Defrost shrimp; cook broccoli. Arrange broccoli on bottom of a 2 quart baking dish. Sprinkle with shredded cheese. Preheat oven to 350°. Sauté onion in ½ cup butter until transparent. Stir in flour, curry powder and salt. Gradually stir in milk. Cook, stirring constantly, over low heat until sauce is thickened. Stir in lemon juice; add shrimp and pour over broccoli. Melt ¼ cup butter, mix with bread crumbs, and sprinkle on top. Bake 30 minutes.

SEAFOOD

SHRIMP CASSEROLE

Preparation: 15 minutes   Can do ahead   *Yield: 6 servings*
Bake: 45 minutes   Can be frozen

1 pound shrimp, cooked
  peeled and deveined
3 (15 ounce) cans Spanish rice
1 cup commercial sour cream
1 (8 ounce) can sliced water
  chestnuts

⅓ cup sherry
½ cup slivered almonds, divided
Mushrooms, canned or
  sautéed fresh (optional)

Preheat oven to 350°. Combine Spanish rice, sour cream, sherry and ¼ cup almonds. Add shrimp, water chestnuts and mushrooms. Pour into 9 inch square baking dish. Sprinkle remaining almonds on top. Bake, uncovered, for 45 minutes.

SHRIMP AND SCALLOP BAKE

Preparation: 30 minutes   *Yield: 4 to 6 servings*
Bake: 20 to 30 minutes

Sauce:

6 tablespoons butter
6 tablespoons flour
½ teaspoon salt

2 ⅓ cups milk
⅔ cup dry white wine
10 ounces Swiss cheese, grated

Melt 6 tablespoons butter in large saucepan, add flour and salt and cook until bubbly. Remove from heat and slowly add milk stirring constantly. Add wine. Return to heat and add Swiss cheese and heat until thickened.

3 tablespoons butter
1 pound fresh scallops
  (bay or halved sea scallops)
12 ounces medium shrimp,
  peeled and deveined

8 ounces fresh mushrooms,
  cleaned and sliced
Melted butter
¼ cup dried bread crumbs
Parmesan cheese

Preheat oven to 350°. Sauté scallops, shrimp and mushrooms in 3 tablespoons butter in large frying pan until shrimp is just pink and mushrooms look moist. Put scallops, shrimp and mushrooms into greased 4 quart casserole dish. Top with sauce and stir. Add enough butter melted to moisten ¼ cup bread crumbs. Sprinkle crumbs over casserole. Top with Parmesan cheese to taste. Bake 20 to 30 minutes until cheese bubbles.

SHRIMP AND CRAB CASSEROLE

Preparation: 10 minutes *Can do ahead* *Yield: 6 servings*
Bake: 1 hour

¾ pound small shrimp,
  cleaned
1 ½ pounds crabmeat, cartilage
  removed
1 (8 ounce) can sliced water
  chestnuts
½ green pepper, chopped

⅓ cup chopped parsley
2 cups cooked rice
1 ½ cups mayonnaise
1 (10 ounce) package frozen
  peas
Salt and pepper to taste

Preheat oven to 350°. Combine all ingredients. Toss lightly. Place in greased casserole. At this point may be covered and refrigerated. Bake covered for 1 hour.

SHRIMP CREOLE
from
Guyan Golf and Country Club

Preparation: 20 minutes *Yield: 6 servings*
Cook: 20 minutes

1 ½ to 2 pounds cooked
  shrimp, shelled and deveined
  or 3 (7 ounce) cans shrimp
½ cup chopped onion
½ cup chopped green pepper
½ cup sliced mushrooms
  (optional)
¼ cup butter or margarine

2 tablespoons flour
3 (8 ounce) cans tomato sauce
½ teaspoon salt
⅛ teaspoon pepper
¼ teaspoon monosodium
  glutamate
Bay leaf or pinch of dried
  basil, if desired
2 cups cooked rice

If using canned shrimp, rinse in cold water and drain. Make sauce: cook onion, green pepper and mushrooms in butter for 5 minutes. Stir in flour, cook until bubbly; add tomato sauce, salt, monosodium glutamate, pepper and either bay leaf or dried basil. Cook about 10 minutes. Toss in shrimp and mushrooms, bring sauce to boil, then simmer 5 minutes until shrimp are heated through. Serve over rice.

Note: To prepare in a casserole: place shrimp in buttered casserole, add sauce, mix well. Heat at 350° for 30 minutes or until heated through.

SEAFOOD

HERBED SHRIMP OLÉ

Preparation: 45 minutes   Can do ahead   *Yield: 6 servings*
Cook: 30 to 45 minutes

24 large shrimp, peeled
   and deveined
4 tablespoons butter, divided
3 cloves garlic, peeled
1 tablespoon Dijon mustard
1 teaspoon capers
½ cup white wine

1 teaspoon chopped fresh
   parsley
1 teaspoon chopped fresh
   chives
1 tablespoon chopped fresh dill
Juice of one-half lemon
6 flour tortillas

In large skillet melt 2 tablespoons butter; add garlic, shrimp, mustard and capers. Heat and stir until shrimp is pink. Add ½ cup white wine. Reduce liquid over high heat, watching closely so it doesn't burn. Mix herbs together and place on top of shrimp. Add the lemon juice and toss to heat thoroughly. Remove garlic cloves. Heat 2 tablespoons butter in an iron skillet until hot. Fry flour tortillas, one at a time, until light brown. Place tortillas on tray. Put 4 shrimp on each tortilla and pour sauce over all and serve.

Note: This may be used as an appetizer with tortillas cut into wedges.

SHRIMP LUNCHEON DISH

Preparation: 30 minutes   Can do ahead   *Yield: 8 servings*
Cook: 25 minutes   Can be frozen

3 tablespoons butter
3 tablespoons flour
2 cups milk
1 (10 ¾ ounce) can cream
   of chicken soup, undiluted
10 ounces sharp cheese,
   shredded
4 hard boiled eggs, sliced

1 pound shrimp, cooked, peeled
   and deveined
¼ cup chopped green pepper
2 tablespoons sherry flavoring
   or sherry
Chinese noodles
Baking shells

Melt butter; add flour and cook 2 to 3 minutes. Stir in milk and cook until thick. Add soup, cheese, eggs, shrimp, green pepper and sherry; heat through. Serve over Chinese noodles in seafood shells.

SHRIMP SAGANAKI

Preparation: 30 minutes   *Yield: 6 servings*
Cook: 10 minutes

1 pound raw medium-sized
  shrimp
1 (8 ounce) package frozen
  artichoke hearts
½ cup olive oil
¼ pound small, whole
  mushrooms (about ¾ inch
  in diameter)

2 cloves garlic, finely minced
½ teaspoon salt
Freshly ground pepper
½ teaspoon crumbled dried
  oregano
2 tablespoons fresh lemon juice
2 tablespoons finely chopped
  parsley

Peel and devein shrimp. Blanch artichoke hearts in boiling, salted water for 2 minutes, then drain. Heat olive oil in frying pan, add shrimp and mushrooms and cook, stirring, until shrimp turn pink. Add artichoke hearts, garlic, salt, pepper and oregano; heat thoroughly. Sprinkle with lemon juice and stir lightly to blend flavors. Sprinkle with parsley.

Note: Serve from heatproof dish over a candle warmer or chafing dish as an entrée or appetizer.

SHRIMP SAVORY

Preparation: 20 minutes   *Can do ahead*   *Yield: 6 servings*
Bake: 30 minutes   *Can be frozen*

1 teaspoon butter
1 small onion, chopped
1 cup cream
1 cup shrimp
1 cup cooked rice

1 teaspoon Worcestershire
  sauce
⅓ cup chili sauce <u>or</u> ketchup
Salt and pepper
¾ cup buttered bread crumbs

Preheat oven to 350°. Sauté onion in butter until golden brown; add other ingredients. Put in greased baking dish. Cover with buttered bread crumbs. Bake 30 minutes or until golden brown in moderate oven.

SEAFOOD

CHOPSTICK TUNA

Preparation: 10 minutes   *Yield: 4 to 5 servings*
Bake: 15 minutes

1 (10 ¾ ounce) can cream of
 mushroom soup, undiluted
¼ cup water
1 (3 ounce) can chow mein
 noodles (about 2 cups)

1 can tuna (6 ½, 7 or 9 ¼
 ounces)
1 cup sliced celery
½ cup salted toasted cashews
¼ cup chopped onion
1 can mandarin orange sections

Preheat oven to 375°. Combine soup and water. Add 1 cup noodles (reserve
1 cup), tuna, celery, cashews and onion; toss lightly. Place in ungreased 10 x 6
inch baking dish. Sprinkle remaining noodles on top. Bake for 15 minutes or
until heated through. Garnish with mandarin orange sections.

Poultry

POULTRY

BREASTS OF CHICKEN
WITH MUSHROOMS AND CREAM

Preparation: 30 minutes   *Yield: 4 servings*

4 chicken breasts, boned
½ teaspoon fresh lemon juice
¼ teaspoon salt
Pinch of white pepper
5 tablespoons butter

1 tablespoon minced green
  onion
¼ pound mushrooms, diced or
  sliced
⅛ teaspoon salt

Preheat oven to 400°. Rub chicken breasts with drops of lemon juice and sprinkle lightly with salt and pepper. Heat 5 tablespoons butter in a heavy ovenproof 10 inch casserole over moderate heat until foaming. Stir in minced green onion and sauté a moment; do not brown. Stir in mushrooms and cook lightly for a few minutes without browning. Sprinkle with salt. Quickly roll the chicken breasts in the casserole, then top with a round of buttered waxed paper, cover casserole and place in hot oven. After 6 minutes, press top of chicken breasts with finger. If still soft, return to oven for a few minutes. When the meat is springy to the touch, it is done. Remove chicken to a warm platter and cover while making the sauce.

Sauce:

¼ cup white stock or canned
  beef bouillon
¼ cup dry white vermouth,
  port or Madeira

1 cup whipping cream
Salt, pepper and lemon juice
  to taste
2 tablespoons fresh minced
  parsley

Pour the stock or bouillon and wine into the casserole with the mushroom mixture and boil down quickly over high heat until liquid is syrupy. Stir in the cream and boil down again over high heat until cream has thickened slightly. Remove from heat, taste carefully for seasoning and add drops of lemon juice to taste. Pour the sauce over the chicken breasts, sprinkle with parsley and serve at once.

Note: Very quick. An elegant entrée when having little time for preparation. Good with broccoli flowerets and glazed baby carrots with a chocolate mousse for dessert or fresh fruit!

CHICKEN WITH CHIVES

Preparation: 10 minutes   *Yield: 4 servings*
Cook: 50 minutes

½ cup dry bread crumbs
2 tablespoons grated Parmesan
  cheese
½ teaspoon thyme
½ teaspoon oregano
½ teaspoon garlic powder

2 chicken breasts, boned,
  halved and skinned
½ cup butter, melted
½ cup dry white wine
⅛ cup freeze-dried chives

Preheat oven to 375°. Combine bread crumbs, Parmesan cheese, thyme, oregano and garlic powder. Dip chicken in butter then coat by rolling in bread crumb mixture. Place in baking dish. Bake for 30 minutes. Combine wine, chives and remaining butter, stirring well. Pour over chicken; continue to bake for about 20 minutes or until done.

CHICKEN JUBILEE

Preparation: 30 minutes   *Can do ahead*   *Yield: 8 servings*
Cook: 1 hour

2 broiler-fryers, cut up
1 teaspoon salt
½ teaspoon pepper
¼ cup butter or margarine,
  melted
1 (28 ounce) can sliced
  peaches, drained

1 (17 ounce) can dark sweet
  pitted cherries, drained
1 (8 ounce) bottle sweet 'n
  sour sauce
2 medium onions, sliced
½ cup chili sauce

Preheat oven to 325°. Place chicken skin side up in a baking dish. Broil until brown. Sprinkle with salt and pepper and drizzle with butter. Combine peaches, cherries, sweet 'n sour sauce, onions and chili sauce. Pour over chicken and bake 1 hour.

Note: May be served with rice.

POULTRY

CHICKEN IN WHITE WINE

Preparation: 20 minutes   *Yield: 8 to 12 servings*
Cook: 20 minutes

½ cup finely minced green
  onions
6 tablespoons butter
6 tablespoons flour
2 cups boiling milk
½ cup dry white wine or dry
  white vermouth
½ teaspoon salt

Dash of pepper
½ teaspoon oregano
½ to ¾ cup heavy cream
3 cups cooked diced chicken
¼ cup minced parsley
½ cup grated imported Swiss
  cheese (Gruyere)
2 tablespoons butter

Preheat oven to 425°. Cook onion in butter in heavy saucepan over low heat for about 5 minutes, until onions are tender but not browned. Stir in the flour, and cook slowly for 2 minutes without coloring. Remove from heat, beat in boiling milk, wine and seasonings. Bring to a boil over medium heat, stirring. Boil several minutes to evaporate the alcohol in the wine and to allow the sauce to thicken. Thin sauce to medium consistency with tablespoons of cream. Taste for seasoning. Fold the chicken and parsley into the sauce and check seasonings again. Spread in a shallow baking dish, 1 ½ to 2 inches deep. Sprinkle cheese on top and dot with butter. Bake in upper third of oven for 15 to 20 minutes, or until top is nicely browned.

Variation: Fold in sautéed mushrooms with the chicken.

Note: This is a delightful brunch or luncheon entrée. Serve with dry white wine. Fresh asparagus is a nice accompaniment.

HINT: *Properly wrapped chicken will keep for 2 days in the coldest part of the refrigerator.*

COMPANY CHICKEN

Preparation: 10 minutes   *Yield: 8 servings*
Crockpot cook: 5 ½ to 6 ½ hours
Oven cook: 1 hour

8 chicken breasts, boned and halved

2 tablespoons melted butter <u>or</u> margarine (more may be needed)

1 (6 ounce) package Italian salad dressing mix

1 (10 ¾ ounce) can cream of mushroom soup

6 ounces cream cheese (3 ounces oven method)

½ cup white wine

1 tablespoon chopped onion

Rice (oven method)

Brush chicken with melted butter. Sprinkle generously with dressing mix. Layer in a crockpot. Cook on high temperature for 5 to 6 hours. Three-quarters of an hour before serving combine soup, cream cheese, wine and onion in saucepan. Cook until smooth. Pour over chicken in crockpot and continue cooking 30 minutes or until hot. Will stay if not quite ready to serve -does not separate or curdle. Turn down to low if desired.

VARIATION: Oven Method

Preheat oven to 325°. Reserve ½ teaspoon of salad dressing mix to use for rice. In large skillet, combine remaining dressing mix with butter. Add chicken and brown slowly until golden. Place in casserole. Blend soup, wine and 3 ounces of cream cheese. Spoon over chicken. Bake, uncovered for 1 hour basting once or twice with sauce while baking. Serve over rice.

For rice: Prepare according to package directions adding reserved salad dressing mix to water.

HINT: Leave transparent wrap on prepacked poultry - it is designed to control moisture losses properly.

POULTRY

DIFFERENT CHICKEN ROLL-UPS

Preparation: 30 minutes   *Can do ahead*   *Yield: 6 servings*
Cook: 45 minutes

6 chicken breasts, halved,
  skinned and boned
6 thin slices Danish ham
6 slices Mozzarella cheese
1 large tomato, seeded and
  chopped

½ teaspoon ground sage
4 tablespoons margarine
⅓ cup fine dry bread crumbs
2 tablespoons grated Parmesan
  cheese
2 tablespoons parsley

Preheat oven to 350°. Place chicken breast between waxed paper and pound with mallet until very thin. Place 1 slice ham and 1 slice cheese on each breast. Mix sage and tomato and place a tablespoon of mixture in the center of cheese. Roll up and secure with toothpick. Melt margarine. Combine bread crumbs, parsley and cheese. Dip the rolled breast in the margarine, then roll in the bread crumbs, parsley and cheese combination. Place in baking dish. Bake 40 to 45 minutes.

JANE'S CHICKEN ROSEMARY

Preparation: 45 minutes   *Can do ahead*   *Yield: 8 servings*
Cook: 45 minutes

4 whole chicken breasts
3 (10 ounce) packages frozen
  asparagus
1 cup mayonnaise
1 (10 ¾ ounce) can cream of
  celery soup

¼ pound almonds, chopped
1 teaspoon rosemary
1 cup white wine
Salt and pepper to taste

Preheat oven to 325°. Boil chicken 30 minutes, drain and dice. Cook asparagus according to package directions. Arrange asparagus in the bottom of a greased 3-quart casserole. Mix chicken with wine, mayonnaise, soup, rosemary, salt and pepper. Pour over asparagus. Top with nuts. Bake for 45 minutes.

GOURMET CHICKEN

Preparation: 15 minutes   *Can do ahead*   *Yield: 8 servings*
Cook: 45 minutes

8 chicken breast halves, boned
  and skinned
2 tablespoons margarine or
  butter
½ teaspoon salt
Pepper
2 to 4 tablespoons minced
  onion

2 tablespoons parsley flakes
1 (1 ⅞ ounce) package sour
  cream sauce mix
1 (4 ounce) can mushroom
  pieces and stems, drained
4 tablespoons sherry or white
  wine

Preheat oven to 375°. Brown chicken pieces in margarine in a skillet. Transfer to baking pan when brown. Season each with salt, pepper and green onion. Sprinkle parsley evenly over chicken. Sprinkle the sour cream sauce mix over the chicken, and top with mushrooms. Spoon on the wine. Cover the pan with heavy duty foil, sealing around the edges. Bake 35 to 40 minutes or until chicken is tender.

Note: The dry sour cream mix doesn't make an actual sauce - it's more like a flavorful coating on the chicken.

MICROWAVE CRUNCHY PARMESAN CHICKEN

Preparation: 20 minutes   *Yield: 4 servings*
Cook: 15 minutes

¾ cup grated Parmesan cheese
1 (3 ounce) can french fried
  onions, crushed
¼ cup dry bread crumbs
1 teaspoon paprika
Dash of pepper

½ teaspoon salt
1 egg, beaten
1 tablespoon milk
2 ½ to 3 pound fryer, cut up or
  chicken breasts
¼ cup margarine, melted

Combine cheese, onion, crumbs and seasonings. Dip chicken in combined egg and milk. Coat with cheese mixture. Place in baking dish. Pour margarine over chicken. Bake on High — covered with waxed paper for 10 minutes. Uncover and bake for 5 more minutes.

POULTRY

PARMESAN BAKED CHICKEN

Preparation: 15 minutes   *Yield: 4 to 6 servings*
Cook: 1 hour

½ cup grated Parmesan cheese
2 cups dry bread crumbs
⅓ cup chopped fresh parsley
1 (3 ounce) can french fried
   onions, crushed
Pinch of white pepper

½ cup unsalted margarine
2 garlic cloves, crushed
1 teaspoon Worcestershire
   sauce
¾ teaspoon dry mustard
8 chicken breast halves, boned
   and skinned

Preheat oven to 350°. Line baking dish with foil. Combine cheese, bread crumbs, parsley, crushed onions and white pepper in a shallow bowl and mix well. Melt the margarine in a saucepan, add the garlic and sauté about one minute. Remove pan from heat. Stir in Worcestershire sauce and mustard. Dip the chicken in the margarine mixture and then in the bread crumb mixture. Coat chicken pieces well and transfer to the foil-lined baking dish. Drizzle the remaining butter mixture over the top. Bake uncovered about 50 to 60 minutes, or until chicken is tender and done.

REUBEN CHICKEN

Preparation: 20 minutes   *Yield: 4 servings*
Cook: 1 ½ hours

2 chicken breasts, halved
   and boned
¼ teaspoon salt
⅛ teaspoon pepper
1 (16 ounce) can sauerkraut,
   drained (press out excess
   liquid - Very Important!)

4 slices (each about 4 inches
   x 6 inches) natural Swiss
   cheese
1 ¼ cup thousand island
   dressing
1 tablespoon parsley

Preheat oven to 325°. Place chicken breasts in a greased 9 x 13 x 2 inch baking pan. Sprinkle with salt and pepper. Place sauerkraut over chicken; top with Swiss cheese. Pour dressing evenly over the cheese and smooth to cover surface. Cover with foil and bake for 1 ½ hours. Sprinkle with parsley and serve.

PEACHY CHICKEN BREASTS

Preparation: 30 minutes   *Yield: 6 servings*
Cook: 45 minutes

6 whole chicken breasts,   ½ cup chopped onion
  boned and skinned   ½ cup coarsely chopped
1 ½ teaspoons salt   cashews
⅛ teaspoon pepper   ⅛ teaspoon ground ginger
3 fresh peaches, peeled and   ½ cup butter or margarine
  diced

Preheat oven to 375°. Place each chicken breast on a sheet of waxed paper. Flatten to ¼ inch thickness; sprinkle salt and pepper over inside of breasts. Set chicken aside. Combine peaches, onion, cashews and ginger, stirring well. Place ¼ cup filling in center of each breast; fold side of chicken over filling and secure with a toothpick. Melt butter in a 13 x 9 x 2 inch baking pan; place breasts top side down in butter. Bake for 25 minutes; turn chicken and bake 20 additional minutes. Serve with Peach Sauce.

Peach Sauce:

2 fresh peaches, peeled and   ½ cup firmly packed brown
  sliced   sugar
1 (8 ounce) carton commercial   2 teaspoons Dijon mustard
  sour cream   1 tablespoon brandy
                                  ¼ teaspoon salt

Combine all ingredients in a saucepan; place over low heat for 8 minutes or until heated thoroughly. Yield: 2 cups.

HINT: *Brownish areas on frozen birds are the result of freezer burn, which indicates dehydration or long or improper storage.*

POULTRY

TARRAGON CHICKEN IN WINE SAUCE

Preparation: 1 hour   *Can do ahead*   *Yield: 4 servings*

2 whole chicken breasts,
   boned and skinned
½ teaspoon salt
½ teaspoon pepper
1 ½ tablespoons cornstarch
1 ½ tablespoons vegetable oil
1 egg white, unbeaten

2 (10 ounce) packages frozen
   spinach
6 tablespoons butter or
   margarine
2 cups sliced mushrooms
⅔ cup white wine
1 cup heavy cream
1 tablespoon dried tarragon

Slice chicken into ¼ inch strips. Combine chicken with salt, pepper, cornstarch, oil and egg white in medium bowl. Let stand 10 minutes, or prepare early in the day and let stand in refrigerator. Meanwhile cook spinach according to package directions, drain and keep covered. Melt butter in a large skillet over medium heat. Add chicken and cook until golden (8 to 10 minutes). Remove chicken. Add mushrooms to pan and cook until tender. Add wine, cream and tarragon to pan along with chicken. Simmer over medium heat, stirring occasionally, until sauce is the consistency of heavy cream. Arrange cooked spinach on platter. Spoon chicken and sauce over spinach.

Variation: Rice may be substituted for spinach.

Note: If the sauce is too thin, add a teaspoon of cornstarch dissolved into ½ cup milk to the sauce and it will thicken quickly.

HINT: A 3 ounce skinless broiled chicken breast has only 115 calories - no meat has a lower fat content than chicken.

SWISS BAKED CHICKEN BREASTS

Preparation: 10 minutes   *Yield: 8 servings*
Cook: 50 minutes

¼ cup butter **or** margarine,
   melted
8 chicken breast halves,
   boned and skinned
2 tablespoons chopped chives
1 (6 ounce) package sliced
   Swiss cheese

1 (10 ¾ ounce) can cream of
   chicken soup, undiluted
¼ cup dry white wine
1 cup herb seasoned stuffing
   crumbs, crushed

Preheat oven to 350°. Melt butter in a small saucepan. Set aside. Arrange the chicken in a buttered 13 x 9 x 2 inch baking dish. Sprinkle the chives over the chicken. Place ½ slice of Swiss cheese on each chicken breast half. Mix together the soup and wine. Spread the sauce over the chicken evenly. Sprinkle top with crushed stuffing mix. Drizzle butter over the crumbs. Bake for 45 to 55 minutes, uncovered.

AMARETTO CHICKEN SALAD

Preparation: 45 minutes   *Can do ahead*   *Yield: 6 servings*

½ cup slivered almonds
¼ cup butter
4 cups cubed cooked chicken
   (white meat recommended)
1 (15 ¼ ounce) can crushed
   pineapple, drained

1 cup chopped celery
1 ½ cups mayonnaise
1 teaspoon salt
¼ cup Amaretto
6 lettuce leaves and/or
   pineapple slices

Sauté almonds in butter until golden brown. Drain well. Combine ¼ cup of the almonds, the cubed chicken, crushed pineapple, celery, ½ cup mayonnaise and salt. Cover and chill. Combine remaining 1 cup mayonnaise and Amaretto to make dressing. Chill. When ready to serve, put chicken salad on lettuce leaf or on lettuce leaf and pineapple slice. Generously cover with dressing and sprinkle with remaining ¼ cup almonds.

POULTRY

CELESTIAL CHICKEN SALAD

Preparation: 1 hour   *Can do ahead*   *Yield: 8 to 10 servings*

4 cups cooked, cubed chicken
  breasts or turkey
2 cups very finely chopped
  celery
½ cup pecan halves, toasted

4 slices crisply cooked bacon,
  crumbled
1 cup Hellmann's mayonnaise
1 cup commercial sour cream
1 teaspoon lemon juice

Mix all ingredients. Toss lightly. Chill. Serve on lettuce cups.

Note: If recipe is doubled - do not double lemon juice.

CHICKEN CHUTNEY SALAD

Preparation: 20 minutes   *Can do ahead*   *Yield: 4 servings*
Chill: 1 to 2 hours

2 cups diced, cooked chicken
1 cup pineapple tidbits, drained

1 cup diagonally sliced celery
¼ cup sliced green onion

Dressing:

½ cup Hellmann's mayonnaise
2 tablespoons chopped chutney
½ teaspoon grated lime rind
2 tablespoons lime juice

⅓ teaspoon salt
½ teaspoon curry powder
1 cup salted peanuts for garnish

Toss together chicken, pineapple, celery and green onion. In a separate bowl, combine the dressing ingredients. Stir into chicken mixture. Chill. Serve on greens and top with peanuts.

HINT: If chicken is poached, boning is easier.

FRUITED CHICKEN SALAD

Preparation: 30 minutes　　　*Can do ahead*　　　*Yield: 4 to 6 servings*

3 cups cooked, cubed chicken
　breasts
1 cup seedless grapes
3 cups diced celery
½ cup pineapple tidbits,
　drained
1 tablespoon lemon juice

½ cup chopped almonds <u>or</u>
　pecans (optional)
½ teaspoon salt
¼ teaspoon paprika
1 cup mayonnaise
½ cup heavy cream

Combine chicken, grapes, celery, pineapple, lemon juice and nuts. Chill. In a separate bowl, combine salt, paprika, mayonnaise and cream. Chill. Just before serving combine with chicken mixture. Serve on lettuce and top with nuts.

HOT CHICKEN SALAD #1

Preparation: 15 minutes　　　*Can do ahead*　　　*Yield: 4 to 6 servings*
Cook: 35 minutes

2 cups cooked and shredded
　chicken
½ cup sliced almonds
1 (8 ounce) can sliced water
　chestnuts, drained
1 (2 ounce) jar chopped
　pimentos, drained

½ teaspoon celery seed
1 teaspoon salt
⅛ teaspoon pepper
2 tablespoons lemon juice
1 cup Miracle Whip
¾ cup grated Cheddar cheese
1 (3 ounce) can french fried
　onion rings

Preheat oven to 350°. Mix chicken, almonds, water chestnuts, pimentos, celery seed, salt, pepper, lemon juice and Miracle Whip. Place in casserole and top with cheese. Bake 30 minutes. Add onion rings and bake an additional 5 minutes.

HINT: Use dental floss to truss the bird's legs together when roasting.

POULTRY

HOT CHICKEN SALAD #2

Preparation: 30 minutes   *Can do ahead*   *Yield: 6 to 8 servings*
Cook: 35 minutes

2 cups cooked, cubed
  chicken
1 cup cooked rice
1 (4 ounce) can sliced
  mushrooms
1 tablespoon lemon juice
1 teaspoon salt
1 (8 ounce) can sliced
  water chestnuts, drained
1 cup chopped celery

¾ cup mayonnaise
1 tablespoon chopped
  onion
1 (10 ¾ ounce) can cream
  of chicken soup
4 ounces Mozzarella
  cheese, grated
1 cup crushed corn flakes
½ cup slivered almonds
¼ cup melted butter

Preheat oven to 350°. Combine chicken, rice, mushrooms, lemon juice, salt, water chestnuts, celery, mayonnaise, onion, soup and cheese. Place in a greased 1-quart casserole. Combine corn flakes, almonds and butter. Sprinkle over chicken mixture. Bake 35 minutes.

HOT TURKEY SALAD SOUFFLÉ

Preparation: 20 minutes   *Yield: 10 to 12 servings*
Stand: 1 hour
Cook: 1 ½ hours

6 slices white bread
2 cups diced, cooked
  turkey or chicken
½ cup chopped onion
½ cup chopped green
  pepper
½ cup chopped celery
½ cup mayonnaise

¾ teaspoon salt
Pepper to taste
2 eggs, beaten
1 ½ cups milk
1 (10 ¾ ounce) can cream
  of mushroom soup
½ cup shredded Cheddar
  cheese

Grease baking dish. Cube 2 slices of bread and trim crusts from remaining 4 slices of bread. Place cubed bread in bottom of baking dish. Combine turkey, onion, green pepper, celery, mayonnaise, salt and pepper. Spoon over cubed bread. Arrange the 4 slices of bread over turkey mixture. Combine milk and eggs and pour over ingredients. Cover and chill 1 hour. Preheat oven to 350°. After 1 hour spread mushroom soup over casserole - do not spread to edge of pan. Bake 1 hour. Add cheese and bake an additional 15 minutes.

178

BARBECUED CHICKEN

Preparation: 15 minutes   *Can do ahead*
Cook: 1 hour
Grill: 15 minutes

2 cups ketchup
3 cups water
2 cups sugar
1 cup vinegar
¼ cup margarine
¼ cup butter

1 tablespoon Tabasco
¼ cup mustard
3 tablespoons salt
2 teaspoons pepper
3 pounds skinned and
    boned chicken pieces

Mix together all ingredients except chicken in a large Dutch oven. Bring to boil. Add chicken. Cook over low heat for one hour. Refrigerate until ready to grill. Do early in the day or the day before.

Note: This recipe may be halved. The amount of chicken depends on the number of people served. This also works well with country ribs.

BRUNSWICK STEW

Preparation: 1 hour   *Yield: 10 to 12 servings*
Cook: 5 hours

1 ½ pounds stew beef
1 stewing chicken
4 medium potatoes, diced
½ head of small cabbage,
    thinly sliced
1 (10 ounce) package
    frozen lima beans
4 medium onions, finely
    chopped

4 cups fresh corn (approx-
    imately 8 ears) <u>or</u>
    2 (10 ounce) packages
    frozen corn
1 (20 ounce) can tomatoes
Salt
Pepper
Piece of dried red pepper
1 (8 ounce) can peas (optional)
½ cup butter

Cook beef and chicken together until tender, at least 2 hours. Pull chicken and beef from bones cutting into small pieces, and return to broth. Add potatoes, cabbage, lima beans, onions, corn, tomatoes, salt, pepper and a small piece of dried red pepper. Cook 1 hour covered, then uncover and cook down until thick (approximately 2 hours). If too much fat on top, skim off and add butter.

POULTRY

CHICKEN BREASTS OVER RICE

Preparation: 35 minutes   Can do ahead   *Yield: 8 servings*
Cook: 1 hour

1 (6 ounce) package seasoned
  long-grained and wild rice
8 chicken breast halves,
  boned and skinned
3 tablespoons butter or
  margarine
¼ cup chopped onion
½ cup slivered almonds

1 (4 ounce) can mushroom
  pieces and stems, drained
½ (10 ¾ ounce) can cream of
  mushroom soup, undiluted
½ cup chicken broth
1 (8 ounce) carton commercial
  sour cream

Preheat oven to 375°. Prepare rice according to package directions. While rice is cooking brown the chicken in margarine in a large skillet. Remove chicken pieces and sauté the onions in the same pan until they are translucent. Add the almonds and sauté briefly. Add drained mushrooms and cooked rice. Mix well. Transfer the rice mixture to a buttered casserole. Put the breasts on top of the rice. Mix the soup, broth and sour cream. Pour over the chicken and rice. Bake covered for 45 minutes and then uncovered for 15 minutes. If rice looks dry, add more chicken broth.

CHICKEN CASSEROLE

Preparation: 1 hour   Can do ahead   *Yield: 6 servings*
Cook: 1 hour   Can be frozen

2 or 3 raw chicken breasts or
  2 whole chickens
1 (8 ounce) package wide
  noodles
1 (8 ounce) package cream
  cheese, softened
1 cup commercial sour cream

2 (10 ¾ ounce) cans cream of
  chicken soup
1 small onion, minced
½ teaspoon garlic powder
½ teaspoon salt
1 cup dry bread crumbs
⅓ cup melted butter

Boil chicken ½ hour or until tender. Strain the broth and cook noodles in the broth according to the package directions. While the noodles are cooking, skin, debone and cut the chicken into bite sized pieces and set aside. Drain noodles. Preheat oven to 325°. Cut cream cheese in pieces and add to hot noodles. Cover and let stand for 5 minutes. Stir. Add sour cream, soup, onion, garlic powder and salt. Stir and add chicken. Stir again. Put in greased casserole. Add bread crumbs to melted butter and sprinkle over chicken mixture. Bake 1 hour.

CHICKEN CACCIATORE

Preparation: 45 minutes   *Yield: 4 to 6 servings*
Cook: 30 minutes

4 medium carrots, cut into
  3 inch strips
3 medium stalks celery, cut
  into 3 inch strips
⅓ cup chopped fresh parsley
1 cup chopped onion
1 cup sliced fresh mushrooms
¼ pound butter

1 clove garlic, minced
6 chicken breasts, boned
Seasoning salt
1 ½ teaspoons oregano
1 teaspoon sweet basil
1 (16 ounce) can tomato sauce
½ cup dry sherry

Prepare carrots and celery. Chop parsley, onion and mushrooms. Set aside. Brown minced garlic in butter in fry pan over low heat. Sprinkle seasoning salt over boned chicken breasts and place in frying pan to brown. Add prepared carrots, celery, parsley, onion, mushrooms, oregano and sweet basil. Cover and steam for 10 minutes over low heat. Add tomato sauce and dry sherry. Stir lightly and simmer uncovered for 20 minutes.

Note: May be served over hot spaghetti or Dumplings Italian Style (see Index).

CHICKEN CASSEROLE WITH ALMONDS

Preparation: 10 minutes   *Yield: 20 servings*
Cook: 1 hour

2 (4 pound) chickens, boiled,
  cooled, meat removed and
  cut up (reserving broth)
4 (10 ¾ ounce) cans cream of
  mushroom soup, undiluted
3 cups chicken broth

4 (3 ounce) cans chow mein
  noodles
1 (2 ¾ ounce) package almond
  slices
4 cups chopped celery
¾ cup chopped onions
1 (2 ounce) jar pimentos,
  chopped

Preheat oven to 300°. Heat soup in large saucepan. Add 3 cups reserved chicken broth and the rest of the ingredients. Mix well. Pour into two greased 9 x 13 inch casseroles. Bake for 1 hour.

POULTRY

CHICKEN AND CHEESE CASSEROLE

Preparation: 30 minutes   *Do ahead*   *Yield: 6 servings*
Chill: Overnight
Stand: 1 hour
Cook: 1 hour

7 slices bread
3 or 4 whole chicken breasts,
  cooked and cubed
2 (4 ounce) packages grated
  Cheddar cheese

3 eggs
2 ½ cups milk
1 teaspoon salt
1 teaspoon paprika

Trim crusts from bread, spread with butter and cut in cubes. Line the bottom of a 9 x 13 inch baking dish with cubes. Place chunks of chicken over bread and cover with cheese. Combine eggs, milk and salt. Mix and pour over casserole. Sprinkle with paprika. Let stand in refrigerator overnight. Remove from refrigerator one hour before baking. Bake in 325° oven for one hour.

Note: Ham and/or turkey may also be used.

CHICKEN MACIEL

Preparation: 15 minutes   *Can do ahead*   *Yield: 3 to 4 servings*
Cook: 30 minutes   *Can be frozen*

2 pounds cold boiled chicken
3 ounces butter
½ teaspoon paprika
1 heaping teaspoon curry
  powder
1 pint heavy cream

1 heaping teaspoon cornstarch
2 ounces sherry
1 cup cooked rice
Salt
½ cup grated Swiss cheese

Preheat oven to 350°. Dice chicken into 1 inch pieces. Sauté 5 minutes in melted butter with paprika and curry. Bring 1 pint of cream to a boil. Add cornstarch that has been dissolved in sherry. Stir constantly until mixture thickens. Fold in chicken and rice. Salt to taste. Sprinkle top with grated Swiss cheese. Bake 25 or 30 minutes.

CHICKEN-SAUSAGE MARENGO

Preparation: 20 minutes
Cook: 1 hour

Yield: 6 to 8 servings

1 pound sweet sausage
2 tablespoons butter
2 tablespoons salad <u>or</u> olive oil
2 broiling chickens cut in
   pieces
1 (1 pound 12 ounce) can
   tomato purée
1 (6 ounce) can sliced
   mushrooms, reserving liquid
1 (8 ounce) can pitted ripe
   black olives, sliced, reserving
   liquid

¼ cup sweet pepper flakes
1 tablespoon parsley flakes
2 teaspoons celery flakes
1 ½ teaspoons Italian seasoning
1 teaspoon instant minced
   onion
½ teaspoon salt
¼ teaspoon pepper
1 bay leaf
½ cup liquid from mushrooms
¼ cup liquid from olives

Cook sausage until brown. Cut in small pieces and place on paper towel to drain. Add butter and oil to the drippings. Brown chicken and remove to paper towel to drain. Skim off any fat and add tomato purée, mushrooms, olives, sweet pepper flakes, celery flakes, Italian seasoning, minced onion, salt, pepper, bay leaf and liquids. Return the chicken and sausage and simmer covered 30 to 40 minutes or longer.

CROCKPOT CHICKEN

Preparation: 5 minutes
Cook: Crockpot 4 to 10 hours

Yield: 4 to 6 servings

Various chicken pieces,
   8 to 10
1 (15 ounce) can tomato sauce

1 (1 ½ ounce) package dry
   spaghetti sauce mix
1 (4 ounce) can mushroom
   pieces, with liquid

Place chicken pieces in crockpot. Combine tomato sauce, spaghetti sauce mix and mushrooms. Mix well. Pour over chicken. Cook on Low 8 to 10 hours or cook on High for 4 hours.

Note: Serve with spaghetti noodles, tossed salad and French bread.

POULTRY

CHICKEN AND SPINACH NOODLE CASSEROLE

Preparation: 1 ½ hours   *Can do ahead*   *Yield: 8 servings*
Cook: 45 minutes   *Can be frozen*

4 pounds chicken breasts
½ cup margarine
1 cup chopped bell pepper
1 cup chopped celery
1 cup chopped onion
½ pound processed cheese
1 (6 ounce) jar stuffed
   olives, drained

1 (6 ounce) can sliced
   mushrooms, drained
1 (6 ounce) package spinach
   noodles
4 cups chicken stock
1 (10 ¾ ounce) can cream of
   mushroom soup, undiluted

Boil chicken breasts in seasoned water (lightly salted, onion, thyme, celery).
Use enough water to have 4 cups of chicken stock. Save stock. Bone chicken
and cut in large pieces. This can be done in advance. Sauté in margarine the
bell pepper, onion and celery. Stir in cheese, cut in cubes. Add whole olives
and mushroom slices and then stir in chicken. Boil spinach noodles in three
cups of stock, until stock is absorbed. Add mushroom soup to the noodles.
Mix all ingredients together in 2-quart casserole and serve hot. One cup of
stock may be used to moisten the mixture if needed.

Note: If prepared ahead, reheat at 300° for about 45 minutes. It is even better
reheated.

CURRIED HONEY CHICKEN

Preparation: 15 minutes   *Yield: 6 servings*
Cook: 1 ½ hours

2 (3 pound) frying chickens,
   cut up
¼ cup melted butter
½ cup honey

¼ cup prepared mustard
1 teaspoon salt
1 teaspoon curry powder

Preheat oven to 375°. Dip chicken in mixture of butter, honey, mustard, salt
and curry powder. Place in roasting pan, meaty side up. Bake for 1 ½ hours.
Baste occasionally with drippings in pan. Serve with rice.

CHICKEN AND WILD RICE

Preparation: 30 minutes   *Yield: 6 to 8 servings*
Cook: 25 to 35 minutes

1 ½ cups chicken broth
1 ½ cups light cream
¼ cup flour
½ cup butter, softened
1 ½ teaspoons salt
½ teaspoon pepper
1 small onion

1 (2 ounce) jar pimentos,
   drained
8 sprigs parsley
1 cup cooked wild rice
1 (8 ounce) can mushrooms,
   drained
3 cups cubed, cooked chicken
½ cup slivered almonds

Preheat oven to 350°. Put chicken broth, cream, flour, butter, salt, pepper, onion, pimento and parsley in a blender. Blend until vegetables are chopped. Transfer to pan and cook over low heat until thickened. Mix sauce with prepared rice, mushrooms and cooked chicken. Pour into buttered 2-quart casserole. Top with ½ cup slivered almonds. Bake 25 to 35 minutes.

MEXICAN CHICKEN CASSEROLE

Preparation: 10 minutes   *Can do ahead*   *Yield: 6 servings*
Cook: 45 minutes   *Can be frozen*

1 chicken, cooked and boned
1 (10 ¾ ounce) can cream of
   mushroom soup
1 (10 ¾ ounce) can cream of
   chicken soup
1 pound grated Colby or
   Cheddar cheese
2 cups chicken broth

2 to 3 green chilies (use
   according to taste)
2 teaspoons chili powder
1 (4 ounce) jar pimentos,
   chopped
1 onion, chopped
½ of 1 (8 ounce) package taco
   flavored tortilla chips

Preheat oven to 325°. Mix all the ingredients together. Place in a large casserole. Bake for 45 minutes.

HINT: *Freeze leftover pieces of chicken in a heavy duty freezer bag or plastic container to have on hand for future recipes.*

POULTRY

SARAH'S CHICKEN CASSEROLE

Preparation: 10 minutes   *Can do ahead*   *Yield: 20 servings*
Cook: 30 minutes

6 to 8 cups cooked chicken
  chunks
2 ½ cups thin diagonally cut
  celery
¼ cup grated onion
1 ½ tablespoons salt
1 tablespoon pepper
1 cup sliced water chestnuts

3 (6 ounce) boxes wild rice,
  cooked
¼ cup lemon juice
2 ½ cups mayonnaise
1 cup chicken broth
2 cups grated mild
  Cheddar cheese

Preheat oven to 350°. Mix all ingredients and place in 2 (9 x 13 inch) casseroles. Bake for 30 minutes until thoroughly heated and cheese is melted.

Note: Good for a buffet supper party.

SOUFFLÉD CHICKEN SUPREME

Preparation: 30 minutes   *Yield: 6 servings*
Cook: 40 minutes

1 (10 ¾ ounce) can cream of
  mushroom soup
1 cup milk
2 cups diced cooked chicken
3 tablespoons butter <u>or</u>
  margarine

¼ cup flour
¾ cup milk
4 eggs, separated
1 teaspoon salt
Few drops Tabasco
¼ teaspoon cream of tartar

Preheat oven to 375°. Blend soup with 1 cup milk. Add chicken and pour into 2-quart shallow baking dish. Melt butter or margarine in small saucepan. Blend in flour; cook, stirring constantly, until bubbly. Stir in ¾ cup milk; continue cooking and stirring until mixture thickens and bubbles 1 minute; cool. Beat yolks with salt and pepper seasoning in a large bowl. Beat in hot mixture. Beat whites with cream of tartar just until stiff peaks form. Fold whites, ½ at a time, into yolk mixture just until well combined. Spoon souffle mixture over chicken in baking dish. Bake for 40 minutes, or until puffed and browned.

MEATS

BEEF TENDERLOIN À LA BURGUNDY

Preparation: 30 minutes   *Yield: 8 to 10 servings*
Roast: 50 to 70 minutes

1 whole beef tenderloin,
  trimmed (3 ½ to 6 pounds)
Suet, sliced thinly to cover
  tenderloin
Burgundy wine (½ to 1 bottle) -
  do not use a commercially
  made cooking wine
¼ cup butter

1 small onion, chopped
1 (8 ounce) can sliced
  mushrooms
3 tablespoons flour
1 (10 ½ ounce) can beef broth,
  if needed
¼ to ½ teaspoon gravy
  browning sauce, optional
Salt and pepper to taste

Preheat oven to 400°. Place whole trimmed tenderloin in roasting pan. Completely cover surface of meat with suet slices. Insert meat thermometer at least 2 inches from end of roast. Put in oven and roast until edges of suet slices curl back (about 15 minutes). Remove the suet and pour ½ bottle of Burgundy over the meat. Reduce oven temperature to 325° and roast with repeated bastings of pan drippings until desired doneness; 140° internal temperature for rare or 160° internal temperature for medium, approximately 50 to 70 minutes at the 325° setting, adding more wine if necessary. While meat is roasting start sauce preparation.

Sauce:

In a large skillet melt butter and sauté chopped onion. Drain mushroom liquid into a 2 cup measure. Add drained mushrooms and flour to butter and onions. Brown slightly, stirring constantly about 3 to 5 minutes on medium heat. The sauce can be set aside at this point until the meat is ready. After taking the meat from the oven, pour the wine and drippings into the 2 cup measure until full. If more liquid is needed to make 2 cups, add wine or beef broth. Pour liquid into the warm onion-mushroom mixture and cook, stirring constantly, until hot and smooth; approximately 3 minutes. If a browner color is desired, add ¼ to ½ teaspoon gravy browning sauce. Salt and pepper to taste. Serve sauce separately with the meat.

Note: The temperatures used in this recipe are contrary to all instructions for roasting tenderloin. With the repeated bastings the meat stays juicy and flavorful.

BEEF TENDERLOIN

Preparation: 10 minutes   *Yield: 6 to 8 servings*
Bake: 30 minutes

1 beef tenderloin, 3 ½ to 6   **Garlic salt**
pounds   **Soy sauce**
½ cup margarine, melted

Melt margarine in iron skillet. When cool, roll whole tenderloin in margarine. Rub garlic salt all over and pour soy sauce over all sides. Let meat sit until room temperature. Bake at 450° for 30 minutes for medium rare tenderloin.

MEAT MARINADE FOR BEEF TENDERLOIN OR FLANK STEAK

Preparation: 5 minutes   *Yield: 6 to 8 servings*
Marinate: 4 hours or overnight

½ cup real butter   **2 tablespoons Worcestershire**
½ cup olive oil   **sauce**
¼ cup vinegar   **½ teaspoon dried red pepper**
Juice of 2 lemons   **flakes**
½ to 1 teaspoon garlic powder

Combine all ingredients in a saucepan and bring to a boil. Pour over a 3 ½ to 4 pound beef tenderloin. Marinate for 2 to 4 hours. Bake at 375° about 30 minutes for medium rare.

Note: This marinade is also used for flank steak or shish kabobs. Marinate steak overnight, then grill 4 ½ minutes on each side for medium rare.

HINT: A meatloaf can be cooked more quickly if it is placed in a tube pan rather than a loaf pan.

MEATS

ROAST BEEF DIJON

Preparation: 10 to 15 minutes   *Yield: 12 servings*
Roast: 2 to 3 hours

2 cups soft white bread
  crumbs
½ cup chopped parsley
2 cloves garlic, crushed
1 rounded teaspoon salt
½ teaspoon pepper

½ teaspoon thyme leaves
6 pounds rib eye roast
4 tablespoons Dijon-style
  mustard
½ cup butter or margarine,
  melted

Preheat oven to 325°. Make bread crumbs with 3 to 4 slices of fresh white bread, using a blender or food processor. Combine bread crumbs, parsley, garlic, salt, pepper and thyme. Wipe roast with damp paper towels and put in open roasting pan. Spread mustard over top of roast. Press seasoned crumb mixture into mustard. Drizzle with melted butter and insert meat thermometer into the center of roast. Roast uncovered until meat thermometer registers 140° for rare or 160° for medium, approximately 2 to 2 ¼ hours or 2 ¼ to 3 hours respectively. For easier carving, let roast stand for 15 minutes while preparing mushroom gravy.

Mushroom Gravy:

¼ cup meat drippings
3 tablespoons flour
1 (10 ½ ounce) can condensed
  beef broth, undiluted

1 (4 ounce) can sliced
  mushrooms
Salt and pepper to taste

Pour off drippings in roasting pan, returning ¼ cup drippings to pan. Stir in the flour until smooth. Brown over low heat, stirring to loosen any brown bits in pan. Drain mushrooms, reserving liquid. Add mushroom liquid to beef broth to make 2 cups liquid, adding water, if necessary. Slowly stir into flour mixture. Add sliced mushrooms. Bring to boil, stirring until smooth and mushrooms are heated. Makes 2 ¼ cups.

Note: The crumb topping works well with other types of beef roasts. For smaller roasts use proportionate amounts of crumb mixture, mustard, etc.

HINT: *Dry wine serves as a tenderizer for meat.*

BEEF ROULADEN

Preparation: 1 hour *Can do ahead* *Yield: 8 servings*
Cook: 45 minutes

3 pound sirloin tip roast,
sliced ¼ inch thick
2 large onions, finely
chopped
10 tablespoons butter or
margarine
1 ½ pounds mushrooms
¾ pound cooked ham, sliced
⅜ inch thick

¾ cup grated Parmesan cheese
1 cup dry red wine
1 cup beef broth
1 teaspoon salt
Freshly ground pepper
2 tablespoons each cornstarch
and cold water
2 tablespoons chopped fresh
parsley

Cut away fat from each meat slice. Place 1 slice at a time between pieces of waxed paper and pound lightly with smooth side of a mallet until meat is about ¹⁄₁₆ inch thick. Then cut each piece into rectangles about 4 by 6 inches. In large skillet, cook onions in 2 tablespoons of the butter until limp; transfer to a bowl. Finely chop half the mushrooms (save smallest ones for the sauce) and cook chopped mushrooms in 2 tablespoons of butter; add to onions. Cut ham into julienne strips about ½ inch long and ⅛ inch wide and add to mushroom mixture along with cheese; mix lightly. Place 1 heaping tablespoon of filling on each meat rectangle; fold the long sides of meat over the filling about ½ inch on each side and roll up meat; secure with toothpick. Repeat until all meat rolls are filled.

Using two large skillets, melt 2 tablespoons butter in each pan and brown meat rolls, turning to brown all sides. Pour in wine and broth and season with salt and pepper. Cover and simmer gently until meat is fork tender, about 10 to 15 minutes. Remove toothpicks from meat rolls and transfer to ovenproof serving dish. Combine wine juices in a single skillet and bring to boil. Stir in cornstarch blended with water and cook, stirring, until thickened. In other skillet, cook remaining whole mushrooms (slice if larger than bite size) in 2 tablespoons of butter for about 5 minutes, and add to meat sauce. Pour the mushroom and meat sauce over the meat rolls. (Can make ahead to this point, let cool, cover and refrigerate.) Heat at 375°, covered, for 20 minutes. (If refrigerated, heat for 45 to 50 minutes or until heated through.) Sprinkle with parsley before serving.

MEATS

BOUNTIFUL BEAST

Preparation: 15 minutes   *Yield: 6 to 8 servings*
Marinate: 24 hours
Grill to taste

Meat tenderizer, unflavored
1 (2 to 3 inch) lean chuck steak
1 clove garlic
1 cup Burgundy wine
¼ cup red wine vinegar

½ cup safflower or olive oil
Lots of cracked black pepper
Pinch of oregano
Pinch of basil
1 large sliced onion

Put tenderizer on both sides of beef and pierce with fork. Mix remaining ingredients in bowl. Put tenderized beef in bowl with ingredients. Let marinate for 24 hours, turning meat every 3 to 4 hours. Cook over hot charcoal fire until pink all the way through. Slice thin and serve hot or cold.

EASY ROSEMARY ROAST

Preparation: 15 minutes   *Yield: 8 to 10 servings*
Cook: 2 hours 45 minutes

1 (4 to 5 pound) chuck roast
2 tablespoons vegetable oil
½ cup water
½ cup ketchup
¼ cup red wine vinegar
2 tablespoons Worcestershire
   sauce

1 teaspoon dried rosemary
   leaves
½ teaspoon salt
1 small piece bay leaf
1 large onion, thinly sliced
6 medium potatoes
6 carrots

In a large Dutch oven, brown roast on all sides in hot oil. Combine water, ketchup, vinegar, Worcestershire sauce, rosemary, salt and bay leaf. Pour over roast. Add sliced onion; cover and simmer 2 hours. Peel and quarter potatoes. Peel carrots and cut into 1 ½ inch lengths. Add potatoes and carrots to roast. Cover and cook about 45 minutes longer or until potatoes and carrots are tender.

BARBECUED BEEF BRISKET

Preparation: 15 minutes 　　　　*Yield: 6 to 8 servings*
Marinate: Overnight
Bake: 4 ½ hours

Beef Brisket, 3 to 4 pounds

Marinade:

½ teaspoon onion salt　　　　2 tablespoons liquid smoke
½ teaspoon celery salt　　　　¼ cup plus 2 tablespoons
¼ teaspoon garlic salt　　　　　Worcestershire sauce

Sprinkle dry ingredients on meat, add liquid and cover with foil. Refrigerate overnight, turning once. Preheat oven to 275°. Put drained brisket in covered baking pan, reserving the marinade for sauce. Bake for 4 ½ hours.

Sauce:

2 tablespoons light brown　　　¼ teaspoon pepper
　sugar　　　　　　　　　　　1 cup chili sauce
2 tablespoons vinegar　　　　　½ cup reserved meat marinade
½ teaspoon salt

Combine all ingredients for sauce in medium saucepan and bring to a boil. Simmer 10 minutes or until sauce thickens. Pour over meat and serve.

FLANK STEAK MARINADE

Preparation: 15 minutes　　　　*Yield: 4 servings*
Marinate: 4 hours or longer
Broil: 10 minutes

¼ cup soy sauce　　　　　　　2 tablespoons cider vinegar
½ cup oil　　　　　　　　　　1 tablespoon honey
½ teaspoon ginger　　　　　　2 to 4 pounds flank steak,
½ teaspoon garlic powder　　　　scored
½ teaspoon onion powder

Mix together soy sauce, oil, ginger, garlic powder, onion powder, vinegar and honey. Score flank steak deeply and marinate steak for 4 hours or longer, turning often. Broil steak about 5 minutes on each side.

MEATS

FLANK STEAK AND BACON TOURNEDOS

Preparation: 30 minutes　　　　　　　　　　　　*Yield: 4 servings*
Grill: 15 minutes, covered

1 to 1 ½ pounds flank steak
　(ask butcher to run it
　through meat tenderizer
　machine)
Instant non-seasoned meat
　tenderizer

½ pound bacon
1 teaspoon garlic salt
½ teaspoon ground pepper
2 tablespoons snipped parsley
1 (1 ¾ ounce) envelope
　Bernaise sauce mix

Preheat grill. Sprinkle tenderizer on flank steak. If butcher cannot tenderize it, then pound it to an even thickness of about ½ inch. Cook bacon until almost done but not crisp. Sprinkle steak with garlic salt and pepper. Score steak diagonally. Place bacon strips lengthwise on flank steak. Sprinkle with parsley. Roll up, starting at narrow end. Skewer with wooden picks at 1 inch intervals. Cut in 1 inch slices (8 slices). Grill over medium coals, 15 minutes, turning once for rare. Prepare Bernaise sauce according to directions on package. Serve sauce with steaks.

GRILLED STEAK ROLL-UPS

Preparation: 30 minutes　　　　*Can do ahead*　　　　*Yield: 6 servings*
Grill: 20 minutes, covered

6 sirloin tip steaks, sliced
　very thinly
2 teaspoons Worcestershire
　sauce
2 teaspoons prepared mustard

6 kosher dill pickle spears,
　drained and patted dry
½ cup grated Cheddar or
　Colby cheese
½ cup cooked, crumbled bacon

Preheat a covered grill. Mix Worcestershire sauce and mustard together. Spread mustard mixture on steaks with a spoon. Place 1 pickle spear on end of each steak. Sprinkle with cheese and bacon. Roll in jelly roll fashion from pickle end to tip and secure with pick. Place on covered grill at medium heat for 10 minutes. Turn and cook 10 minutes longer.

Note: Have the butcher slice the steaks as thinly as possible.

MICROWAVE STIR-FRY BEEF DELIGHT

Preparation: 30 minutes to 1 hour *Yield: 4 to 6 servings*
Cook: 15 minutes

Marinade:

¼ cup soy sauce
1 tablespoon cornstarch
2 tablespoons vegetable oil
1 teaspoon ground ginger
⅛ teaspoon garlic powder
¼ teaspoon pepper
2 cups sliced fresh
  mushrooms

1 (6 ounce) package frozen
  pea pods (defrost in
  package 1 to 2 minutes -
  DO NOT COOK)
1 small onion, sliced and
  separated into rings
1 pound beef flank or sirloin
  steak cut in ⅛ to ¼ inch strips
  1 ½ to 2 inches long

Combine marinade ingredients in order given and stir in meat to coat well. Marinate at room temperature 20 to 30 minutes or marinate in refrigerator several hours. Preheat 10-inch browning dish at 100% power for 5 ½ minutes. Add meat and marinade quickly, stir 30 seconds. Add lid and cook on 100% power until pink color is lost. DO NOT OVERCOOK. Add remaining ingredients, stir well. Cook at 5 ½ to 8 minutes on 100% power until vegetables are tender crisp and meat is done. Stir every 2 minutes.

Tip: Excellent served over a bed of rice and topped with Chinese noodles.

Note: May increase marinade by adding 2 to 3 tablespoons dry sherry.

Variation: Omit pea pods and substitute 1 large green pepper cut in strips.

HINT: Sprinkle a fry pan with salt to keep meat from sticking without adding extra calories.

MEATS

MARINATED BARBECUED CHUCK STEAK

Preparation: 10 minutes   *Yield: 2 servings*
Marinate: Overnight
Grill: 16 to 20 minutes

1 tablespoon chili powder
2 teaspoons ground ginger
1 teaspoon salt
1 clove garlic, minced
2 tablespoons minced onion

⅓ cup lemon juice
¼ cup olive oil
1 (2 pound) chuck steak,
   about 1 inch thick

Combine first 7 ingredients; stir. Place steak in a large shallow bowl, pour marinade over steak. Turn steak to coat both sides with marinade, cover and refrigerate 10 hours or overnight. Remove steak from marinade and place on grill over hot coals. Cook 8 to 10 minutes on each side or until desired degree of doneness.

MAMA'S STROGANOFF

Preparation: 30 minutes   *Can do ahead*   *Yield: 4 servings*
Cook: 1 ½ hours   *Can be frozen*

¼ cup olive oil
2 medium onions, sliced
   thinly
½ pound fresh mushrooms,
   sliced or 2 (4 ounce) cans
   mushrooms
1 pound lean beef (top or
   bottom round), cut in strips

2 tablespoons flour
1 (16 ounce) can tomatoes
   and juice
1 teaspoon salt
⅛ teaspoon pepper
¼ cup Worcestershire sauce
½ cup commercial sour cream

Sauté onions in olive oil, add mushrooms and sauté for 5 minutes. Remove mushrooms and onions and set aside. Brown beef in remaining olive oil. Add flour to beef and stir until absorbed. Add tomatoes (put through blender), salt, pepper and Worcestershire sauce to beef. Cook 1 hour, covered. After 1 hour, add onions, mushrooms and sour cream. Cook uncovered 30 minutes. Serve over wild rice or noodles.

STEAK PIZZAIOLA
from
Chef Geoffrey Fennessey of La Pola's Italian Restaurant
Hilton Head, South Carolina

Preparation: 10 to 15 minutes   *Yield: 1 to 2 servings*
Cook: 20 to 30 minutes

1 cup tomato purée
1 clove garlic, pressed
½ teaspoon dry basil
1 (12 ounce) sirloin strip steak
Salt and pepper
1 clove garlic, mashed
1 tablespoon cooking oil
½ medium onion, chopped

6 mushrooms, sliced
½ medium zucchini, cut in
   bite size pieces (about 1 cup)
2 ounces dry red wine
   (Valpolicella or Beaujolais)
1 to 2 servings of pasta, cooked
   and drained

Simmer tomato purée, pressed garlic and basil in a small saucepan for 15 minutes. While sauce is simmering, season steak with salt, pepper and rub meat with garlic. Pan fry in hot oil, searing steak to desired doneness. Add onions, mushrooms and zucchini. Cook until soft. Add tomato-basil sauce and simmer 4 minutes. Add wine and simmer 2 minutes longer. Serve vegetable-tomato sauce over steak and cooked pasta. Garnish with parsley sprig.

SHERRIED BEEF

Preparation: 15 minutes   *Can do ahead*   *Yield: 6 to 8 servings*
Bake: 3 hours

3 pounds sirloin
2 (10 ¾ ounce) cans cream of
   mushroom soup
¾ cup sherry

1 envelope dry onion soup mix
⅓ cup slivered almonds
1 (8 ounce) can mushrooms,
   drained

Preheat oven to 325°. Trim fat from sirloin. Cut in strips. Place in 3 quart casserole. Mix all other ingredients. Pour mixture over meat. Mix all together. Bake for 3 hours in covered casserole dish. Serve with rice or noodles.

MEATS

TOURNEDOS

Preparation: 1 hour   *Yield: 6 servings*
Cook: 30 minutes

6 crustless rounds of white
  bread
3 to 4 tablespoons clarified
  butter
½ pound fresh mushrooms,
  cleaned and sliced
2 tablespoons butter
1 tablespoon oil
2 tablespoons minced shallots
  or onion
¼ teaspoon salt
Dash of pepper

6 filet mignons (1 inch thick
  and 2 ½ inches in diameter)
6 slices bacon
2 tablespoons butter
1 tablespoon oil
Salt and pepper to taste
1 cup beef bouillon
2 tablespoons tomato paste
¼ cup red wine
1 tablespoon cornstarch
2 tablespoons minced parsley

Brown bread rounds in hot butter on each side. Wrap in foil and reheat in oven just before serving. In same skillet, sauté mushrooms in hot butter and oil for five minutes to brown them lightly. Stir in onions and cook slowly for 2 more minutes. Season and set aside.

Dry steaks on paper towel and wrap a slice of bacon around each steak. Place butter and oil in skillet and set on moderately high heat. When butter foam begins to subside, sauté steaks 3 to 4 minutes on each side (longer for medium and well done). Remove from skillet, season with salt and pepper and place on a warm serving platter.

Pour off fat; stir in the mixture of bouillon and tomato paste. Boil rapidly, stirring to loosen any brown bits in the pan; reduce liquid a little. Mix the cornstarch with red wine and add to the bouillon mixture; boil rapidly for a minute to evaporate the alcohol and to thicken sauce lightly. Add minced parsley and mushroom and onion mixture; simmer a minute more. Place steaks on top of bread rounds and pour sauce over each steak.

HINT: *To keep fats in the frying pan from spattering, sprinkle salt in the bottom of the pan.*

198

BOEUF BOURGUIGNON

Preparation: 30 to 40 minutes   *Do ahead*   *Yield: 4 servings*
Cook: 2 hours   *Can be frozen*

2 pounds top round steak
  (plain round, sirloin, <u>or</u>
  tenderized chuck)
2 tablespoons margarine
3 tablespoons flour for
  thickening
½ cup sherry, heated
24 small canned onions

5 slices diced bacon
1 cup Burgundy wine
2 tablespoons tomato paste
2 bay leaves
¾ cup beef consommé
¼ cup water
1 pound fresh sliced mushrooms

Cut beef in 1 inch cubes, removing gristle; brown in margarine, put in Dutch oven and add flour and heated sherry. Sauté onions with diced bacon and add to meat (reserve bacon grease for mushrooms). Add Burgundy, tomato paste, bay leaves, consommé and water. Cook over low heat at least two hours. Sauté mushrooms in bacon grease; add during last ½ hour of cooking. Chives, thyme, tarragon and parsley may also be used. Serve over or with rice.

BEEF WINE STEW

Preparation: 10 minutes   *Can do ahead*   *Yield: 4 to 6 servings*
Bake: 3 hours   *Can be frozen*

½ cup red wine
1 (10 ½ ounce) can consommé
¼ cup herbed poultry stuffing,
  finely crushed
¼ cup flour, sifted
½ teaspoon bouquet garni

½ teaspoon salt
¼ teaspoon pepper
1 medium onion, sliced
2 pounds lean, boneless stewing
  beef
Parsley

Preheat oven to 300°. Mix wine and consommé together in a 2 quart casserole dish. Mix the stuffing mix, flour, bouquet garni, salt and pepper together and add to liquid. Beat with a wire whisk, mixing well. Stir in onion and beef. Cover tightly and bake 3 hours. Stir at least once during the baking time. Sprinkle with parsley before serving.

Note: May be served on bed of rice.

MEATS

JUNIOR LEAGUE OVEN STEW

Preparation: 15 to 20 minutes   *Can do ahead*   *Yield: 6 to 8 servings*
Bake: 3 ½ to 5 hours   *Can be frozen*

6 small carrots
3 medium potatoes
2 pounds stew meat
1 (28 ounce) can tomatoes
1 tablespoon sugar
1 diced onion

1 ½ teaspoons salt
½ cup water
½ cup chopped celery
1 tablespoon tapioca
1 slice bread, cubed
½ cup red wine

Preheat oven to 325°. Cut carrots in strips, peel and quarter potatoes. Combine all ingredients. Do not brown meat. Pour into 3 quart casserole. Bake covered in oven for 3 ½ hours. May add more onion, potatoes or carrots depending on personal preference. To serve more, extra meat may be added. Broth amount remains the same.

Variation: Eliminate the water and increase the wine to 1 cup for a tastier broth. Cheddar cheese croutons may be substituted for the bread.

Note: Reduce heat to 275° and bake for 5 hours if gone for the day.

CHEESEBURGER LOAF

Preparation: 30 minutes   *Can do ahead*   *Yield: 6 servings*
Bake: 1 hour
Stand: 5 to 10 minutes

½ cup evaporated milk
1 egg
1 cup cracker crumbs
1 ½ pounds ground beef
   (chuck preferred)

2 tablespoons finely chopped
   onion
1 ½ teaspoons salt, or to taste
1 teaspoon dry mustard
1 tablespoon ketchup
1 cup grated American cheese

Preheat oven to 350°. Combine all ingredients except cheese in bowl and mix thoroughly. Lightly grease a loaf pan. Put ⅓ of meat mixture in the bottom of pan and spread out evenly. Put ½ cup of cheese on top, keeping cheese away from the edge of the pan (to prevent sticking). Repeat layers (⅓ meat - ½ cup cheese - ⅓ meat). Bake one hour. Let loaf stand for 5 to 10 minutes before placing on a platter.

CORN BREAD PIE

Preparation: 30 minutes   *Yield: 8 servings*
Bake: 20 minutes

Filling:

1 pound ground beef	Dash pepper
1 large onion, chopped	1 tablespoon chili powder
1 (10 ½ ounce) can tomato soup	1 (12 ounce) can whole kernel
1 can water	corn
½ teaspoon salt	½ cup green pepper, chopped

Brown ground beef and onion in large skillet. Add tomato soup, water, salt, pepper, chili powder, corn and green pepper. Cook 15 minutes on medium heat.

Topping:

¾ cup corn meal	1 egg
1 tablespoon sugar	½ cup milk
1 tablespoon flour	1 tablespoon bacon drippings,
1 ½ teaspoons baking powder	melted

Preheat oven to 350°. Mix all ingredients together and drop by spoonfuls over meat-vegetable mixture. Bake for 20 minutes.

MUSHROOM MEAT LOAF

Preparation: 30 minutes   *Can do ahead*   *Yield: 4 to 6 servings*
Bake: 1 hour   *Can be frozen*
Stand: 15 minutes

1 ½ pounds ground chuck	¼ cup chopped celery
1 cup soft bread crumbs	1 ½ teaspoons salt
½ pound fresh mushrooms	⅛ teaspoon pepper
3 slices bacon, diced	½ cup milk
¼ cup chopped onion	2 eggs, slightly beaten

Preheat oven to 350°. Mix bread crumbs with meat before adding other ingredients. Chop mushrooms. Cook bacon in skillet until almost crisp. Add chopped mushrooms, onion and celery. Cook until almost wilted. Mix all ingredients together. Pack in 9 x 5 x 3 inch pan and bake 1 hour. Let stand in pan 15 minutes before slicing.

MEATS

ROLLED MEAT LOAF

Preparation: 25 minutes   *Can do ahead*   *Yield: 4 to 6 servings*
Bake: 1 hour   *Can be frozen*

1 ½ pounds ground beef
1 cup fresh bread crumbs
1 egg
1 small onion, chopped
1 teaspoon salt or to taste
1 teaspoon oregano

1 (15 ounce) can tomato sauce
1 ½ cups Mozzarella cheese,
    shredded
1 (4 ounce) can sliced
    mushrooms, drained

Preheat oven to 375°. Mix together beef, bread crumbs, egg, onion, salt, oregano and ½ can tomato sauce. Press mixture into a rectangle on waxed paper. Sprinkle with cheese and mushrooms. Lift and roll meat up in jelly roll fashion. Place seam side down in pan and bake 30 minutes. Drain, top with remainder of tomato sauce and bake an additional 30 minutes.

BARBECUE GLAZED HAM

Preparation: 25 minutes   *Can do ahead*   *Yield: 8 to 10 servings*
Cook: 2 hours

1 (4 pound) can fully cooked
    ham
½ cup applesauce
1 (6 ounce) can apricot
    nectar, undiluted

⅛ cup chili sauce
1 ½ tablespoons Worcester-
    shire sauce
¼ teaspoon dry mustard
Whole cloves

Sauté ham in a large Dutch oven over low heat for 10 minutes, turning on all sides. Remove ham. Drain and reserve cooking liquid. Return 3 tablespoons to Dutch oven. With a sharp knife, make diagonal cuts, ⅛ inch deep and 1 inch apart, to form diamond pattern on top and sides. Return ham to Dutch oven. Over medium heat, gently brown ham on all sides, about 15 minutes. If necessary, add some of reserved cooking liquid to keep from sticking. Combine applesauce with rest of ingredients, except whole cloves; spoon mixture over ham. Simmer, covered, over low heat for 2 hours, basting every 20 minutes. Remove to platter and stud surface of ham with cloves. Serve with the sauce in pan.

HAM AND SPINACH ROLL-UPS

Preparation: 30 minutes　　　*Can do ahead*　　　*Yield: 8 to 10 servings*
Bake: 35 minutes
Stand: 10 minutes

1 (10 ¾ ounce) can cream of
　celery soup
1 cup commercial sour cream
2 tablespoons Dijon mustard
1 cup quick cooking rice,
　uncooked
1 (10 ounce) package frozen
　chopped spinach, thawed,
　drained and patted dry
　with paper towels

1 cup small curd cottage cheese
2 eggs
½ cup chopped onion
¼ cup unsifted flour
18 thin (about ⅛ to ¼ inch) ham
　slices
2 to 3 tablespoons butter,
　melted
2 tablespoons parsley
⅔ cup fine bread crumbs
Paprika

Preheat oven to 350°. In small bowl, thoroughly mix soup, sour cream and mustard. In a medium bowl, combine ½ cup soup mixture, rice, spinach, cottage cheese, eggs, onion and flour; mix well. Place about 2 heaping tablespoons of spinach mixture on each ham slice. Roll up and place close together, seam side down, in 11 x 7 inch baking dish. Spoon remaining soup mixture over ham rolls. Melt butter in small saucepan. Add bread crumbs and parsley and toss lightly. Place over top of soup mixture. Sprinkle lightly with paprika. Bake uncovered 30 to 35 minutes. Let stand 10 minutes before serving.

Note: If prepared ahead, return to room temperature before baking.

HINT: *Put water in the bottom of the broiler pan to prevent grease from spattering and catching fire.*

MEATS

HAM WELLINGTON

Preparation: 1 hour
Bake: 30 to 45 minutes, 325°
   30 to 35 minutes, 400°

Yield: 8 servings

1 (3 pound) Polish ham
¼ cup maple syrup

½ cup prepared mustard

Preheat oven to 325°. Place ham on rack. Mix together syrup and mustard. Bake 30 to 45 minutes, basting every 15 minutes with mustard sauce. Cool ham. Mix pastry and prepare paté.

Pastry:

3 ¾ cups flour
1 teaspoon salt
1 cup butter, cold

2 tablespoons shortening
¾ cup ice water

Combine flour and salt in bowl. Cut in butter and shortening. Add water, 1 tablespoon at a time, to make a stiff dough. Cover and chill.

Paté:

½ pound finely chopped
   mushrooms
2 tablespoons chopped green
   onion
2 tablespoons butter, melted
¼ teaspoon salt

⅛ teaspoon marjoram
1 teaspoon flour
Dash black pepper
2 tablespoons beef broth
1 tablespoon chopped parsley

Sauté mushrooms and onions in butter until liquid evaporates. Stir in salt, marjoram, flour, pepper and broth. Cook, stirring constantly, until mixture comes to a boil and thickens. Remove from heat, stir in parsley and cool.

To Assemble Wellington:

1 egg, well beaten
1 tablespoon water

Sesame seeds

Preheat oven to 400°. Set aside a small portion of pastry (about 1 cup) to use as cutouts for decoration. Roll remaining pastry into a 12 inch square. Press paté into pastry, leaving 2 inches uncovered on all edges. Place ham on

204

HAM WELLINGTON (Continued)

pastry; mold to surface; remove excess pastry. Place seam side down on a baking sheet. Make cutouts from remaining pastry; arrange on loaf. Brush pastry with egg beaten with water and sprinkle with sesame seeds. Bake for 30 to 35 minutes or until lightly browned. Let stand a few minutes before slicing.

Note: Can prepare ham and paté a day ahead. Be careful removing ham from baking sheet to serving platter.

QUICK LAMB CURRY

Preparation: 20 minutes   *Can do ahead*   *Yield: 4 servings*
Cook: 10 minutes

1 teaspoon sugar
¼ cup diced onion
1 teaspoon curry powder or
   to taste
3 cups cooked, cubed lamb
   or veal
1 ¼ teaspoons salt
¼ teaspoon pepper

¼ lemon, grated rind only
3 ½ cups boiling water
3 tablespoons flour
3 tablespoons butter or
   margarine
½ cup evaporated milk
Cooked rice

Caramelize sugar in large frying pan. When golden brown, add onion and curry powder. Stir until well mixed. Add cooked, cubed meat, stirring until slightly browned. Add salt, pepper, lemon rind; mix well. Pour in boiling water. Blend flour and butter until smooth. Add to meat and liquid. Heat until sauce is thickened. Add evaporated milk, mixing well. Serve over cooked rice.

Note: May be served with small bowls of peanuts, grated coconut, chutney, chopped green onions and sieved egg yolk.

HINT: Dry food with a paper towel before browning for best results.

MEATS

GIGOT D'AGNEAU à la BRETONNE
(LEG OF LAMB WITH WHITE BEANS
AND TOMATOES)

Soak: Overnight   *Yield: 6 to 8 servings*
Preparation: 1 hour
Cook: 2 ½ hours (if beans and lamb are prepared simultaneously)

Bean and Tomato Mixture:

1 pound dried white beans,
  soaked overnight in cold
  water
1 onion, studded with 4 cloves
1 carrot
Bouquet garni (sprig of thyme,
  bay leaf and fresh parsley)
Stalk of celery
Salt and pepper

2 tablespoons butter
2 onions, finely chopped
1 clove garlic, minced
1 ½ pounds tomatoes, peeled,
  seeded and chopped (4 large
  or 6 medium)
⅓ cup white wine
Salt and pepper
2 to 3 tablespoons fresh parsley

Soak the beans overnight in cold water. Drain and put in large pot with clove-studded onion, carrot, bouquet garni, celery and enough water to cover by at least 1 inch. Bring to boil and simmer for 1 ½ hours or until beans are very tender, adding salt and pepper halfway through cooking. Add more hot water as it evaporates to keep beans covered with liquid. At the end of cooking, beans should be moist but not soupy. Discard the onion, carrot and bouquet garni.

While beans are simmering, cook tomatoes. Melt butter in sauté pan or shallow saucepan. Add chopped onions and garlic and cook slowly, stirring often, for 4 to 5 minutes or until soft but not browned. Add tomatoes, white wine, salt and pepper. Cook over medium heat, stirring often, for 15 to 20 minutes or until nearly all moisture has evaporated. Add the tomatoes to the cooked beans and taste for seasoning.

Leg of Lamb:

6 pound leg of lamb
2 tablespoons oil
1 onion, quartered
1 carrot, quartered

1 clove garlic, cut in 4 to 5
  slivers (optional)
2 teaspoons rosemary (optional)

Preheat oven to 450°. Trim away all but a thin layer of fat and the skin from

206

GIGOT D'AGNEAU à la BRETONNE (Continued)

the lamb. Pour oil into roasting pan. Add quartered onion and carrot and put lamb on top. Make several incisions in lamb with point of a knife and insert slivers of garlic so the flavor will permeate the meat. Sprinkle lamb with rosemary, salt and pepper. Sear meat in a hot oven 10 to 15 minutes or until browned; lower heat to 400° and continue roasting. Baste the lamb often during cooking and, if the pan juices start to brown too much, add a little broth or water. Roast 9 to 11 minutes per pound for rare, 13 to 15 minutes per pound for medium well. Transfer the lamb to a warmed platter and let stand in a warm place for 15 to 20 minutes before carving.

Gravy:

½ cup white wine   Salt and pepper
1 cup broth or water

Discard excess fat from roasting pan, leaving onion and carrot. Add wine and stock to roasting pan and boil, stirring to dissolve the pan juices. Simmer for 5 to 10 minutes or until well flavored. Strain gravy into small saucepan. Skim off excess fat. Bring to boil and taste for seasoning. Keep hot until ready to serve. If necessary, reheat the bean and tomato mixture.

To serve: carve the lamb and replace it on the bone. Stir 2 tablespoons chopped parsley into beans, spoon them around the lamb and decorate the platter with parsley; or place the uncarved leg on platter, garnish and carve at the table and serve beans separately, sprinkled with more chopped parsley. Spoon a little gravy over meat to moisten it and serve the rest in a sauceboat.

Note: Leg of lamb and gravy may be prepared alone, if preferred.

MEATS

BROILED SKEWERED LAMB

Preparation: 30 minutes   *Do ahead*   *Yield: 4 servings*
Marinate: Overnight
Broil: 10 to 30 minutes

2 pounds lean, boneless leg
   of lamb
1 large onion
2 tablespoons olive oil
4 tablespoons fresh lemon
   juice
1 tablespoon salt

½ teaspoon freshly ground
   black pepper
1 large firm ripe tomato,
   quartered or cherry tomatoes
1 large green pepper, seeded
   and quartered
2 tablespoons heavy cream

Have the butcher debone a portion of a leg of lamb, trim excess fat and cut into 2 inch cubes. Peel onion, cut into ⅛ inch slices, separate into rings and place in a deep bowl. Sprinkle onion rings with olive oil, lemon juice, salt and pepper. Mix well. Add lamb cubes, turning the pieces with a spoon to coat well. Marinate at room temperature at least 2 hours or in the refrigerator at least 4 hours, turning lamb occasionally. Before cooking have meat at room temperature. Heat charcoal grill or oven broiler. Remove lamb from marinade. String the cubes of meat tightly on 3 to 4 skewers. Brush meat evenly on all sides with cream just before broiling. Alternately, thread the tomato and green pepper on a separate skewer. Place meat and vegetables on a charcoal grill. If using an oven broiler suspend the skewers of meat and vegetables in a 9 x 13 x 2 inch pan so that the bottom of the pan is 1 inch below the meat. Broil the meat and vegetables 4 inches from the heat, turning skewers occasionally. Watch vegetables closely since they cook faster than the lamb. Remove skewer of vegetables when done and keep warm. Lamb will need 10 to 30 minutes broiling time depending on degree of doneness desired; on a charcoal grill approximately 10 minutes for rare lamb and 15 minutes for well done lamb.

BARBECUED PORK ROAST

Preparation: 10 minutes   *Yield: 6 servings*
Roast: 3 hours

1 (4 to 5 pound) pork loin roast
1 teaspoon salt
½ teaspoon pepper
1 teaspoon garlic powder
¾ cup barbecue sauce
1 (10 ounce) jar pure apple jelly

2 (1 pound) cans small whole
    potatoes, drained
1 (1 pound) can small whole
    carrots, drained
1 (1 pound) can small whole
    onions, drained

Preheat oven to 325°. Place meat, fat side up, on rack in open pan. Sprinkle salt, pepper and garlic powder over meat and rub into meat well. Roast for 3 hours or until meat thermometer registers 170°. During the last half hour of roasting, add potatoes, carrots and onions. Combine barbecue sauce and jelly; simmer over low heat. Use to baste roast and vegetables during last half hour. Serve with remaining sauce.

BEER BRAISED LOIN OF PORK

Preparation: 45 minutes   *Yield: 8 servings*
Bake: 2 ½ hours

1 (5 pound) pork loin roast
5 cups chopped onion
1 pound carrots, diced
1 (12 ounce) bottle of beer

2 teaspoons salt
¼ teaspoon pepper
Bay leaf
5 whole cloves

Preheat oven to 350°. Brown roast well on all sides in ovenproof pan. Remove. Sauté onions and carrots in pork drippings until soft. Stir in beer, salt, pepper, bay leaf and whole cloves. Return pork to pan and cover. (A cooking bag with pork and other ingredients may be used.) Bake for 2 ½ hours or until pork is tender. Remove to platter and keep warm. Pour cooking liquid and vegetables from pan into a large bowl. Skim off fat and remove bay leaf and cloves. Place the liquid and vegetables in blender and blend on low speed until smooth. Pour sauce into small pan. Bring to boil, stirring often. Generously spoon sauce over sliced pork.

MEATS

SPANISH PORK

Preparation: 1 hour   *Yield: 8 servings*
Cook: 3 to 4 hours

1 (3 pound) pork loin roast   **1 tablespoon salt**

In 4 quart Dutch oven, boil pork roast in enough water to cover roast halfway. Cook until meat falls off bones. Check periodically to see if there is enough water for 3 or more cups broth. Add water, if needed. Remove meat from broth and completely cool. Reserve broth for dressing and gravy.

Dressing:

4 cups bread crumbs   **½ to 1 teaspoon sage**
½ cup broth   **1 cup finely chopped celery**
1 teaspoon salt   **2 to 3 tablespoons grated onion**

Mix ingredients lightly with fork. Season to taste.

Gravy:

¼ cup broth   **2 cups boiling broth**
¼ cup flour   **¼ teaspoon salt**

Leave ¼ cup of broth in pan, reserving rest of broth. Put Dutch oven on stove over low heat. Add flour. Stir and blend until flour is brown (about 2 minutes). Add boiling broth slowly, stirring constantly. Bring mixture to simmering point. Add salt. Cook about 5 minutes.

Combination of above ingredients:

Preheat oven to 350°. After pork roast is completely cooled, remove all bone and cut the meat into small pieces. In a 9 x 13 inch baking dish, layer dressing, gravy and pork. Repeat layers. Bake until well browned.

PORK NORMANDE

Preparation: 35 to 50 minutes
Cook: 40 to 50 minutes

Yield: 4 servings

1 tablespoon oil	3 tablespoons Calvados
1 tablespoon butter	(Apple Jack)
2 pork tenderloins,	1 tablespoon flour
¾ pound each	1 ½ cups chicken broth, canned
2 medium onions, sliced	Salt and pepper
2 tart apples, peeled, cored	⅓ cup heavy cream or crème
and sliced	fraîche

Heat oil and butter in a shallow casserole or large frying pan with lid and brown tenderloins on all sides over medium heat. Remove. Add onions and cook until soft, but not brown. Add sliced apples and continue cooking over moderately high heat until apples and onions are golden brown. Return tenderloins to the pan, pour calvados over them and flame. Stir flour into juices. Add broth, salt and pepper and bring to a boil. Cover and simmer, stirring occasionally, for 40 to 50 minutes or until meat is tender when pierced with a skewer. When meat is nearly tender, prepare caramelized apple garnish.

Caramelized apple slices:

2 tart apples, unpeeled	2 tablespoons sugar
2 tablespoons butter	

Core and thickly slice apples, leaving skin. Heat butter in a frying pan. Dip one side of each apple slice in sugar and place it sugared side down in hot butter. Cook over high heat for 4 to 5 minutes or until caramelized. Sprinkle rest of the sugar on apples, turn them over and brown on other side. Cover and keep warm.

When the pork is tender, remove it from the pan and carve it diagonally in medium slices. Arrange slices overlapping on a platter and cover to keep warm while finishing sauce.

Strain the cooking juices into a small pot pressing to purée apples. Bring to a boil and, if necessary, reduce to a coating consistency. Add cream, bring just back to a boil and taste for seasoning. Spoon some of sauce over pork and garnish dish with caramelized apple slices. Serve the remaining sauce separately.

MEATS

MANDARIN PORK ROAST

Preparation: 15 minutes   *Yield: 8 to 10 servings*
Cook: 3 hours

1 (4 pound) boneless pork
  loin roast
1 teaspoon salt
¼ teaspoon pepper
½ teaspoon garlic powder
2 tablespoons Dijon mustard
1 (11 ounce) can mandarin
  oranges

¼ cup light brown sugar
¼ cup vinegar
1 chicken bouillon cube
1 tablespoon soy sauce
2 tablespoons cornstarch
½ cup water
1 medium onion, chopped
⅓ cup chopped green pepper

Preheat oven to 325°. Trim fat from roast. Sprinkle roast with salt, pepper and garlic powder. Spread mustard over roast; place in large Dutch oven. Cover and bake until meat thermometer registers 170° (about 2 ½ hours). Increase oven temperature to 400°. Drain mandarin oranges, reserving liquid. Combine liquid, brown sugar, vinegar, bouillon cube, soy sauce, cornstarch and water in a saucepan; cook over medium heat, stirring constantly until smooth and thickened. Remove from heat; stir in onion, green pepper and oranges. Spoon sauce over roast. Bake uncovered for 30 minutes, basting occasionally. Slice pork and serve with pan drippings.

PORK TENDERLOIN

Preparation: 15 minutes   *Yield: 2 to 4 servings*
Marinate: Overnight
Bake: 60 to 75 minutes

Marinade:

¼ cup soy sauce
1 tablespoon brown sugar
¼ cup bourbon

1 garlic clove, minced
1 pork tenderloin

Mix all ingredients thoroughly. Add tenderloin and marinate overnight.

Sauce:

⅓ cup commercial sour
  cream
1 tablespoon dry mustard
½ teaspoon vinegar

Salt to taste
⅓ cup mayonnaise
1 tablespoon finely chopped
  green onion

Mix all ingredients together and refrigerate until ready to use.

Preheat oven to 325°. Drain tenderloin. Bake covered for 1 to 1 ¼ hours. Check after 45 minutes. Baste occasionally with marinade while cooking. Remove cover during last few minutes of cooking. Slice diagonally and spoon sauce over top.

PORK CHOPS FLORENTINE
from
Guyan Golf and Country Club

Preparation: 50 minutes   *Yield: 6 servings*
Bake: 15 minutes

6 (½ inch thick) pork chops   3 (10 ounce) packages frozen
Flour   chopped spinach, cooked
Salt and pepper   according to package
                                                            directions

Dredge chops with flour, salt and pepper. Brown in non-stick skillet or use 1 tablespoon of oil in skillet. Cover skillet and cook chops slowly 30 minutes or until tender. Preheat oven to 375°. Drain spinach, season with salt and pepper.

Cream Sauce:

1 (10 ½ ounce) can chicken   6 tablespoons butter or
   broth, undiluted   margarine
1 onion, sliced   6 tablespoon flour
1 carrot, sliced   1 ¾ cups milk
½ bay leaf   2 egg yolks, lightly beaten
                                                    1 cup grated natural Swiss
                                                       cheese

Simmer chicken broth with onion, carrot and bay leaf in a covered saucepan for 10 minutes. Strain. Melt butter, add flour; when bubbly add strained broth and milk, stirring constantly. Cook until thickened. Whisk a small amount of sauce into egg yolks; return yolk mixture to remaining cream sauce whisking constantly. Grease large shallow baking dish, spread spinach on bottom; place chops on top. Pour sauce over chops; sprinkle with cheese. Bake for 15 minutes or until cheese is browned and melted.

PORK-APPLE BAKE

Preparation: 15 minutes   *Yield: 6 servings*
Bake: 1 ½ hours

6 pork loin <u>or</u> rib chops,   2 tablespoons soy sauce
   cut ¾ inch thick   2 tablespoons ketchup
½ teaspoon salt   2 teaspoons cornstarch
¼ teaspoon pepper   ¼ teaspoon ground cinnamon
1 ½ cups apple juice   1 large red apple
2 tablespoons light brown sugar

About 1 ¾ hours before serving, preheat oven to 350°. In a 13 x 9 inch baking
dish, arrange pork chops in one layer; sprinkle with salt and pepper. Bake for
1 ¼ hours, turning pork chops once. In small saucepan, combine apple juice,
brown sugar, soy sauce, ketchup, cornstarch and cinnamon. Heat mixture
to boiling and slightly thickened. Remove from heat. Core apple and cut into
6 slices. Remove pork chops from oven. Skin fat and place an apple slice on
each chop. Pour apple juice mixture over top. Bake an additional 15 minutes
or until chops are fork tender, basting occasionally with sauce in dish.

SAUSAGE PIZZA

Preparation: 45 minutes   *Can do ahead*   *Yield: 6 to 8 servings*
Bake: 15 minutes   *Can be frozen*

Crust:

1 package yeast
¾ cup warm water
1 teaspoon sugar
½ teaspoon salt

2 tablespoons dried skim milk
2 cups unsifted flour
1 tablespoon cooking oil

Dissolve yeast in warm water. Add sugar, salt, dried milk and flour. Knead oil into dough. Let rise in warm place 30 minutes. Roll on floured surface to 1 inch larger than 12 x 17 inch cookie sheet. Place on ungreased sheet, forming rim for crust. Preheat oven to 450°.

Sauce:

1 (15 ounce) can tomato sauce
2 tablespoons Italian seasoning

¼ cup Parmesan cheese

Combine ingredients and spread over dough.

Topping:

1 pound sausage, fried, drained
and crumbled

3 cups shredded Mozzarella
cheese

Sprinkle with sausage and Mozzarella cheese. Bake 15 minutes or until brown.

VEAL FRICASSEE WITH PAPRIKA

Preparation: 1 hour   *Can do ahead*   *Yield: 6 servings*
Bake: 1 ¼ to 1 ½ hours

3 pounds veal stew meat,
  cut in 2 inch pieces
3 cloves garlic, peeled
3 tablespoons Hungarian
  paprika
¼ cup peanut oil (more if
  needed)
1 ½ teaspoons salt
Freshly ground pepper

1 pound onions, peeled and
  sliced
¼ cup bourbon or Cognac
1 ½ cups dry white wine
2 cups chicken or beef broth
Bouquet garni of parsley,
  thyme, bay leaf
⅓ cup commercial sour cream
1 tablespoon finely chopped
  fresh parsley

Trim meat of fat and gristle. Cut the garlic in slivers. Using a small, pointed knife, make an incision in each piece of meat and insert a piece of garlic. Pat meat dry with paper towels, and turn each piece in paprika to coat it evenly. Preheat oven to 375°. Heat oil in 6 to 8 quart ovenproof casserole over medium-high heat. Sear pieces of veal in single layer without crowding; if necessary, do this in two or three lots. As meat is lightly browned on all sides, remove from pan and season with salt and pepper. Lower heat slightly and, if needed, add an extra tablespoon or two of oil to pan. Add onions and cook for 8 to 10 minutes, stirring occasionally, until lightly browned. Return meat to pan, pour on bourbon or Cognac, and set it alight, shaking gently over heat until all alcohol is flamed away. Pour on white wine and bring it to a simmer. Add broth and bouquet garni. Place a piece of waxed paper or baking parchment directly on surface of meat, cover, then set casserole in oven. Cook 1 ¼ to 1 ½ hours, until meat is tender, turning pieces once halfway through cooking. Discard bouquet garni. Using slotted spoon or skimmer, remove the meat and onions to serving dish; cover lightly and keep warm. Skim fat from cooking liquid; boil down rapidly to about 1 cup. Remove from heat and strain liquid. Swirl in sour cream and correct seasoning. Ladle spoonfuls of sauce over the meat and onions. Sprinkle with parsley and serve. Pass remaining sauce in sauceboat.

Note: To make in advance (up to a day ahead), remove casserole from oven when meat is almost done; cool to room temperature. Store, still covered in the refrigerator. Remove 1 hour before serving. Rewarm by returning cooking liquid to a simmer on top of the stove, then set casserole in 375° oven for 10 to 15 minutes. Finish sauce by boiling down and stirring in sour cream as directed above.

PARMESANED VEAL

Preparation: 15 to 20 minutes   *Yield: 4 servings*
Cook: 30 minutes

1 ½ pounds veal cutlet, cut
   in 2 inch pieces
½ cup Parmesan cheese
2 tablespoons olive oil
1 clove garlic, minced
1 cup beef stock
½ cup white wine

1 tablespoon lemon juice
¼ teaspoon marjoram
¼ teaspoon thyme
Salt and pepper to taste
Cooked spaghetti
Parsley flakes (optional garnish)

Sprinkle both sides of veal pieces with Parmesan cheese and pound both sides. Brown slowly in olive oil with garlic. Add remaining ingredients to meat. Cover and simmer until very tender and all but about 6 tablespoons of the liquid is absorbed, about 30 minutes. Serve over cooked spaghetti.

VEAL PICCATA
from
Chef Geoffrey Fennessey of La Pola's Italian Restaurant Hilton Head, South Carolina

Preparation: 5 minutes   *Yield: 1 serving*
Cook: 10 minutes

6 ounces veal scallops
Flour
Salt
Pepper
6 tablespoons butter

1 lemon, cut in half
2 ounces dry white wine
   (Sauterne)
Cooked Spaghetti

Tenderize the veal scallops. Salt and pepper and dredge lightly in flour. Sauté the floured veal in hot butter until brown. Remove the veal to a warm plate. Add the wine to the butter remaining in the pan to deglaze. Add the juice of ½ lemon. Pour the sauce over the veal and serve immediately. Garnish with parsley and a thin lemon slice from the remaining ½ lemon.

Note: La Pola's serves cooked spaghetti on the plate with the veal and uses the veal sauce over the spaghetti.

Sauces & Accompaniments

SPRUCE KNOB

SAUCES

ADELLE'S BARBECUE SAUCE

Preparation: 30 minutes   *Can do ahead*   *Yield: 4 to 5 cups*
                                Can be frozen

2 onions, chopped
1 cup chopped celery
1 clove garlic
2 tablespoons vinegar
2 tablespoons Worcestershire
   sauce
1 teaspoon salt
1 teaspoon paprika

1 teaspoon chili powder
¼ teaspoon red pepper
8 ounces ketchup
2 cups water
¼ cup brown sugar
1 (4 to 5 pound) chuck <u>or</u>
   pork roast

Mix all ingredients together. Pour over roast and cook until meat is tender.
Shred meat and serve for delicious barbecues.

EXCELLENT BARBECUE SAUCE

Preparation: 10 minutes   *Can do ahead*   *Yield: 1 ¾ cups*
Cook: 25 minutes

¼ cup vinegar
½ cup water
2 tablespoons sugar
1 tablespoon prepared mustard
½ teaspoon pepper
½ to ¾ cup honey
1 ½ teaspoons salt
¼ teaspoon cayenne pepper

Juice from 1 large whole lemon
1 onion, peeled and sliced
   into rings
¼ cup butter (only if cooked
   in oven and not on the grill)
1 cup ketchup
2 tablespoons Worcestershire
   sauce

Mix together in saucepan vinegar, water, sugar, prepared mustard, pepper,
honey, salt, cayenne pepper, lemon juice and onion. Add the ¼ cup butter if
using this sauce in the oven and not on the grill. Simmer uncovered for 20
minutes. Add ketchup and Worcestershire sauce and bring to a boil.

EGG SAUCE

Preparation: 30 minutes   *Yield: 10 servings*

3 hard boiled eggs, whites of
    eggs chopped; yolks pressed
    through sieve. (Prepared
    ahead and set aside)
1 ½ tablespoons butter <u>or</u>
    margarine
2 tablespoons flour

1 teaspoon salt
⅛ teaspoon pepper
½ cup vegetable liquid (reserved
    from boiled vegetables)
¾ cup evaporated milk <u>or</u>
    whole milk
¾ cup mayonnaise

Melt butter, blend in flour. Add salt and pepper. Stir in vegetable liquid and
bring to boil, cooking slowly 2 minutes and stirring constantly. Add chopped
egg whites and ¾ cup evaporated or whole milk. Remove from heat and stir in
mayonnaise. Pour sauce over vegetable and sprinkle egg yolks on top.

Note: Excellent served over cauliflower, broccoli or asparagus.

Microwave:

Melt butter on 100% power for 20 to 30 seconds or until melted. Add flour,
salt and pepper and blend well. Stir in vegetable liquid and bring to a boil on
100% power stirring every minute. After boil is reached reduce power to 50%
and continue to cook until mixture thickens, stirring every minute. Add
chopped egg whites and ¾ cup of evaporated or whole milk. Stir well. Add
mayonnaise. Pour sauce over vegetable and sprinkle egg yolks on top.

HAM BASTING SAUCE

Preparation: 10 minutes   *Can do ahead*

¾ cup brown sugar
1 tablespoon vinegar
1 teaspoon prepared mustard

2 tablespoons pineapple, apple
    <u>or</u> other fruit juice <u>or</u> water
Whole cloves
Pineapple slices (optional)

Mix the brown sugar, vinegar and mustard. Add just enough juice to make
the mixture pouring consistency. Stud ham with whole cloves and cover with
pineapple slices, if desired. Baste ham during the last 30 to 45 minutes of
baking time.

SAUCES

MICROWAVE HOLLANDAISE SAUCE

Preparation: 10 minutes   *Yield: 1 cup*
Cook: 2 to 3 minutes

½ cup butter <u>or</u> margarine   ½ teaspoon dry mustard
½ cup half and half   ½ teaspoon salt
2 egg yolks   Dash of hot sauce
2 tablespoons lemon juice

Place butter in 4-cup glass measure. Microwave at HIGH 1 minute to melt. Stir in remaining ingredients with a wire whisk. Microwave at MEDIUM 1 to 1 ½ minutes. Stir at 20 second intervals. Beat thoroughly at end of cooking time. Serve with fish or vegetables.

MOCK HOLLANDAISE

Preparation: 15 minutes   *Yield: 1 ¼ cups*

1 cup commercial sour cream   ½ teaspoon salt
Juice of 1 lemon   ¼ teaspoon paprika
2 egg yolks

Mix all ingredients over hot water in double boiler until thick. Serve warm over cauliflower, asparagus or broccoli.

HORSERADISH SAUCE

Preparation: 10 minutes   *Yield: 2 cups*

1 cup whipping cream   2 tablespoons prepared
                                       horseradish

Whip cream until stiff. Fold in horseradish until mixed well. Chill before serving. Serve with hot or cold ham or roast beef.

JEZEBEL SAUCE

Preparation: 5 minutes   *Can do ahead*   *Yield: 6 cups*

1 (18 ounce) jar pineapple
  preserves
1 (18 ounce) jar apple jelly

1 (5 ounce) jar prepared
  horseradish
1 (1 ounce) can dry mustard
1 teaspoon black pepper

Combine ingredients and whirl in blender. Keeps indefinitely when refrigerated but horseradish mellows, so add more if necessary.

Note: Excellent with ham, lamb, venison and beef.

LEMON BUTTER SAUCE

Preparation: 5 minutes   *Yield: ¾ cup*
Cook: 2 minutes

½ cup butter
4 tablespoons lemon juice
⅛ teaspoon garlic powder

¼ teaspoon oregano
¼ teaspoon salt
¼ teaspoon pepper

Combine all ingredients and heat to just a boil and remove from heat.

Note: Excellent over vegetables and seafood.

MUSTARD SAUCE FOR HAM

Preparation: 1 hour   *Can do ahead*   *Yield: 20 servings*

1 teaspoon cornstarch
⅓ cup sugar, divided
1 tablespoon dry mustard
½ teaspoon salt
1 cup light cream

2 egg yolks
¼ cup cider vinegar
Dash ground cloves
1 cup whipping cream, whipped

Mix cornstarch with half the sugar in small pan. Add dry mustard, salt and cream and heat slowly until it thickens. Beat the egg yolks with the rest of the sugar. Add a little of the hot mixture to the yolks, then combine the two mixtures and cook two minutes. Add vinegar slowly. Cook a minute longer. Add cloves and cool. When cool, fold in whipped cream and serve with dash of cloves on top.

SAUCES

MUSHROOM SAUCE FOR STEAK

Preparation: 10 minutes   *Yield: 1 cup*
Cook: 15 minutes

2 tablespoons butter <u>or</u>
  margarine
1 (8 ounce) can sliced
  mushrooms, drained

¼ teaspoon coarsely ground
  black pepper
2 teaspoons finely minced onion
¾ teaspoon cornstarch
¼ cup sherry

Heat butter in medium skillet. Sauté the drained mushrooms with pepper until the mushrooms are golden brown, about 5 minutes. Add onion during the last minute or so of sautéing. Combine cornstarch and sherry. Stir into mushrooms. Cook, stirring constantly until the mixture comes to a boil. Sauce should be thick and translucent. Serve immediately.

SEAFOOD COCKTAIL SAUCE

Preparation: 10 minutes   *Can do ahead*   *Yield: 1 cup*

¾ cup chili sauce
1 tablespoon Worcestershire
  sauce
1 to 2 tablespoons prepared
  horseradish

¼ teaspoon salt
1 ½ tablespoons lemon juice
1 teaspoon grated onion
Tabasco sauce (few drops)

Mix all ingredients and chill thoroughly.

Note: Good for shrimp, crabmeat or oyster cocktails.

SHRIMP COCKTAIL SAUCE

Preparation: 5 minutes   *Can do ahead*   *Yield: 1 cup*

½ teaspoon prepared
  horseradish
1 teaspoon water
¾ cup ketchup
1 teaspoon minced onion
1 tablespoon white wine
  vinegar with tarragon

1 teaspoon Worcestershire
  sauce
½ teaspoon Beau Monde
  seasoning
Dash cayenne pepper

Mix all ingredients well. Chill before serving.

STEAK ONION-PARSLEY BUTTER

Preparation: 10 minutes *Can do ahead* *Yield: ½ cup*

2 tablespoons grated onion
2 tablespoons chopped parsley
¼ teaspoon seasoned salt
¼ to ½ teaspoon cracked
   black pepper

¼ teaspoon dry mustard
2 teaspoons Worcestershire
   sauce
3 tablespoons softened butter
   or margarine

Combine all ingredients. Blend well. Refrigerate covered until ready to use. Excellent spread over steak just before serving.

MING'S SWEET AND SOUR SAUCE FOR COOKING
from
Ming's Restaurant

Preparation: 5 minutes *Yield: 10 ounces*

3 ounces apple cider vinegar
3 ounces cold water
¼ cup sugar

2 tablespoons brown sugar
2 tablespoons orange juice
4 teaspoons cornstarch

Mix together vinegar, water, sugars and orange juice. The sauce may be refrigerated until needed. When ready to use, add cornstarch and mix well. Add sauce, pineapple chunks and green pepper squares to browned chunks of pork, chicken, scallops or shrimp. Bring to a boil for 1 minute, reduce heat and cook until sauce is thickened and vegetables are crisp tender.

Note: Other ingredients that can be added to this dish are sweet pickle chunks, tomato wedges, carrot matchsticks.

SAUCES

BASIC TOMATO SAUCE
from
Rocco's Ristorante

Preparation: 20 minutes   *Can do ahead*   *Yield: 1 gallon*
Cook: 50 minuites   *Can be frozen*

1 medium onion
2 carrots
2 celery stalks
4 garlic cloves
2 tablespoons salt
3 tablespoons basil, dried

1 (16 ounce) can tomato paste
7 pounds peeled tomatoes,
    Italian style
¾ cup olive oil
3 tablespoons butter

Chop onions, celery, carrots and garlic in fine pieces. Melt butter in large pot, add salt and olive oil. Add vegetables to this mixture and sauté until they are soft. Add basil, tomato paste and tomatoes, crushing tomatoes in pot. Simmer mixture 30 to 40 minutes.

Note: Serve over pasta or Dumplings Italian Style. (See index.)

HOT CURRIED FRUIT

Preparation: 20 minutes   *Can do ahead*   *Yield: 8 to 10 servings*
Cook: 1 hour

½ cup melted margarine
¾ cup firmly packed brown
   sugar
1 ½ teaspoons curry powder
1 (29 ounce) can pear halves,
   drained
1 (20 ounce) can pineapple
   tidbits, drained

1 (30 ounce) can apricot
   halves, drained
1 (29 ounce) can sliced
   peaches, drained
1 (8 ounce) jar maraschino
   cherries, drained
2 bananas, sliced

Preheat oven to 300°. Combine margarine, sugar and curry powder and heat, stirring until well blended. Combine pears, pineapples, apricots, peaches, cherries and bananas in a shallow 2-quart casserole; add margarine mixture. Bake for 1 hour.

Note: Take juices and put in blender with ½ to 1 cup ice and blend for a frosty, refreshing drink.

HOT SPICED FRUIT

Preparation: 30 minutes   *Yield: 8 to 10 servings*
Chill: Overnight
Cook: 30 minutes

1 (16 ounce) can mandarin
   oranges
1 (29 ounce) can sliced
   peaches
1 (29 ounce) can sliced pears
1 (16 ounce) can pineapple
   chunks
1 (16 ounce) can stewed prunes

1 cup syrup from fruit
¼ to ½ cup brown sugar
2 tablespoons butter
½ teaspoon nutmeg
1 teaspoon cinnamon
¼ teaspoon ground cloves

Drain and layer fruits in casserole. Bring to a boil 1 cup syrup from fruit, brown sugar and butter. Add nutmeg, cinnamon and ground cloves. Pour over fruit and refrigerate overnight. Bake 350° for 30 minutes.

ACCOMPANIMENTS

MARY'S FRUIT COMPOTE A L'ORANGE

Preparation: 15 minutes   *Can do ahead*   *Yield: 10 servings*
Chill: Several hours

2 (20 ounce) cans pineapple
  chunks, well drained
1 pint strawberries, halved
1 cup seedless green grapes

½ cup Grand Marnier
½ cup strained fresh <u>or</u>
  reconstituted frozen orange
  juice

In a 2 ½ to 3 quart bowl, combine the drained pineapple chunks, halved strawberries and seedless grapes. Combine the Grand Marnier and strained orange juice. Pour over the fruit. Toss to coat well. Cover and refrigerate for several hours or overnight, stirring once or twice.

Note: There's enough juice to add more grapes or strawberries if desired to increase the number of servings. You may substitute any fruit of your choice that is complemented by orange flavor.

SUMMER RUM FRUIT

Preparation: 20 minutes   *Can do ahead*   *Yield: 16 servings*
Cook: 5 minutes
Chill: 1 hour

4 cups sliced peaches, fresh
  <u>or</u> frozen
1 cup raspberries, fresh <u>or</u>
  frozen
2 cups pineapple chunks,
  fresh <u>or</u> frozen

4 cups melon
¾ cup water
10 to 12 mint leaves
1 cup sugar
¼ cup light dry rum

Place fruit in freezer for 1 to 1 ½ hours. Near end of freezing time, place sugar and water on medium high heat for about 5 minutes. Crush mint into syrup; discard leaves. Syrup will be thin and light. Allow to cool for about 10 minutes. Add rum. Stir well. Remove fruit from freezer. Pour rum syrup over fruit and toss. Place in serving bowl; decorate with mint leaves and strawberries.

Note: Any fresh summer fruit may be substituted.

GRAN'S HOT DOG CHILI

Preparation: 15 minutes   *Can be frozen*
Cook: 1 ½ hours

1 pound ground beef
1 medium onion
1 (6 ounce) can tomato paste
3 (6 ounce) cans water

½ cup ketchup
1 teaspoon cider vinegar
1 ½ to 2 tablespoons chili
   powder
1 teaspoon salt

Do not brown hamburger! Combine all ingredients, adding 1 can water at a time. Mix well. Cook slowly for 1 ½ hours. Serve over hot dogs.

HOT DOG SAUCE

Preparation: 15 minutes   *Can do ahead*   *Yield: Large quantity*
Cook: 4 to 5 hours   *Can be frozen*

6 pounds ground chuck
2 cups dried onion flakes
3 teaspoons salt
3 teaspoons pepper
3 teaspoons dried mustard
6 teaspoons Worcestershire
   sauce

3 teaspoons garlic salt
3 teaspoons Italian seasoning
2 bay leaves
4 shakes of crushed red pepper
2 (6 ounce) cans tomato paste
2 (46 ounce) cans tomato juice

Brown meat in large pan (soup kettle). Add remaining ingredients in order and let simmer on stove for 4 to 5 hours. (If too thick, add water.)

ACCOMPANIMENTS

BAKED RASPBERRIED PEACHES

Preparation: 10 minutes   *Can do ahead*   *Yield: 8 servings*
Cook: 30 minutes

1 (29 ounce) can cling peach
  halves, drained
3 tablespoons butter <u>or</u>
  margarine

4 tablespoons red raspberry
  jelly
1 tablespoon sugar
1 tablespoon ground cinnamon

Preheat oven to 300°. Place drained peach halves, cut side up, in a shallow baking pan. Dot the centers with butter. Fill the centers with jelly. Mix sugar and cinnamon together and sprinkle over peaches. Heat in oven until juice bubbles in center, about 30 minutes.

Note: Excellent colorful garnish with a roast ham, poultry or for an omelette or luncheon plate.

STRAWBERRY BUTTER

Preparation: 10 minutes   *Can do ahead*   *Yield: 2 ½ cups*

1 pound softened sweet butter
¾ cup finely chopped fresh
  strawberries

3 to 5 tablespoons powdered
  sugar

Combine all ingredients in blender or food processor with steel blade. Whip until light. Use on biscuits or rolls for luncheon.

YORKSHIRE PUDDING

Preparation: 10 minutes   *Yield: 9 servings*
Cook: 40 minutes

1 cup flour
½ teaspoon salt
1 cup milk

2 eggs
½ cup drippings from beef

Beat flour, salt, milk and eggs until <u>just</u> smooth. Heat square pan and meat drippings in 425° oven until drippings pop. Pour in batter and bake 35 minutes. Pudding will puff high during baking, then collapse, leaving high, crisp edges. Excellent with roast beef.

Desserts

STATE CAPITOL
·CHARLESTON·

CAKES

BLUEBERRY CHEESECAKE

Preparation: 20 to 30 minutes   *Can do ahead*   *Yield: 9 to 12 servings*
Bake: 18 to 20 minutes
Cool: 30 minutes   *Chill: 2 ½ hours*

Crust:

¾ cup flour
⅓ cup butter
¼ cup sugar

⅛ teaspoon salt
1 egg, slightly beaten

Crust: Preheat oven to 350°. Cut butter into flour. Stir in sugar, salt and egg. Press firmly into bottom of 9 inch square baking dish (or bottom of spring form pan). Bake for 18 to 20 minutes. Cool completely.

Filling:

1 tablespoon lemon juice
1 teaspoon unflavored gelatin
2 (8 ounce) packages cream
   cheese, softened
½ teaspoon vanilla

1 cup powdered sugar
1 cup whipping cream
1 (21 ounce) can blueberry
   pie filling

Filling: While crust is baking, dissolve gelatin in lemon juice over low heat. Beat cheese, powdered sugar and vanilla until fluffy, about 5 minutes. Add gelatin. Whip cream and fold into cheese mixture. Spread over crust. Chill 2 to 2 ½ hours. Spread pie filling over top and return to refrigerator until ready to serve.

Note: Other flavored pie fillings may be used.

HINT: *Flavoring should be added to the creamed mixture of a cake in order to achieve maximum flavor.*

CREAM CHEESECAKE

Preparation: 20 minutes   *Can do ahead*   *Yield: 6 to 8 servings*
Bake: 35 minutes
Stand: 20 minutes

2 (8 ounce) packages cream
  cheese, softened
3 eggs
⅔ cup sugar
½ teaspoon almond extract **or**
  rum extract

1 cup commercial sour cream
1 teaspoon vanilla
3 tablespoons sugar
Slivered almonds

Preheat oven to 350°. Beat cream cheese, eggs, ⅔ cup sugar and almond extract together very thoroughly until smooth, thick and lemon colored. Pour into greased 9 inch pie plate. Bake for 25 minutes. Cool 20 minutes. Beat sour cream, 3 tablespoons sugar and vanilla together. Pour this mixture over top of cheesecake. Return to 350° oven and bake 10 minutes. Cool. Sprinkle slivered almonds on top.

Note: Even better the next day.

PETITE CHERRY CHEESECAKES

Preparation: 40 minutes   *Can do ahead*   *Yield: 24 servings*
Bake: 20 minutes
Chill: 1 hour

2 (8 ounce) packages cream
  cheese
¾ cup sugar
2 eggs
1 tablespoon lemon juice

1 teaspoon vanilla
24 vanilla wafers
1 (21 ounce) can cherry pie
  filling

Preheat oven to 375°. Beat together cream cheese, sugar, eggs, lemon juice and vanilla until light and fluffy. Line small muffin pan with paper baking cups and place one vanilla wafer in the bottom of each cup. Fill the cups ⅔ full with cream cheese mixture. Bake for 15 to 20 minutes, or until set. Top each with one tablespoon of the pie filling. Chill 1 hour.

CHOCOLATE ECLAIR CAKE

Preparation: 30 minutes   *Can do ahead*   *Yield: 15 servings*
Chill: Overnight

Cake:

1 (14 ounce) box graham
  crackers
2 (3 ⅝ ounce) packages French
  vanilla pudding, cooked
  according to instructions
  but with only 3 cups milk

1 (8 ounce) package frozen
  whipped topping, thawed

Place a layer of graham crackers in bottom of lightly buttered 9 x 13 inch pan, covering bottom completely. Cook pudding, let cool and mix with whipped topping. Spread one-half of this on graham crackers, add another layer of graham crackers, remainder of pudding and whipped topping. Cover with another layer of graham crackers.

Frosting:

2 ounces unsweetened
  chocolate, melted
2 tablespoons white corn syrup

1 ½ cups powdered sugar
Milk to thin frosting

Combine frosting ingredients, using enough milk to thin. Spread over graham cracker cake and refrigerate overnight before serving.

HINT: To keep frozen berries from bleeding in batter, only partially thaw them before adding them to the batter.

CHOCOLATE TORTE WITH RASPBERRY SAUCE

Preparation: 45 minutes   *Can do ahead*   *Yield: 2 (9 inch) pies*
Bake: 30 to 35 minutes   *Can be frozen*

4 ounces unsweetened chocolate	⅛ teaspoon salt 1 cup chopped macadamia nuts
1 cup butter	1 (10 ounce) package frozen
4 eggs	raspberries
2 cups sugar	Vanilla ice cream
2 teaspoons vanilla	Chocolate curls
1 cup unsifted flour	

Preheat oven to 325°. Melt chocolate and butter in top of a double boiler over simmering water. Cool. Beat eggs until thick and lemon-colored and gradually beat in sugar, 1 tablespoon at a time, until very thick. Beat in vanilla. Mix in the melted chocolate mixture and the flour and salt, mixing just until blended. Fold in chopped nuts. Turn into two buttered 9 inch pie pans and bake for 30 to 35 minutes, or until the top springs back when lightly touched. Let cool. (May be packaged and frozen at this point.) Before serving, let layers thaw completely at room temperature. Purée thawed raspberries in a blender with syrup, then pour through a wire strainer to remove seeds. Pour into a pitcher. To serve each torte, top with balls of ice cream, allowing about 1 quart for each pie. Sprinkle with chocolate curls. At the table, pour the raspberry sauce over the torte and cut into wedges to serve.

HINT: *If you're using a pastry bag and need to change tips, slip the new one over the one you've been using, and hold it on with your hand as you work.*

CAKES

MAHOGANY CAKE

Preparation: 1 ½ hours   *Can do ahead*   *Yield: 8 to 10 servings*
Bake: 40 to 45 minutes   *Can be frozen*

Cake:

1 cup shortening
2 ½ cups sugar
2 eggs
2 ½ cups sifted flour
½ cup cocoa

2 teaspoons baking soda
¼ teaspoon salt
1 cup milk
1 cup boiling water

Preheat oven to 350°. Grease and flour pan(s). Cream together shortening and sugar. Add eggs. Sift flour, cocoa, soda and salt. Add sifted mixture to shortening mixture a little at a time, alternating with milk. Beat until smooth; add boiling water. Pour into 13 x 9 inch pan or three 8 inch cake pans. Bake about 40 to 45 minutes for oblong pan; check 8 inch cake pans at 25 minutes. Frost the cake with Mocha Frosting.

Mocha Frosting:

6 tablespoons cocoa
6 tablespoons hot coffee
6 tablespoons butter

1 teaspoon vanilla
3 cups powdered sugar

Mix all ingredients together and beat until smooth.

HINT: *When a recipe calls for citrus rind, use only the colored layer which yields the flavor-giving oils.*

RED VELVET CAKE

Preparation: 1 hour   *Can do ahead*   *Yield: 8 to 12 servings*
Bake: 30 to 35 minutes

Cake:

½ cup shortening <u>or</u> butter
1 ½ cups sugar
2 eggs
2 tablespoons red food coloring
2 tablespoons water
2 tablespoons cocoa

1 cup buttermilk
2 to 2 ¼ cups flour
1 teaspoon salt
1 teaspoon vanilla
1 tablespoon vinegar
1 to 1 ½ teaspoons baking soda

Preheat oven to 350°. Cream shortening and sugar. Add eggs and blend. Add coloring, water and cocoa. Blend in buttermilk; add flour and salt gradually. Add vanilla and beat until mixed. Mix vinegar and soda together and stir in last. Do <u>not</u> beat. Pour into two 9 inch, greased and floured pans. Bake 30 to 35 minutes.

Fluff Frosting:

1 cup milk
¼ cup flour
1 cup sugar

½ cup shortening
½ cup butter
1 teaspoon vanilla
Dash of salt

Cook milk, flour and salt until thickened. Cool. Cream butter, sugar and shortening. Add flour mixture and beat; add vanilla. Frost cake when cooled.

HINT: Use direct heat from gas burner to warm egg whites before beating. Egg whites at room temperature beat up to a larger volume.

CAKES

TURTLE CAKE

Preparation: 1 hour   *Can do ahead*   *Yield: 20 servings*
Bake: 30 to 35 minutes

1 (18 ¼ ounce) box German
  chocolate cake mix
¾ cup butter <u>or</u> margarine,
  softened
⅔ cup sweetened condensed
  milk, divided

1 (14 ounce) package of
  caramels
1 (6 ounce) package of
  chocolate chips
1 cup chopped pecans

Preheat oven to 350°. Mix cake according to directions on the box. To this mixture add margarine and ⅓ cup of the condensed milk. Beat well. Pour half of mixture into 9 x 13 inch pan and bake for 15 minutes. In double boiler, melt caramels with remaining ⅓ cup of condensed milk. Pour over hot cake. Sprinkle chocolate chips and nuts over top. Pour rest of batter over top and bake 15 to 20 minutes longer.

Note: Unwrapping all those caramels takes longer than one would think. It helps if this is done ahead of time.

CREAM CHEESE POUND CAKE

Preparation: 20 minutes   *Can do ahead*   *Yield: 15 to 20 servings*
Bake: 1 to 1 ½ hours

3 cups sugar
1 ½ cups butter, softened
6 eggs
1 (8 ounce) package cream
  cheese, softened

3 cups flour
1 teaspoon vanilla extract
1 teaspoon butter flavoring

Preheat oven to 325°. Cream sugar and butter. Add eggs one at a time, beating after each addition. Blend in softened cream cheese. Add flour and mix well. Add vanilla and butter flavoring. Bake in slightly greased tube pan. Check for doneness after one hour. Do not overbake.

GERMAN CHOCOLATE POUND CAKE

Preparation: 30 minutes   *Can do ahead*   *Yield: 20 servings*
Bake: 1 ½ hours

2 cups sugar
½ cup shortening
½ cup butter
4 eggs
2 teaspoons vanilla

1 cup buttermilk
3 cups flour
½ teaspoon soda
1 teaspoon salt
1 (4 ounce) bar German
   chocolate, melted

Preheat oven to 300°. Cream sugar and shortening; add eggs, vanilla and buttermilk. Sift dry ingredients. Add to creamed mixture. Beat well. Add chocolate to batter; blend well. Pour into greased and floured tube pan. Bake 1 ½ hours. Place in tight fitting cake cover while hot, leave until cold.

MRS. SHINGLETON'S BUTTERMILK POUND CAKE

Preparation: 20 minutes   *Can do ahead*   *Yield: 10 to 12 servings*
Bake: 1 ½ hours

3 cups sugar
1 cup butter
½ cup shortening
4 eggs
1 teaspoon vanilla

3 cups flour
½ teaspoon soda
½ teaspoon salt
1 cup buttermilk
1 cup chopped pecans

Preheat oven to 325°. Grease and flour a 10 inch tube pan. Cream together sugar, shortening and butter until light and fluffy. Add eggs, one at a time, beating after each. Add vanilla. Sift soda, salt and flour together. Add sifted dry ingredients alternately with buttermilk to creamed mixture, beating after each addition. Line greased and floured pan with chopped nuts. Pour cake batter on top of nuts. Bake for 1 ½ hours. Cool cake in pan for 10 minutes. Remove from pan and cool on rack.

Note: Best alone, but may be served with berries and cream or ice cream.

CAKES

GERMAN APPLE CAKE

Preparation: 30 minutes *Can do ahead* *Yield: 12 servings*
Bake: 45 to 50 minutes

Cake:

1 cup salad oil
3 eggs
2 cups sugar
1 teaspoon vanilla
2 cups flour

1 teaspoon baking soda
½ teaspoon salt
2 teaspoons cinnamon
4 cups thinly sliced peeled
  apples
1 cup nuts

Preheat oven to 350°. Beat salad oil and eggs until very fluffy. Add sugar and vanilla. Mix well. Gradually add flour, soda, salt and cinnamon. Blend well. Fold in apples and nuts. Pour into greased and floured 9 x 13 inch pan. Bake 45 to 50 minutes. Cake may be served plain or with Cream Cheese or Penuche Icing.

Cream Cheese Icing:

1 (3 ounce) package cream
  cheese, softened
1 ½ teaspoons soft butter

1 teaspoon vanilla
¾ cup powdered sugar

Blend all ingredients and spread over cake.

Penuche Icing:

½ cup butter
1 cup brown sugar

¼ cup milk
1 ¾ cups sifted powdered sugar

Melt butter. Add brown sugar; boil over low heat for about 2 minutes. Stirring constantly, add milk and bring to a boil. Cool to lukewarm. Gradually add powdered sugar and beat with mixer until thick. If topping becomes too thick, add a little hot water or if not thick enough, add more powdered sugar.

HINT: *Your cake won't stick to the plate if you have sprinkled powdered sugar on the plate.*

APPLE TART

Preparation: 45 minutes *Can do ahead* *Yield: 6 to 8 servings*
Bake: 45 minutes

½ cup butter, softened
⅓ cup sugar
¼ teaspoon vanilla
1 cup sifted flour
1 (8 ounce) package cream
  cheese
¼ cup sugar

1 egg, slightly beaten
½ teaspoon vanilla
4 cups thinly sliced peeled
  apples (about 4 medium)
½ teaspoon ground cinnamon
⅓ cup sugar
¼ cup sliced almonds

Preheat oven to 450°. Beat butter, ⅓ cup sugar and ¼ teaspoon vanilla with electric mixer until well blended. Slowly stir in flour until mixture forms a soft dough. Press into bottom and 1 ½ inches up sides of ungreased 9 inch spring form pan. Beat cream cheese and ¼ cup sugar with electric mixer. Add egg and vanilla and beat until just smooth. Pour into prepared spring form pan. Combine apples, cinnamon and remaining sugar. Layer evenly over cream cheese mixture. Sprinkle with almonds. Bake 10 minutes. Lower heat to 400° and bake for 25 more minutes. Cool in pan on rack before removing sides of pan. Serve at room temperature or chilled.

BLUEBERRY TORTE

Preparation: 30 minutes *Yield: 8 to 10 servings*
Bake: 1 hour

½ cup butter, softened
1 cup flour
5 egg whites
1 cup sugar
1 teaspoon vanilla

1 teaspoon white vinegar
1 ½ to 2 cups fresh or frozen
  blueberries
Whipped cream for top

Preheat oven to 325°. Mix butter and flour together and pat in bottom of a round spring form pan. Beat egg whites until dry. Slowly add sugar, vanilla and white vinegar. Mix in blueberries. Pour egg white mixture on top of flour and butter crust. Bake 1 hour. Let cool. Meringue will fall when removed from oven. Serve with whipped cream.

SAUCY CHERRY CAKE

Preparation: 15 minutes   *Can do ahead*   *Yield: 12 to 16 servings*
Bake: 45 minutes

Cake:

2 cups sugar
2 cups flour
2 teaspoons baking soda
¼ teaspoon salt
2 eggs, beaten

2 tablespoons melted butter or
   margarine
1 (1 pound) can pitted pie
   cherries and juice
2 cups chopped pecans or
   walnuts

Preheat oven to 350°. Grease and flour 9 x 13 inch cake pan. Sift together sugar, flour, baking soda and salt. Combine the beaten eggs and slightly cooled, melted butter. Add to dry ingredients. Add cherries and juice. Mix thoroughly, using a mixer; add nuts. Pour into prepared pan. Bake for 45 minutes. Cool and cut into squares.

Sauce:

½ pint whipping cream
1 cup sugar

½ cup butter or margarine
2 teaspoons vanilla

Mix the whipping cream, sugar, butter and vanilla in saucepan. Cook slowly to the boiling point, stirring constantly. Do not boil. Pour the hot sauce over the cut cake. Cover and refrigerate. Remove from refrigerator about 15 minutes before serving.

Note: This is a very rich cake. Serve small pieces.

HINT: *Freeze large pieces of citrus peel to be used for zest, when needed.*

FIG PRESERVE CAKE

Preparation: 30 minutes   *Can do ahead*   *Yield: 20 servings*
Bake: 1 hour 15 minutes

Cake:

1 ½ cups sugar
2 cups flour
1 teaspoon baking soda
1 teaspoon salt
1 teaspoon nutmeg
1 teaspoon cinnamon
½ teaspoon allspice
½ teaspoon cloves

1 cup oil
3 eggs
1 cup buttermilk
1 tablespoon vanilla
1 cup fig preserves, chopped
½ cup chopped pecans or
    walnuts

Preheat oven to 350°. Combine dry ingredients. Add oil and eggs, beating well after each egg. Add buttermilk and vanilla, mixing thoroughly. Stir in preserves and nuts. Pour batter into greased and floured 10 inch tube pan. Bake for 1 hour 15 minutes. Cool 10 minutes. Remove from pan. Pour warm buttermilk glaze over cake.

Buttermilk Glaze:

¼ cup buttermilk
½ cup sugar
¼ teaspoon baking soda

1 ½ teaspoons cornstarch
¼ cup margarine
1 ½ teaspoons vanilla

Combine buttermilk, sugar, soda, cornstarch and margarine in a saucepan; bring to a boil and remove from heat. Cool slightly and stir in vanilla.

HINT: Keep cake filling from soaking into cake by sprinkling layers lightly with powdered sugar before spreading the filling.

CAKES

GROOMS CAKE

Preparation: Difficult, but worth it.
Bake: 1 hour 45 minutes

Make cakes the day before and freeze to make assembling easier.

Pound Cake:

1 (16 ounce) pound cake mix
⅔ cup water

1 teaspoon lemon peel
2 eggs

Date Cake:

1 (14 ounce) box date bar mix
½ cup hot water
½ cup chopped walnuts

2 eggs
1 teaspoon baking powder
Fruit liqueur for flavor

Fillings:

1 (8 ounce) jar cranberry jelly
1 (16 ounce) can apricots

1 (16 ounce) can plums

Butter Cream Icing:

1 cup butter, softened
2 pounds powdered sugar

¼ cup plus 2 tablespoons
   strong coffee
1 tablespoon vanilla

Chocolate Icing:

⅓ cup shortening
1 tablespoon butter
1 cup powdered sugar, divided

Dash salt
½ teaspoon vanilla
¼ cup cocoa
Water

Pound Cake: Blend cake mix, water, eggs and lemon peel in large bowl and beat 3 minutes. Spread 2 ⅓ cups batter in a greased and floured 8 inch cake pan (you will have batter left over). Bake 45 to 55 minutes. Cool. Split in half and freeze. Do not defrost before assembling cake.

Date Cake: Mix date filling from date mix in ½ cup hot water. Stir into the crumbly mix two eggs, baking powder and nuts. Spread in a greased and

GROOMS CAKE (Continued)

floured 8 inch cake pan. Bake 15 minutes at 350°. Decrease oven temperature to 325° and bake 30 to 35 minutes more. Cool. Split and freeze. Do not defrost before assembling cake.

Butter Cream Icing: Mix butter and sugar. Stir in hot coffee and vanilla. Beat until spreading consistency.

Chocolate Icing: Beat shortening, butter, ½ cup sugar, salt and vanilla until smooth. Gradually add ½ cup sugar and cocoa. Stir in water 1 teaspoon at a time until spreading consistency.

Fillings: Stir cranberry jelly to break; set aside. Drain apricots thoroughly, mash and sieve; set aside. Drain and pit plums, mince and drain well; set aside.

Assembly: Start with split date nut layer. Spread with thin layer of butter cream icing, then ¼ cup cranberry filling. Sprinkle with fruit liqueur. Top with layer of pound cake. Spread with thin layer of butter cream icing, then ¼ cup apricot filling. Sprinkle with fruit liqueur. Top with date cake, spread with butter cream icing, then ¼ cup plums. Sprinkle with liqueur. Top with remaining pound cake. Sprinkle with liqueur. Frost top and sides with butter cream icing. Decorate with chocolate icing.

GRAHAM CRACKER KARETHOPETA

Preparation: 30 minutes   *Yield: 6 to 8 servings*
Bake: 40 minutes

½ cup butter	½ cup flour
6 eggs, separated	¼ teaspoon cinnamon
1 cup nuts	3 teaspoons baking powder
9 ½ whole graham crackers	¼ teaspoon cloves
1 ½ cups sugar	1 ½ cups milk

Preheat oven to 350°. Beat butter until fluffy. Add egg yolks and beat well. Crush nuts and crackers with rolling pin. Sift together sugar, flour, spices and baking powder. Combine with nuts and crackers. In a separate bowl alternately add dry ingredients with milk. Beat egg whites until stiff and fold into mixture. Spoon into greased 9 x 13 inch pan and bake for about 40 minutes, until done. Cool, cut and serve.

Note: May be served with whipped topping.

CAKES

HUMMINGBIRD CAKE

Preparation: 1 hour　　　*Can do ahead*　　　*Yield: 8 to 12 servings*
Bake: 30 minutes

Cake:

3 cups flour
2 cups sugar
1 teaspoon salt
1 teaspoon baking soda
1 teaspoon ground cinnamon
3 eggs, beaten
1 ½ cups salad oil

1 ½ teaspoons vanilla extract
1 (8 ounce) can crushed
　pineapple, undrained
2 cups chopped pecans or
　walnuts, divided
2 cups chopped bananas

Preheat oven to 350°. Combine dry ingredients in a large mixing bowl, add eggs and salad oil, stirring until dry ingredients are moistened. Do not beat. Stir in vanilla, pineapple, 1 cup chopped nuts and bananas. Spoon batter into 3 well greased and floured 9 inch cake pans. Bake for 25 to 30 minutes or until cake tests done. Cool in pans 10 minutes, remove from pans and cool completely.

Cream Cheese Frosting:

1 (8 ounce) package cream
　cheese, softened
½ cup butter or margarine,
　softened

1 (16 ounce) package powdered
　sugar
1 teaspoon vanilla extract

Combine cream cheese and butter; and cream until smooth. Add powdered sugar, beating until light and fluffy. Stir in vanilla. Spread frosting between layers and on top and sides of cake. Sprinkle with 1 cup chopped nuts.

HINT: *When blending liquid and dry ingredients for a cake, always begin and end with the dry ingredients.*

MANDARIN ORANGE CAKE

Preparation: 30 minutes   *Can do ahead*   *Yield: 8 to 10 servings*
Bake: 35 minutes

Cake:

1 cup sugar	½ teaspoon salt
1 egg	1 teaspoon vanilla
1 cup flour	1 (11 ounce) can mandarin
1 teaspoon baking soda	oranges, drained

Preheat oven to 350°. Combine all ingredients and mix two minutes at medium speed. Bake in a 9 inch square pan 30 to 35 minutes.

Topping:

¾ cup brown sugar	3 tablespoons butter
3 tablespoons milk	Whipped cream

Combine topping ingredients in a saucepan. Bring to a boil, stirring occasionally. Pour over hot cake. Add one recipe topping when serving warm cake. Top with whipped cream.

Note: This recipe can be doubled for a 9 x 13 inch pan. Also double the syrup recipe.

MINT CHOCOLATE ANGEL FOOD CAKE

Preparation: 1 hour   *Do ahead*   *Yield: 12 to 16 servings*
Bake: 30 to 40 minutes
Cool: 1 hour

Angel food cake mix	Dash of salt
1 quart whipping cream	1 teaspoon peppermint extract
1 cup sugar	Bitter chocolate, grated
4 heaping tablespoons cocoa	

Prepare cake according to package directions. Let cool. Slice cake crosswise in 4 layers. Set aside. Mix together cream, sugar, cocoa, salt and peppermint extract. Refrigerate 1 hour then whip to proper consistency for icing. Put cake together by icing between each layer. Ice sides and top. Lightly sprinkle grated bitter chocolate on top of frosted cake. Make one day ahead and refrigerate overnight.

CAKES

WALNUT TORTE

Preparation: 1 hour   *Can do ahead*   *Yield: 8 servings*
Bake: 1 hour

Torte:

8 eggs, separated	**1 ¾ cups ground walnuts**
1 cup sugar	**1 cup dry bread crumbs**

Preheat oven to 300°. In a large bowl beat egg yolks until thick and lemon colored (high speed about 2 minutes). Gradually add sugar until mixture is thick and falls from beaters in heavy ribbons (about 2 minutes). In a separate bowl beat egg whites until stiff. Fold nuts and crumbs into yolk mixture. Gently fold egg whites in yolk mixture. Bake 50 to 60 minutes, in a greased and floured 8 inch cake pan. Let cool 10 minutes.

Mocha Rum Frosting:

1 ½ cups butter	**2 tablespoons instant coffee**
2 ½ cups powdered sugar	**powder**
1 egg	**2 tablespoons rum**

Beat butter until pale and fluffy. Gradually add sugar and then egg, beating on high speed the whole time. <u>Must be light and fluffy</u> (at least 10 to 15 minutes on high). Add rum and coffee after dissolving together.

Note: You can also add other liqueurs like Amaretto.

HINT: Roll raisins and other dried fruits in flour to keep them from sticking together or sinking to the bottom during baking.

CARIBBEAN FUDGE PIE

Preparation: 30 minutes *Can do ahead* *Yield: 8 servings*
Bake: 25 minutes

¼ cup butter
¾ cup brown sugar, packed
3 eggs
1 (12 ounce) package semi-
  sweet chocolate pieces,
  melted
2 teaspoons instant coffee
  powder

1 teaspoon rum extract
¼ cup flour
1 cup coarsely broken walnuts
1 (9 inch) unbaked pie shell
½ cup walnut halves for
  decoration

Preheat oven to 375°. Cream butter with sugar; beat in eggs, one at a time. Add melted chocolate, instant coffee and rum extract. Stir in flour and broken walnuts, and turn into pie shell. Top with remaining ½ cup walnut halves. Bake for 25 minutes. Cool. Top with whipped cream, if desired.

CHOCOLATE CHEESE PIE

Preparation: 30 minutes *Can do ahead* *Yield: 10 servings*
Chill: 5 hours

5 whole graham crackers
½ cup butter, melted
2 eggs, separated
1 (8 ounce) package cream
  cheese, softened
1 (6 ounce) package semi-
  sweet chocolate morsels

1 teaspoon vanilla
½ cup sugar, divided
1 cup whipped topping
Extra whipped topping
  for garnish
Pinch salt

Crush graham crackers. Mix with butter. Pat into large, deep pie plate. Melt chocolate in double boiler over moderate heat. Remove from heat. Beat cream cheese until smooth, add vanilla and ¼ cup sugar. Add egg yolks one at a time, beating well. Add chocolate and beat. In a separate dish, beat egg whites and add salt. Beat until soft peaks form and add remaining ¼ cup sugar. Beat until firm but not dry. Fold whipped topping into chocolate mixture, then fold in egg whites. Pour into pie pan. Refrigerate 5 hours or overnight.

Note: To serve add extra Cool Whip and chocolate curls.

PIES

HEAVENLY PIE

Preparation: Takes a long time, but is well worth the effort.
Do ahead   *Yield: 2 (10 inch) pies*

Meringue:

4 egg whites at room   1 teaspoon vanilla extract
   temperature   1 cup sugar
1 teaspoon apple cider vinegar

Preheat oven to 250°. Lightly grease bottoms, sides and rims of two 10 inch
pie pans. Beat egg whites in a large, deep mixing bowl until stiff. While
continuing to beat, add vinegar and vanilla; then, while still beating, add sugar
in small amounts at a time. Beat until the egg white mixture forms stiff, shiny
peaks. Fill both pie pans with the meringue, shaping as pie crust. Handle the
meringue gently so as not to break down the egg whites. Bake for 45 minutes;
turn off oven, leaving door closed for 15 more minutes. Open oven door but
leave pie pans in oven to completely cool.

Filling:

1 (6 ounce) package semi-   2 tablespoons strong coffee
   sweet chocolate morsels   1 ½ cups whipping cream
2 tablespoons butter   ¾ cup powdered sugar, unsifted
                              1 ½ teaspoons vanilla extract

Melt the chocolate morsels, butter and coffee together over double boiler,
stirring until well mixed. Let cool. Mixture will become thick and very stiff.
Whip the whipping cream in a large, deep, pre-chilled mixing bowl. When the
cream begins to thicken, quickly add the powdered sugar and vanilla, beating
only until the sugar disappears. Gently fold the whipped cream into the
chocolate mixture. Pour this filling evenly into both pie shells. Lightly cover
with plastic wrap and refrigerate, allowing to set overnight.

Topping:

1 ½ cups whipping cream   1 ½ teaspoons vanilla extract
¾ cup powdered sugar, unsifted

Whip the whipping cream in a large, deep, pre-chilled mixing bowl. When the
cream begins to thicken, quickly add the powdered sugar and vanilla, beating

HEAVENLY PIE (Continued)

only until the sugar disappears. Spread the whipped cream topping evenly over both pies, which have set overnight in the refrigerator.

Note:

1. Be sure the egg white bowl is completely dry inside before adding the egg whites.

2. Do not allow the beating of the egg whites to stop.

3. Do not try on a humid day.

CHOCOLATE CHESS PIE

Preparation: 10 minutes　　　　*Can do ahead*　　　　*Yield: 8 servings*
Bake: 40 minutes

1 (9 inch) unbaked pie shell
½ cup butter
1 ½ squares unsweetened
　chocolate
1 cup brown sugar
½ cup sugar

1 tablespoon flour
2 eggs
½ egg shell of milk
1 teaspoon vanilla
2 to 3 drops mint flavoring

Bake crust at 475° for 3 minutes. Melt butter and chocolate together. Add remaining ingredients to chocolate mixture and mix well. Pour into pie shell and bake at 325° for 35 to 40 minutes.

Note: When ready to serve, top with whipped cream and accent with red cherries.

HINT: *Cake mixes are better if the mix is sifted before assembling the batter.*

PIES

FRENCH SILK PIE

Preparation: 45 minutes   *Can do ahead*   *Yield: 12 servings*
Bake: 12 to 15 minutes   *Can be frozen*
Chill: 3 hours

Crust:

½ cup brown sugar
1 cup flour

½ cup butter (no substitution)
½ cup chopped pecans

Preheat oven to 400°. Mix all ingredients and press in 9 x 13 inch pan. Bake until slightly brown, about 12 to 15 minutes. When cool enough to handle crush with hands and pat back in same pan.

Filling:

1 cup butter, softened
   (no substitution)
1 ½ cups sugar
3 ½ squares unsweetened
   chocolate, melted

4 eggs
1 tablespoon vanilla
Whipping cream (optional)

Cream together butter and sugar. Add vanilla and chocolate. Add eggs 1 at a time and beat 3 minutes after each addition. Pour over crust and chill for at least 3 hours. Serve plain or with whipped cream. Decorate with shaved chocolate or chocolate curls and nuts.

BEST EVER APPLE PIE

Preparation: 20 minutes   *Can do ahead*   *Yield: 8 servings*
Bake: 1 hour

1 pie shell
5 to 6 cups sliced apples,
   peeled
1 ½ cups sugar
⅛ teaspoon salt

½ teaspoon cinnamon or more
   to taste
½ cup plus 5 tablespoons flour
3 tablespoons water
½ cup margarine

Preheat oven to 425°. Place apples in pie shell. Sprinkle 1 cup sugar, salt, cinnamon, 5 tablespoons flour and water on top of apples. Combine ½ cup sugar, ½ cup flour and ½ cup margarine to make crumbly mixture. Sprinkle on top of pie. Place pan in large brown paper bag; bind airtight with paper clips or staples. Bake for 1 hour.

BERRY PIE

Preparation: 1 hour   *Can do ahead*   *Yield: 6 to 8 servings*
Chill: 2 hours

1 (9 inch) cooked and cooled
  pastry
1 quart fresh berries
½ cup sugar
3 tablespoons cornstarch

Juice of ½ lemon <u>or</u> lime
3 ounces cream cheese,
  softened
2 tablespoons milk
½ pint whipped cream

In a saucepan, mix sugar, cornstarch, lemon juice and half the amount of berries. Cook over medium heat until clear. Cream milk and cream cheese in mixing bowl. Spread over bottom of cooled pastry, this will keep crust from becoming soggy. Blend remaining fresh berries with cooked mixture. Turn into pastry and chill. Serve with whipped cream or ice cream.

PEGGY'S CHERRY PIE

Preparation: 30 minutes   *Can do ahead*   *Yield: 8 servings*

Crust:

10 whole cinnamon graham
  crackers

¼ cup melted margarine

Crush graham crackers and mix with margarine. Press in 10 inch pie pan. Chill.

Pie:

1 (14 ounce) can sweetened
  condensed milk
⅓ cup fresh lemon juice
½ cup broken pecans

1 (16 ounce) can water packed
  cherries, drained
½ pint whipping cream, whipped

Mix condensed milk, lemon juice, pecans and cherries together. Fold in whipped cream. Pour into chilled crust and chill at least 1 hour before serving.

LEMON ANGEL PIE

Preparation: 30 minutes   *Can do ahead*   *Yield: 6 servings*
Bake: 1 hour
Chill: 12 hours

Meringue Shell:

3 egg whites   1 cup sugar
¼ teaspoon cream of tartar

Preheat oven to 275°. Beat egg whites with cream of tartar in a medium sized bowl until foamy white. Beat in 1 cup sugar, a tablespoon at a time, until the meringue forms stiff glossy peaks. Lightly butter a 9 inch pie plate. Spoon meringue over bottom and up side to form a shell. Bake for 1 hour. Turn off oven, leave meringue in oven until cool.

Lemon Filling:

5 egg yolks   ⅓ cup lemon juice
⅔ cup sugar   1 cup heavy cream, whipped
1 tablespoon grated lemon rind

Beat egg yolks in top of a double boiler until frothy. Beat in ⅔ cup sugar slowly until mixture is thick and light. Stir in lemon rind and juice. Cook, stirring constantly, over hot, not boiling, water until filling is thick, about 13 minutes; cool. Spoon cooled filling into meringue shell; cover loosely; refrigerate at least 12 hours for meringue and filling to mold. Top with whipped cream; decorate with orange and lemon slices and mint, if desired.

HINT: *To enhance its color, add 1 teaspoon of glycerin to fruit before adding it to the fruit cake mixture.*

PEACH PRALINE PIE

Preparation: 15 minutes   *Can do ahead*   *Yield: 1 pie*
Bake: 50 to 60 minutes

1 (9-inch) pie shell
⅓ cup packed brown sugar
¼ cup flour
3 tablespoons butter
½ cup chopped pecans

1 ½ tablespoons quick cooking
   tapioca
¾ cup sugar
4 cups sliced fresh peaches,
   peeled
1 tablespoon lemon juice

Preheat oven to 425°. Combine brown sugar, flour, butter and pecans with a pastry blender. Sprinkle ⅓ on the pie shell. Combine tapioca and sugar. Mix in peach slices and lemon juice. Turn into pie shell. Top with remaining sugar, flour, butter, pecan mixture. Bake for 15 minutes. Reduce heat to 375° and bake for another 35 minutes.

STRAWBERRY SURPRISE

Preparation: 1 hour   *Can do ahead*   *Yield: 8 to 12 servings*
Bake: 10 minutes
Cook: 20 minutes

2 cups crushed pretzels
   (remove salt) or use
   unsalted pretzels
3 tablespoons sugar
½ cup butter or margarine
1 (2 ¼ ounce) package whipped
   topping mix
½ cup cold milk
½ teaspoon vanilla
½ cup powdered sugar

1 (8 ounce) package cream
   cheese
1 quart strawberries (reserve
   1 cup for topping)
¾ cup water
1 cup sugar
3 tablespoons cornstarch
1 teaspoon lemon juice
Red food coloring

Preheat oven to 400°. Combine pretzels, sugar and butter and press into an 8 x 12 inch ovenproof glass dish. Bake for 10 minutes. Cool. Beat the topping, milk and sugar until thick. Add vanilla and cream cheese. Spread over crumb mixture. Cook berries with water, sugar and cornstarch until thick. Add lemon juice and food coloring. When cooled, spread over cream cheese layer. Cut remaining berries in half and put on top. Refrigerate.

PIES

COCONUT CREAM PIE

Preparation: 20 minutes   *Can do ahead*   *Yield: 1 pie*
Bake: 15 minutes

Baked pie shell	5 egg yolks
¼ cup cornstarch	2 tablespoons butter
⅔ cup sugar	1 teaspoon vanilla
¼ teaspoon salt	1 cup coconut
2 cups milk	

Meringue:

5 egg whites	¼ teaspoon cream of tartar
⅓ cup sugar	½ cup coconut

Preheat oven to 350°. Cook cornstarch, sugar, salt, milk, egg yolks, butter and vanilla over medium-low heat stirring constantly until mixture thickens. Add coconut and pour into baked pie shell. Beat egg whites until fluffy. Gradually add sugar and cream of tartar and beat until soft peaks form. Fold in coconut and spread on top of filling. Bake 15 minutes or until brown.

MYSTERY PECAN PIE

Preparation: 20 minutes   *Can do ahead*   *Yield: 8 to 10 servings*
Bake: 35 to 40 minutes

1 (8 ounce) package cream cheese	4 eggs
	1 (10 inch) pie shell, unbaked
⅓ cup sugar	1 ¼ cups chopped pecans
¼ teaspoon salt	1 cup light corn syrup
2 teaspoons vanilla	¼ cup sugar

Preheat oven to 375°. Combine the ⅓ cup sugar, salt, cream cheese, 1 teaspoon vanilla and one egg. Mix well. Pour into pie crust. Sprinkle pecans on top. Combine remaining eggs, sugar, vanilla and syrup. Mix well. Pour over pecans. Bake 35 to 40 minutes or until center is firm.

OLD FASHIONED PECAN PIE

Preparation: 30 minutes   *Can do ahead*   *Yield: 6 to 8 servings*
Bake: 1 hour

1 cup sugar	1 cup whole pecans
⅔ cup dark corn syrup	¼ cup butter
3 eggs	1 tablespoon flour
¼ teaspoon salt	1 (9 inch) pie shell, unbaked
1 teaspoon vanilla	

Preheat oven to 350°. Combine sugar, butter and syrup until a smooth blend. Add flour, salt and eggs together and beat slightly, then add vanilla and pecans. Bake in an unbaked 9 inch pie shell for 1 hour.

SINFUL TOFFEE PIE

Preparation: 10 minutes   *Can do ahead*   *Yield: 12 servings*
Freeze: At least 2 hours   *Must be frozen*

18 to 32 vanilla wafers	1 cup chopped toffee candy
½ gallon vanilla <u>or</u> vanilla	bars
chocolate ripple ice cream	

Line the sides and bottom of a 9 inch buttered pie plate with whole vanilla wafers. Spoon half of the ice cream into shell, smoothing flat. Sprinkle ½ of chopped toffee candy bars over ice cream. Spoon on remaining ice cream. Store in freezer until serving time.

Sauce:

1 ½ cups sugar	¼ cup light corn syrup
1 cup evaporated milk	Dash salt
¼ cup margarine	

Combine sugar, milk, margarine, corn syrup and salt in saucepan. Bring to a boil over medium heat. Boil 1 minute. Remove from heat. Stir in remaining candy. Cool, stirring occasionally. Serve pie topped with cold or warm sauce.

PIES

PUMPKIN ICE CREAM PIE

Preparation: 20 to 30 minutes   *Do ahead*   *Yield: 1 (9 inch) pie*
                                     Must be frozen

1 cup canned pumpkin
½ cup brown sugar
½ teaspoon each salt,
  cinnamon, ginger

1 quart vanilla ice cream,
  softened
1 (9 inch) graham cracker
  pie crust

Combine pumpkin, sugar, salt and spices. Heat thoroughly; chill well.
Combine ice cream and pumpkin mixture. Spoon into pie crust. Freeze firm.

HINT: After filling a cake pan, tap it firmly on the counter to remove air bubbles. Then tilt all the way around so the batter goes up the sides of the pan about ½ inch. This will keep cake more even and prevent bulge in the center.

HEAVENLY APPLE DUMPLINGS

Preparation: 30 minutes   *Can do ahead*   *Yield: 6 servings*
Bake: 35 minutes   *Can be frozen*

2 cups sugar
2 cups water
¼ teaspoon cinnamon
¼ cup butter
6 apples
2 cups flour
1 teaspoon salt

2 teaspoons baking powder
¾ cup shortening
½ cup milk
Cinnamon
Sugar
Butter

Preheat oven to 375°. For sauce combine sugar, water and cinnamon. Cook 5 minutes. Remove from heat. Add butter and mix. Set aside. Pare and core apples. Sift flour, salt and baking powder together. Cut in shortening. Add milk all at once. Stir just until flour is moistened. Roll ¼ inch thick, cut into 6 inch squares. Place one apple on each square. Sprinkle apple, especially center, generously with cinnamon and sugar mixed together. Dot center with butter. Fold 4 corners of square together over top of apple to seal. Pinch edges together. Repeat with other apples. Place 1 inch apart in a greased baking pan. Pour sauce over dumplings. Bake about 35 minutes or until dumplings are golden. Serve hot with cream or cool and refrigerate, which allows the sauce to thicken.

HOT APPLE SUNDAE

Preparation: 30 minutes   *Can do ahead*   *Yield: 4 servings*

1 cup sugar
½ cup orange juice
¼ cup lemon juice

¼ teaspoon ground cinnamon
3 tart apples (peeled and
    sliced thin)

In a skillet mix together sugar, orange juice, lemon juice and cinnamon. Stir over low heat. Bring to a boil, simmer 5 minutes and add apples then simmer covered 15 minutes longer. Serve over ice cream.

DESSERTS

MOM'S APPLE CRISP

Preparation: 15 minutes   *Can do ahead*   *Yield: 6 servings*
Bake: 40 minutes

⅓ cup butter   1 teaspoon cinnamon
1 cup sugar   1 teaspoon salt
¾ cup flour   ¼ cup water
4 cups peeled and sliced apples

Preheat oven to 350°. Combine flour, sugar and butter. Place apples in greased baking dish. Cover with flour mixture; sprinkle with cinnamon and salt. Pour water over all and bake 40 minutes.

FAVORITE BREAD PUDDING

Preparation: ½ hour   *Can do ahead*   *Yield: 6 to 8 servings*
Bake: 45 minutes

2 ¼ cups milk   ½ teaspoon cinnamon
2 slightly beaten eggs   1 teaspoon vanilla
2 cups day old bread cubes   ¼ teaspoon salt
½ cup brown sugar   ½ cup raisins (optional)

Preheat oven to 350°. Combine milk and eggs. Pour over bread cubes. Stir in sugar, cinnamon, vanilla, salt and raisins. Pour into buttered 8 inch round baking dish. Place baking dish in a shallow pan and pour hot water into pan about 1 inch deep. Bake for 45 minutes.

HINT: *Custards and soufflés will be better if the larger pan containing the water is placed in the oven while it is preheating.*

BLACKBERRY BRANDY SAUCE

Preparation: 10 minutes　　　*Can do ahead*　　　*Yield: 1 ½ cups*

1 cup blackberry jam　　　**¼ to ⅓ cup blackberry brandy**
⅓ cup orange juice

Bring the blackberry jam and orange juice to a boil in a saucepan. Remove from heat, strain and cool slightly. Add brandy to taste. Blend well. Cover and refrigerate until ready to use. Flavor intensifies during storage.

Note: Good served over vanilla ice cream, raspberry sherbet or slices of cake.

Microwave:

Bring blackberry jam and orange juice to a boil in 1 quart glass bowl using 100% power. Remove from heat, strain and cool slightly. Add brandy to taste. Blend well. Cover and refrigerate until ready to use. Flavor intensifies during storage.

CHEF LOUIS' CHOCOLATE SAUCE

Preparation: 30 minutes　　　*Can do ahead*　　　*Yield: 5 ½ cups*

½ cup sweet (unsalted) butter　　　**2 tablespoons cornstarch**
2 cups sugar　　　　　　　　　　　**blended with ½ cup cold**
1 cup Hershey's cocoa　　　　　　**water**
1 cup milk　　　　　　　　　　　　**1 cup Hershey's chocolate**
　　　　　　　　　　　　　　　　　　syrup
　　　　　　　　　　　　　　　　　　½ cup favorite brandy

In a very heavy saucepan, melt butter. Add sugar and cocoa. Stir with wooden spoon until mixture melts and starts to caramelize (at least 5 minutes). Then add milk, stirring constantly. At first there will be some hard lumps of caramelized sugar, but as the milk comes to a boil, they will dissolve. Stir in the cornstarch which has been blended with water; stir it in a slow, even stream into the boiling chocolate mixture, stirring constantly. Remove from heat and let cool. Stir in chocolate syrup and brandy. Keep in a tightly closed container in refrigerator, keeps for months.

DESSERTS

CHOCOLATE MOUSSE

Preparation: 20 minutes   *Can do ahead*   *Yield: 6 servings*

¼ cup sugar
⅓ cup water
1 ½ cups whipping cream
1 (6 ounce) package semi-sweet
  chocolate pieces

3 tablespoons dark rum
3 egg yolks
½ cup toasted almonds

For syrup, combine sugar and water in a small saucepan and boil for 3 minutes. With metal blade in place, add cream to the beaker of the food processor. Process without stopping until a very thick whipped cream forms, about 1 minute. Transfer to a large bowl. Without washing the beaker, reinsert metal blade and add chocolate pieces. Process, turning on and off, for 15 to 20 seconds. Continue processing and gradually pour in hot syrup, rum and egg yolks. Add almonds. Process, turning on and off, until almonds are coarsely chopped and evenly distributed, about 20 seconds. Using a spatula, scrape chocolate-almond mixture over whipped cream and fold together. Pour into individual cups and chill before serving or turn into decorative mold and freeze for 6 hours to serve as a frozen mousse.

HINT: *When frosting a cake, brush cake gently with your hand to remove crumbs. Frost with a thin coat first to seal crumbs, then add a second, thicker layer of frosting.*

SNOW SQUARES CUSTARD

Preparation: 45 minutes   *Can do ahead*   *Yield: 12 servings*
Chill: Overnight

1 envelope unflavored gelatin
4 tablespoons ice water
1 cup boiling water
2/3 cup sugar

3 egg whites, unbeaten
Pinch of salt
1/4 teaspoon vanilla

Sprinkle gelatin in ice water, let soak 5 minutes. Add boiling water, sugar and stir. Set aside and let cool. Put unbeaten egg whites in bowl, add salt, vanilla and cooled gelatin. Beat at high speed until mixture is fluffy and light. Requires a lot of beating. Pour into a 9 x 9 inch glass dish and chill overnight in refrigerator.

Sauce:

3 egg yolks
1/3 cup sugar
3 tablespoons lemon juice

1/3 cup melted butter
1/2 pint heavy cream, whipped
16 graham crackers (rolled finely)

Beat eggs until light in color; add sugar, melted butter and lemon juice. Fold in whipped cream and chill. Cut custard into squares and roll in cracker crumbs. Serve with sauce.

FRESH FRUIT SAUCE

Preparation: 45 minutes   *Can do ahead*
Chill: Overnight

1/2 cup freshly squeezed orange juice
1/2 cup pineapple juice
1/2 cup lemon juice

2 tablespoons cornstarch
1 cup sugar
4 egg yolks
2 (8 ounce) cartons of whipping cream

Mix sugar, cornstarch and fruit juices in double boiler. Beat egg yolks and add to sugar mixture. Cook until thick, stirring constantly to prevent burning. Cool completely overnight in refrigerator. Before serving, whip cream and carefully fold in fruit mixture. Serve with an assortment of seasonal fruit, as a dip or a sauce.

DESSERTS

LEMON ICE CREAM

Preparation: 30 minutes   *Can do ahead*   *Yield: 15 to 20 servings*
Freeze: 30 to 40 minutes   *Must be frozen*

Juice from 9 lemons   **3 cups milk**
4 cups sugar   **Ice**
Pinch of salt   **Ice cream salt**
3 pints half and half cream

Mix lemon juice, sugar and salt. (Can be done in the blender.) Combine half and half with milk. Gradually add lemon juice mixture to the milk mixture, stirring well. Pour into ice cream freezer. Surround with ice and salt and churn until frozen.

Note: Do not use frozen lemon juice. It must be fresh.

ORANGE ICE WITH STRAWBERRIES

Preparation: 45 minutes   *Do ahead*   *Yield: 6 servings*
Freeze: 3 hours   *Must be frozen*

Grated peel from ½ orange   **⅓ cup Grand Marnier or**
4 cups freshly squeezed orange   **Cointreau**
juice   **1 pint fresh strawberries**
1 cup sugar

In food processor or blender, blend 1 cup orange juice, sugar and Grand Marnier until combined. Stir in grated peel and remaining juice, mix well, and pour into 2 ice cube trays and freeze. Slice strawberries and sprinkle with a few drops of Grand Marnier. Just before serving, in food processor with metal blade, add frozen cubes, 1 tray at a time, turning on and off rapidly. A fine ice, free of lumps will form in about 2 or 3 minutes. Serve topped with sliced berries.

HINT: Cut meringue pie better with a knife which has been coated with butter.

PEACH COBBLER

Preparation: 15 minutes   *Can do ahead*   *Yield: 6 to 8 servings*
Bake: 1 hour

¾ cup flour
Pinch of salt
2 teaspoons baking powder
2 cups sugar, divided

¾ cup milk
½ cup butter **or** margarine
2 cups fresh peaches, peeled
    and sliced

Preheat oven to 350°. Sift flour, salt and baking powder together. Mix with 1 cup of sugar. Stir milk in slowly to make a batter. Melt the butter in an 8 x 8 inch baking pan. Pour the batter slowly over the melted butter. Do not stir. Mix the peaches well with the remaining 1 cup of sugar. Carefully spoon them over the batter. Bake for 1 hour. Can be served either warm or cold.

Note: *Apples (add 1 tablespoon cinnamon to the sugar), blueberries, cherries or other fruit may be substituted.*

BROILED PEACHES

Preparation: 30 minutes   *Yield: 6 to 8 servings*
Broil: 10 minutes

1 (28 ounce) can peach halves
¼ cup walnuts **or** pecans
Juice of 1 lemon **or**
    2 tablespoons frozen lemon
    juice
4 tablespoons brown sugar

¼ cup coconut, canned **or**
    packaged
1 tablespoon butter **or**
    margarine
½ pint whipping cream **or**
    commercial sour cream

Drain peaches well. Arrange in shallow baking dish, cut side up. Chop nuts fine and mix with lemon juice, brown sugar and coconut. Stuff peach cavities plump with mixture. Put chunk of butter on top of filling. Broil until slightly brown, about 10 minutes. Serve plain or with whipped or sour cream.

HINT: *To transfer the pastry to the pie pan, fold the pastry round in quarters, place the point at the center of the pie plate and unfold.*

DESSERTS

PEARS A L'ORANGE

Preparation: 30 minutes   *Can do ahead*   *Yield: 6 servings*
Bake: 15 to 20 minutes
Cool: 3 hours

6 pears, peeled, cored and   **⅔ cup Cointreau, Grand**
** quartered**   ** Marnier or other orange**
1 cup water   ** liqueur**
¾ cup sugar   **Whipped cream for garnish**
Grated rind and juice of 1 large
** orange**

Preheat oven to 350°. Place pears in a baking dish. Combine water and sugar and pour over pears. Cover dish and bake for 15 to 20 minutes or until pears are tender but not mushy. Remove from oven. Add grated orange rind and orange juice. Allow to cool at room temperature. Pour over orange liqueur and refrigerate until serving time. Serve garnished with slightly sweetened whipped cream.

SUNSHINE POTS DE CRÉME

Preparation: 15 minutes   *Can do ahead*   *Yield: 6 servings*
Chill: 1 hour

2 eggs, separated   **1 teaspoon grated lemon peel**
1 (14 ounce) can sweetened   **Crumbled lemon cookies,**
** condensed milk**   ** whipped cream, additional**
½ cup fresh lemon juice   ** grated lemon zest (optional**
                                        ** garnish)**

Beat yolks in a medium sized bowl. Add the condensed milk and lemon juice gradually. Add the grated peel and mix well. Beat the egg whites until stiff and fold them into the lemon mixture. Pour into custard cups and chill. Just before serving, garnish with any combination of cookie crumbs, peel or whipped cream if desired.

HINT: *For crispy crust on cherry pie, sprinkle bottom crust with plain bread crumbs before adding filling.*

Cookies & Bars

OGLEBAY

COOKIES

APPLE BARS

Preparation: 20 minutes
Bake: 30 minutes

Yield: 2 dozen

1 cup sifted flour
1 teaspoon baking powder
¼ teaspoon salt
¼ teaspoon ground cinnamon
½ cup butter <u>or</u> margarine
½ cup firmly packed light
   brown sugar

½ cup sugar
1 egg
1 teaspoon vanilla
½ cup finely chopped nuts
½ cup chopped pared cooking
   apples

Preheat oven to 350°. Sift together flour, baking powder, salt and cinnamon. Melt butter in medium pan. Remove from heat. Beat in sugars, egg and vanilla with wooden spoon. Stir in flour mixture, apples and nuts. Spread in greased 8 x 8 x 2 inch pan. Sprinkle with 1 tablespoon of a cinnamon-sugar mixture. Bake for 30 minutes.

Cinnamon-Sugar Mixture:

Combine ½ cup sugar with 1 ½ teaspoons cinnamon. Place in small jar. Shake.

BOURBON OR RUM BALLS

Preparation: 30 minutes
Stand: 1 hour

Do ahead

Yield: 4 dozen

½ pound vanilla wafers, ground
2 tablespoons cocoa
1 cup pecans, chopped
½ cup light corn syrup

2 tablespoons bourbon <u>or</u> rum
2 tablespoons water
¼ pound semi-sweet chocolate,
   finely grated
Powdered sugar

Add nuts to vanilla wafer crumbs. Add cocoa, corn syrup, rum and water and mix well. Coat hands with powdered sugar. Form mixture into balls the size of a quarter. Roll in finely grated chocolate. Let stand 1 hour to dry. Roll again in powdered sugar.

Note: These are better if made ahead of time and refrigerated to allow flavors to blend.

BROWNIES ON THREE LEVELS

Preparation: 30 minutes   *Yield: 2 dozen*
Bake: 35 minutes
Stand: 1 hour

1st Layer:

½ cup flour
¼ teaspoon baking soda
¼ teaspoon salt

1 cup quick oats
½ cup brown sugar
½ cup melted butter <u>or</u>
   margarine

Preheat oven to 350°. Combine flour, baking soda, salt, oats, sugar and margarine. Spread in greased 9 inch square pan. Bake 10 minutes.

2nd Layer:

⅓ cup butter <u>or</u> margarine
2 ounces unsweetened
   chocolate
2 eggs
1 cup sugar

½ teaspoon salt
1 teaspoon vanilla
¾ cup flour
½ cup chopped nuts (optional)

Melt margarine and chocolate together. Beat eggs and stir in sugar, salt and vanilla. Add chocolate mixture, flour and nuts. Spread over baked 1st layer. Bake 25 minutes. Allow to cool before adding 3rd layer.

3rd Layer:

1 ¾ cups powdered sugar
¼ cup butter <u>or</u> margarine,
   softened

2 tablespoons milk
1 teaspoon vanilla

Combine powdered sugar, margarine, milk and vanilla and beat until smooth and creamy. Spread over top.

Note: This recipe may be doubled and baked in a 10 x 15 inch cookie sheet with sides.

COOKIES

BUTTER PECAN "TURTLE" BARS

Preparation: 30 minutes
Bake: 22 minutes

Yield: 3 to 4 dozen

Crust:

2 cups flour
1 cup firmly packed brown
  sugar

½ cup butter, softened

In a 3-quart bowl, combine crust ingredients and mix at medium speed for 2 to 3 minutes or until particles are fine. Pat firmly into ungreased 13 x 9 x 2 inch pan. Sprinkle pecans evenly over unbaked crust.

Caramel Layer:

⅔ cup butter
½ cup firmly packed brown
  sugar

1 cup pecan halves
1 cup milk chocolate chips

Preheat oven to 350°. Prepare caramel layer by combining brown sugar and butter in heavy 1-quart saucepan. Cook over medium heat until entire surface of mixture begins to boil. Boil ½ to 1 minute, stirring constantly. Pour caramel evenly over pecans and crust. Bake at center of 350° oven for 18 to 22 minutes or until entire caramel layer is bubbly and crust is light golden brown. Remove from oven. Immediately sprinkle with chips. Let chips melt slightly (2 to 3 minutes) and slightly swirl them as they melt. Leave some whole for a marbled effect. Do not spread them. Cool completely and cut into bars.

HINT: *Toast oatmeal to be used in oatmeal cookies if you want a nuttier flavor.*

CARAMEL BROWNIES

Preparation: 10 minutes   *Can be frozen*   *Yield: 2 to 3 dozen*
Bake: 20 to 25 minutes

¼ cup butter	1 teaspoon baking powder
1 cup brown sugar	½ teaspoon salt
1 egg	½ teaspoon vanilla
½ cup flour	½ cup nuts (optional)

Preheat oven to 350°. Melt butter over low heat. Pour into bowl and add brown sugar and egg, and stir until mixed well. Sift together flour, baking powder and salt and add to brown sugar mixture. Add vanilla, and nuts if desired. Mix all ingredients and spread in a greased 8 x 8 x 2 inch pan. Bake 20 to 25 minutes.

CHEESE CAKE COOKIES

Preparation: 1 hour   *Yield: 2 dozen*
Bake: 55 minutes

⅓ cup brown sugar	¼ cup sugar
½ cup chopped nuts	1 egg
1 cup flour	1 tablespoon lemon juice
⅓ cup melted butter	1 teaspoon vanilla
1 (8 ounce) package cream cheese	2 tablespoons milk

Preheat oven to 350°. Mix brown sugar, nuts, flour and butter. Mix until crumbly. Remove ½ cup to be used as a topping. Place remainder in an 8 x 8 inch square pan and press firmly. Bake 12 to 15 minutes. Beat cream cheese and sugar until smooth. Beat in egg, lemon juice, vanilla and milk. Pour onto baked crust, top with reserved crumbs and bake 25 minutes. Cool thoroughly, cut in squares. Keep refrigerated.

HINT: Baking sheets should be at least 2 inches narrower and shorter than your oven.

COOKIES

CHOCOLATE CREAM SQUARES

Preparation: 30 minutes   *Can be frozen*   *Yield: 3 dozen*
Chill: 4 hours

Base:

½ cup butter
1 egg
¼ cup sugar
5 tablespoons cocoa

2 cups graham cracker crumbs
1 cup coconut
½ cup walnuts, chopped
1 teaspoon vanilla

Mix together butter, eggs, sugar, cocoa, graham cracker crumbs, coconut, walnuts and vanilla. Pack into a 9 x 9 inch pan.

Filling:

¼ cup butter
2 tablespoons vanilla <u>instant</u>
   pudding

3 tablespoons cream <u>or</u>
   evaporated milk
2 cups powdered sugar

Mix together butter, pudding, cream and powdered sugar and spread over base. Chill.

Icing:

4 squares semi-sweet chocolate   2 tablespoons butter

Melt chocolate and butter for icing, pour over filling. Chill. Cut in small squares.

HINT: To keep cookies from spreading during baking, sprinkle flour on a greased cookie sheet.

CHOCOLATE "CRINKLE" COOKIES

Preparation: 20 minutes   *Yield: 4 dozen*
Chill: Overnight
Cook: 10 to 12 minutes

½ cup vegetable oil (Crisco preferred)
4 (1 ounce) unsweetened chocolate squares, melted
2 cups sugar
4 eggs

2 teaspoons vanilla
2 cups flour
2 teaspoons baking powder
½ teaspoon salt
1 cup powdered sugar

Preheat oven to 350°. Mix together oil, melted chocolate and sugar in a large mixing bowl. Blend in eggs, one at a time until well blended. Add vanilla, mix well; set aside. Sift together flour, baking powder and salt. Add to oil mixture. Chill several hours, or overnight. Drop chilled dough by teaspoonful into powdered sugar. Roll in sugar, shape into a ball. Place two inches apart on greased cookie sheet. Press each ball with fork. Bake for 10 to 12 minutes. Be careful not to overbake.

CREAM CHEESE COOKIES

Preparation: 10 minutes   *Yield: 5 to 6 dozen*
Chill: 1 hour
Bake: 12 to 15 minutes

1 cup margarine
1 (3 ounce) package cream cheese
1 cup sugar
1 egg yolk

2 ½ cups flour
1 teaspoon vanilla
Cherry or pecan halves for decoration

Cream margarine and cream cheese thoroughly. Add sugar, egg yolk, flour and vanilla. Mix well and chill 1 hour. Preheat oven to 325°. Roll in 1 inch balls and lightly press a cherry half or pecan half on top. Bake 12 to 15 minutes.

COOKIES

CONFECTION SQUARES A L'ORANGE

Preparation: 25 minutes *Can be frozen* *Yield: 96 squares*
Chill: 4 hours

1 ¼ cups butter or margarine, divided
½ cup unsweetened cocoa powder
3 ½ cups sifted powdered sugar, divided
1 beaten egg

2 cups graham cracker crumbs
1 teaspoon vanilla
⅓ cup Grand Marnier or Creme de Menthe or Amaretto
1 ½ cups semi-sweet chocolate chips

Bottom layer: In saucepan, melt ½ cup of the butter. Add the cocoa powder and blend well. Remove from heat. Add ½ cup of the powdered sugar, egg and vanilla. Add graham cracker crumbs and mix well. Press into the bottom only of an ungreased baking pan.

Middle layer: Melt ½ cup of the butter. Combine with the liqueur in a mixing bowl. Beat in the remaining 3 cups powdered sugar until smooth, using the low speed of an electric mixer. Spread over the graham cracker layer. Chill 1 to 2 hours.

Top layer: Combine the remaining ¼ cup butter and the chocolate chips in a small saucepan. Heat and stir over low heat until melted. Spread over the liqueur layer. Chill 1 to 2 hours. Cut in small squares.

CRUNCHY BAR COOKIES

Preparation: 15 minutes *Yield: 3 to 4 dozen*

½ cup margarine
1 cup crunchy peanut butter
1 ½ cups graham cracker crumbs

1 cup powdered sugar
1 (12 ounce) bag semi-sweet chocolate chips

Melt together the margarine and peanut butter. Mix graham cracker crumbs and powdered sugar with the margarine and peanut butter. Spread in 9 x 13 inch pan. Melt the chocolate chips and spread over the top of mixture. Let set until chocolate is hard. Cut into squares.

MRS. DENMAN'S ENGLISH DAINTIES

Preparation: 30 minutes   *Yield: 7 dozen*
Bake: 40 minutes

Crust:

1 cup flour   1 tablespoon sugar
½ cup butter

Preheat oven to 325°. Mix flour, butter and sugar until crumbly. Press into a 10 x 14 inch shallow cookie pan and bake at 325° for 10 minutes.

Filling:

2 eggs, well beaten   ½ cup shredded coconut
1 cup brown sugar   1 cup finely chopped nuts
2 scant tablespoons flour   ½ teaspoon baking powder
1 teaspoon vanilla

Raise oven temperature to 350°. Beat eggs, add brown sugar, flour and mix well. Add vanilla, coconut and nuts and mix. Add baking powder and mix. Spread filling over crust, previously baked, and bake for 30 minutes or until brown. (Baked crust will be delicate, filling must be spread with care.)

Icing:

1 cup powdered sugar   Dash of lemon juice
1 to 2 tablespoons butter

Mix powdered sugar and butter and lemon juice. Cover the baked cookie mixture thinly, then cut into 1 ¼ inch squares.

Note: A favorite family Christmas cookie, having been made for more than 50 years. It is light and delicate, but well worth the effort.

HINT: Only grease the cookie sheet if the recipe says to do so.

COOKIES

DATE BALLS

Preparation: 1 hour   *Can be frozen*   *Yield: 40 balls*
Cook: 5 minutes

½ cup butter
1 cup dark brown sugar
1 (8 ounce) package dates,
  chopped

1 cup chopped pecans
1 cup coconut
1 teaspoon vanilla
Powdered sugar

Mix together butter, brown sugar and dates in average sized skillet. Place over heat stirring constantly until bubbly; continue to cook 5 more minutes. Remove from heat and immediately add pecans, coconut and vanilla. Cool to touch. Make into about 40 balls and roll in powdered sugar.

DELMA'S OLD FASHIONED SUGAR COOKIES

Preparation: 15 minutes   *Can be frozen*   *Yield: 4 dozen*
Chill: 2 hours to overnight
Bake: 8 to 10 minutes

2 sticks butter <u>or</u> margarine
1 cup sugar
1 egg
1 teaspoon almond extract

½ teaspoon vanilla extract
2 ⅓ cups unsifted flour
2 teaspoons baking powder
Powdered sugar

Cream butter and sugar. Mix in egg, almond and vanilla. Add flour and baking powder, blend well. Divide dough into 2 parts, roll in waxed paper, chill at least 2 hours or overnight. Slice thin. Bake on greased baking sheets 8 to 10 minutes. Sprinkle with powdered sugar.

Note: These also work well with cookie cutters. Work with dough while cold; roll on floured surface to ⅛ to ¼ inch thickness. If dough gets warm, dough will stick to cutters; re-refrigerate. Be sure to sprinkle dough and cutters with plenty of flour.

HINT: Frozen cookies will keep 9 to 12 months.

DOUBLE CHOCOLATE CHERRY COOKIES

Preparation: 60 minutes   Yield: 3 to 4 dozen
Bake: 10 minutes

1 ½ cups flour
½ cup unsweetened cocoa
¼ teaspoon salt
¼ teaspoon baking powder
¼ teaspoon baking soda
½ cup butter, softened
1 cup sugar

1 egg
1 ½ teaspoons vanilla
1 (10 ounce) jar maraschino
   cherries, reserving juice
1 (6 ounce) bag semi-sweet
   chocolate pieces
½ cup evaporated milk

Preheat oven to 350°. Sift dry ingredients in large bowl. In another large bowl blend softened butter and sugar on low with mixer until fluffy, add egg and vanilla, beat well. Add dry ingredients and mix. Shape dough into 1 inch balls and place on ungreased cookie sheet and press down center. Drain cherries, saving juice. Place a cherry in center of cookies and press down. In a small saucepan combine chocolate pieces and milk, heat until chocolate melts. Stir in 4 teaspoons of cherry juice. Spoon about 1 teaspoon over each cookie spreading to cover cookie. Bake for 10 minutes and cool.

Note: Frosting may be thinned with more cherry juice.

FROSTY LEMON COOKIES

Preparation: 25 minutes   Can be frozen   Yield: 50 to 60 cookies
Chill: 1 to 2 hours
Bake: 10 to 12 minutes

1 (18 ½ ounce) box lemon cake
   mix
1 egg, beaten

1 cup frozen non-dairy
   whipped topping
Powdered sugar

Mix dry cake mix, beaten egg and whipped topping together. Dough should be "just moist"; may need to knead with hands. Chill covered for 1 to 2 hours. Preheat oven to 350°. Form into small balls. Roll in powdered sugar. Slightly flatten with thumb on ungreased cookie sheet. Bake for 10 to 12 minutes.

COOKIES

FILLED ICE BOX COOKIES

Preparation: 1 hour   *Can be frozen*   *Yield: 10 to 12 dozen*
Bake: 8 to 10 minutes

1 pound dates, pitted and
   cut in small pieces
1 ½ cups sugar, divided
1 cup water
1 cup butter
1 cup brown sugar

1 teaspoon vanilla
3 eggs, well beaten
4 cups flour
1 teaspoon soda
½ teaspoon salt
1 cup chopped nuts

Preheat oven to 375°. Mix dates, ½ cup sugar and water. Cook until thick and set aside to cool. Cream butter, add sugars, vanilla and well beaten eggs. Sift flour, soda and salt together and add to creamed mixture. On well floured surface, roll dough to ½ inch thickness and spread with cooled date mixture. Sprinkle with 1 cup chopped nuts and roll as for jelly roll. Chill. Slice ⅜ inch thick and bake for 8 to 10 minutes on greased cookie sheets.

Note: These cookies may be stored in the roll, if well wrapped, in the refrigerator or freezer for 1 month before baking.

HICKORY NUT COOKIES

Preparation: 15 minutes   *Yield: 5 dozen*
Bake: 8 to 10 minutes

1 cup butter
2 cups brown sugar
2 eggs
½ teaspoon cinnamon
1 teaspoon soda

1 tablespoon warm water
½ teaspoon salt
3 ¾ cups flour
1 cup chopped nuts (hickory,
   pecans or walnuts)

Preheat oven to 300°. Cream butter and sugar, add eggs and cinnamon and mix well. Dissolve soda in water and add to creamed butter mixture. Sift together salt and flour and add to butter mixture. Add nuts and mix well. Drop by spoonfuls onto cookie sheets. Bake 8 to 10 minutes or until light brown.

ITALIAN AMARETTI (MACAROONS)

Preparation: 30 minutes   *Can be frozen*   *Yield: 4 ½ dozen*
Bake: 8 minutes

½ cup granulated sugar   1 tablespoon flour
½ cup powdered sugar   2 egg whites
1 cup almond paste   Pine nuts

Preheat oven to 390° (just short of 400°). Mix almond paste and sugars until crumbly. Add flour and egg whites a little at a time. Mix until no lumps remain. Drop by teaspoonfuls onto unglazed brown paper lined cookie sheets. Lightly press pine nuts onto surface of unbaked cookies. Bake in oven for 8 minutes. Check toward end of baking time. Cookies tend to burn on bottom. Remove from oven; slip paper and cookies onto a damp towel for a few minutes to facilitate removal of cookies from the paper.

OATMEAL SPICE COOKIES

Preparation: 30 minutes   *Yield: 5 dozen*
Bake: 12 to 15 minutes

¾ cup shortening   1 teaspoon salt
1 cup brown sugar, packed   1 teaspoon cinnamon
½ cup sugar   ½ teaspoon soda
1 egg   ½ teaspoon cloves
¼ cup water   ¼ teaspoon ground nutmeg
1 teaspoon vanilla   1 teaspoon ground allspice
1 cup flour   3 cups quick cooking oats

Preheat oven to 350°. Cream together shortening, sugars, egg, water and vanilla. Stir in remaining ingredients. Drop dough by rounded teaspoonfuls 1 inch apart onto greased baking sheet. Bake 12 to 15 minutes. Remove from baking sheet and cool. Store in tightly covered container.

HINT: *Dough won't stick to cookie cutters if cutters are dipped into water first.*

COOKIES

MOTHER'S SOUTHERN PECAN BARS

Preparation: 30 minutes
Bake: 40 minutes

Yield: 3 to 4 dozen

Crust:

1 ½ cups sifted flour
½ teaspoon baking powder
⅓ cup butter

½ cup firmly packed brown
  sugar
¼ cup finely chopped pecans

Preheat oven to 350°. Sift flour and baking powder, set aside. Cream butter and brown sugar. Add dry ingredients to creamed ingredients and mix with electric mixer until a coarse meal forms. Stir in the pecans. Pat in a well greased 13 x 9 x 2 inch pan. Bake for 10 minutes.

Topping:

2 eggs
¾ cup dark corn syrup
¼ cup firmly packed brown
  sugar
3 tablespoons flour

½ teaspoon salt
1 teaspoon vanilla extract
¾ cup pecans, coarsely
  chopped

Beat eggs until foamy. Add the corn syrup, brown sugar, flour, salt and vanilla. Mix well. Fold the pecans into the mixture. Pour the topping on the crust. Bake for 25 to 30 minutes more. Cool and cut into squares.

SCOTTISH SHORTBREAD

Preparation: 15 minutes
Chill: Overnight
Bake: 20 minutes

Can be frozen

Yield: 6 dozen

4 cups flour
1 pound butter

1 ⅓ cups sugar
¼ cup shortening

Let butter reach room temperature. Cream together flour, butter, sugar and shortening. Dough is very soft. Divide into 4 portions. Shape into "logs" and wrap in waxed paper. Chill several hours in refrigerator. Slice into cookies ½ inch thick and bake in preheated 300° oven for 20 minutes.

PUMPKIN COOKIES WITH CARAMEL FROSTING

Preparation: 30 minutes   *Yield: 4 dozen*
Bake: 12 minutes

Cookies:

2 cups flour	1 cup sugar
2 teaspoons baking powder	1 cup pumpkin
1 teaspoon soda	1 egg
1 teaspoon cinnamon	½ cup chopped nuts (optional)
½ teaspoon salt	1 teaspoon vanilla
1 cup shortening	

Preheat oven to 350°. Sift dry ingredients together. Cream shortening and sugar. Add pumpkin and egg. Add dry ingredients, nuts and vanilla. Drop by small teaspoon on ungreased sheet. Bake 10 to 12 minutes. Let cookies cool, then frost.

Caramel Frosting:

1 tablespoon butter	1 cup powdered sugar
4 tablespoons milk	¾ teaspoon vanilla
½ cup brown sugar	

Combine butter, milk and brown sugar in a saucepan. Boil 2 minutes, stirring constantly. <u>Cool</u>. Stir in sugar and vanilla. Beat until smooth and creamy and ice the cookies.

SWEET CRESCENT COOKIES

Preparation: 1 hour   *Yield: 3 to 4 dozen*
Cook: 3 minutes

½ cup chopped peanuts	Won ton wrappers
½ cup coconut	1 egg, beaten
½ cup brown sugar	Hot oil in wok
½ cup sugar	

Mix together peanuts, coconut and sugars. Put heaping teaspoon of mixture in center of won ton wrapper. Fold over wrapper and seal edges with beaten egg. Fry in heated oil in wok until browned. Drain on paper towel. Store in airtight container.

COOKIES

ROCKY ROAD FUDGE BARS

Preparation: 1 hour   *Can be frozen*   *Yield: 36 bars*
Bake: 35 minutes

Bar:

½ cup margarine or butter
1 square (1 ounce)
   unsweetened chocolate or
   1 envelope premelted
   unsweetened baking
   chocolate flavor

1 cup sugar
1 cup flour, sifted
½ cup chopped pecans
1 teaspoon baking powder
1 teaspoon vanilla
2 eggs

Filling:

1 (8 ounce) package cream
   cheese, softened (reserve
   2 ounces for frosting)
½ cup sugar
2 tablespoons flour

¼ cup butter or margarine,
   softened
1 egg
½ teaspoon vanilla
¼ cup chopped pecans
1 cup semi-sweet chocolate
   chips

Frosting:

2 cups miniature marsh-
   mallows
¼ cup margarine or butter
1 square (1 ounce) unsweetened chocolate or
   1 envelope premelted
   unsweetened baking
   chocolate flavor

2 ounces reserved cream
   cheese
¼ cup milk
3 cups powdered sugar
1 teaspoon vanilla

Preheat oven to 350°. In saucepan over low heat, melt ½ cup margarine and 1 square chocolate. In large mixing bowl, add remaining bar ingredients to margarine and chocolate; mix well. Spread in greased and floured 9 x 13 inch pan. Set aside. In small mixing bowl, combine 6 ounces of cream cheese with sugar, flour, butter, egg and vanilla. Beat one minute at medium speed until smooth and fluffy; stir in pecans. Spread in pan over chocolate mixture. Sprinkle with chocolate chips. Bake for 25 to 35 minutes. Check with toothpick inserted in center coming out clean. Remove from oven; sprinkle with marshmallows. Bake 2 minutes longer. In saucepan over low heat, melt

ROCKY ROAD FUDGE BARS (Continued)

¼ cup margarine with 1 square chocolate. In small mixing bowl, combine this with cream cheese, milk, powdered sugar and vanilla until smooth. Immediately pour over marshmallows and smooth with back of spoon. Cool. Cut into bars. Store in refrigerator.

SAND TARTS

Preparation: 30 minutes   *Yield: 10 to 12 dozen*
Chill: 30 minutes
Bake: 12 to 15 minutes

2 cups sugar	**3 cups flour**
1 cup butter	**1 teaspoon vanilla**
1 whole egg	**Cinnamon sugar**
1 egg, separated	**Almonds**

Cream butter and sugar well. Add 1 whole egg and 1 egg yolk. Add flour gradually and 1 teaspoon vanilla. Put in refrigerator for 30 minutes. Preheat oven to 350°. Roll thinly on lightly floured board and cut in diamond shapes. Put on cookie sheet. Beat egg white lightly and brush on top of cookies. Sprinkle with cinnamon sugar. Top with almond. Bake for 12 to 15 minutes.

HINT: *Unless otherwise noted in the recipe, always remove cookies from sheet immediately and cool on wire racks.*

COOKIES

"KOLACHES"

Preparation: 2 hours   *Can be frozen*   *Yield: 8 to 10 dozen*
Chill: 1 hour
Bake: 15 minutes

4 cups flour

1 pound top quality **margarine**

Pinch of salt

½ pint commercial sour cream

2 (12 ounce) cans Solo brand
    dessert filling (any flavor)

Powdered sugar

Mix flour, margarine, salt and sour cream as for a pie dough. Refrigerate dough for at least 1 hour. Preheat oven to 400°. Roll out dough to about ¼ inch thickness. Cut into squares with square or diamond-shaped cookie cutter. Put one teaspoonful Solo filling in center of dough squares. Bring 2 opposite corners to center of square to form a pocket; pinch in center to seal. Bake for 15 minutes. When cooled, sprinkle powdered sugar on each kolachy.

Note: Do not use butter or whipped margarine.

NORWEGIAN OATMEAL COOKIES

Preparation: 10 minutes   *Can be frozen*   *Yield: 4 dozen*
Bake: 12 to 15 minutes

1 cup melted butter

2 cups quick oats

1 egg

1 cup sugar

1 cup flour

½ teaspoon baking soda

1 cup pecans

Preheat oven to 375°. Pour melted butter over oatmeal and stir. Beat egg with sugar and stir into oatmeal mixture. Sift flour with baking soda and stir into mixture with pecans. Drop from teaspoon onto baking sheet. Bake for 12 to 15 minutes or until browned.

Note: Do not use margarine.

HINT: *Mail cookies by mailing them in popped, unsalted popcorn.*

Gifts from the Kitchen

DOLLY SODS

GIFTS FROM THE KITCHEN

CHRISTMAS ALMONDS

Preparation: 15 minutes   *Yield: 3 to 4 cups*
Cook: 20 minutes

4 tablespoons butter (do not use margarine)	1 cup sugar
	1 teaspoon vanilla extract
2 cups whole almonds	Salt

Melt butter in large heavy skillet. Add almonds and sugar. Cook over medium low heat stirring constantly until almonds are coated and sugar is golden brown (about 15 to 20 minutes). Carefully add 1 teaspoon vanilla extract, stirring until mixed. Spread nuts on aluminum foil on flat heat-proof surface. Sprinkle salt lightly. Cool. Break into 2 or 3 nut clusters.

HOLIDAY HARD CANDY

Preparation: 1 ½ to 2 hours   *Yield: About 4 cups*

3 ¾ cups sugar	Powdered sugar
1 ½ cups light corn syrup	1 teaspoon flavoring oil
1 cup water	Food coloring

In a large, heavy saucepan mix the sugar, corn syrup and water. Stir over medium heat until sugar dissolves. Boil without stirring until candy thermometer registers 310° or drops of syrup form hard brittle threads in cold water. While the syrup is reaching the proper temperature, place several layers of newspaper on kitchen counter or table. Cover papers with a single 18 x 24 inch sheet of heavy duty aluminum foil. Sprinkle foil liberally with powdered sugar. When the syrup reaches 310°, remove from heat. When boiling has ceased, add flavoring oil and desired amount of food coloring. Mix. Pour immediately on foil. Sprinkle top liberally with more powdered sugar. As candy cools it will become semi-hard, starting at the outside edges first. As each section becomes semi-hard run a pizza cutter over it to score the hardening candy into small squares. When candy is completely cool, snap the scored sheet into small squares.

For Christmas use red food coloring and cinnamon oil, green food coloring and wintergreen, peppermint or spearmint oil.

GRANDMA'S DIVINITY

Preparation: 1 hour   *Can do ahead*   *Yield: 30 to 40 squares*

2 ½ cups sugar
½ cup light corn syrup
½ cup water

2 egg whites, stiffly beaten
1 teaspoon vanilla

Place sugar, corn syrup and water in saucepan over low heat. Stir until sugar is dissolved. Cook without stirring to hard ball stage. Remove from heat. Pour, beating constantly, in a fine stream into stiffly beaten egg whites. Continue beating until gloss is gone and candy holds shape. Add 1 teaspoon vanilla. Put into greased shallow pan or drop on waxed paper. Do not under beat.

Note: This melts in your mouth. It's hard work but well worth the time!

JAN'S QUICK MICROWAVE FUDGE

Preparation: 5 minutes
Cook: 2 ½ minutes
Stand: 30 minutes

1 (16 ounce) box powdered
    sugar
½ cup cocoa
¼ teaspoon salt

½ cup butter <u>or</u> margarine cut
    in 4 equal pieces
¼ cup evaporated milk
2 tablespoons pure vanilla
½ cup chopped pecans

Mix sugar, cocoa and salt and place in 1 ½ to 2-quart glass casserole. Place butter or margarine around casserole with dry ingredients. Make a well (hole) in center of dry ingredients. Mix vanilla and milk and add. Microwave on 100% power for 2 minutes or until liquid bubbles. Stir quickly. Some lumps will remain. That's normal. Add pecans. Stir quickly. Turn out into 8 x 8 inch or 9 x 9 inch buttered container. Refrigerate for 30 minutes to 1 hour or freeze for 20 minutes. Cut. Once cut no need to keep cold.

Variation: 1. Omit cocoa and add extra ½ cup powdered sugar.
             2. Add 2 tablespoons to ¼ cup peanut butter at same time as
                adding nuts.

GIFTS FROM THE KITCHEN

MOLASSES TAFFY

Preparation: 1 ½ hours   *Yield: 1 ½ pounds*

2 cups sugar
1 cup light molasses
¼ cup water

2 teaspoons cider vinegar
2 tablespoons butter
½ teaspoon soda

Butter sides of heavy 2 quart saucepan. Combine sugar, molasses and water. Heat slowly, stirring constantly, until sugar is dissolved. Bring to a boil, add vinegar, and cook to light crack stage (268°). Remove from heat; add butter and sift in soda; stir to mix. Turn out (don't scrape) on buttered platter or large shallow pan. For even cooling use a spatula to turn edges to center. Pull taffy while it's warm, using fingers to pull. If candy sticks, dip fingers into cornstarch. When candy is a light taffy color and getting hard to pull, cut into fourths. Pull each piece into long strands. Cut with buttered scissors. Quickly wrap in pieces of waxed paper.

MUNCHIES

Preparation: 15 minutes   *Yield: 100 pieces*

1 pound white chocolate
2 cups broken pretzels

1 cup peanuts, cocktail <u>or</u>
  dry roasted

Melt chocolate in top of double boiler over hot, but not boiling water. Add pretzels and peanuts. Stir until well coated with chocolate. Drop by small teaspoon on waxed paper. Cool 15 minutes. Store in tin.

Note: Keeps well in tin for a long time.

HINT: *Add one teaspoon cornstarch for each cup of sugar to make creamier fudge.*

PARTY PECANS

Preparation: 30 minutes   *Yield: serves 20*
Cook: 25 minutes

1 pound pecans   **⅛ cup cinnamon**
2 egg whites   **½ teaspoon salt**
½ cup sugar

Preheat oven to 275°. Grease cookie sheet. Beat egg whites until they peak softly. Add pecans, work with hands until well coated. Mix sugar, cinnamon and salt together. Roll pecans in sugar mixture. Bake on greased cookie sheet for 25 minutes.

PEANUT BRITTLE

Preparation: 40 minutes   *Yield: about 4 cups*

3 cups sugar   **2 tablespoons butter**
1 ½ cups white corn syrup   **1 teaspoon soda**
1 ⅓ cups water   **1 teaspoon vanilla**
2 cups unsalted peanuts

In heavy saucepan, mix sugar, corn syrup and water. Stir and bring to a boil. Boil until it reaches 280°. Add peanuts and butter, cook until it reaches 305°. Remove from heat, add soda and vanilla. Stir until well blended. Pour on well buttered cookie sheet. Let cool completely, then crack into pieces.

2-LAYER PEANUT BUTTER FUDGE

Preparation: 20 minutes   *Yield: 8 dozen*

1 (1 pound) box powdered   **1 cup peanut butter, creamy**
sugar   **or crunchy**
1 cup margarine or butter,   **1 (½ pound) milk chocolate bar**
melted

Mix powdered sugar, butter and peanut butter well and spread in bottom of 9 x 13 inch pan. Melt the chocolate bar in the top of a double boiler. Spread on the top of the peanut butter mixture. Cool. Cut into small squares.

GIFTS FROM THE KITCHEN

ENGLISH TOFFEE

Preparation: 3 hours   *Yield: 4 to 5 pounds*

2 cups sugar
1 tablespoon dark corn syrup
1 pound butter
½ cup chopped almonds slices
  or walnuts

½ cup water
1 pound milk chocolate
2 cups finely chopped pecans
  or walnuts

Put sugar, syrup and butter in a preheated pot (medium to medium high heat). Stir and cover. When at a full boil, remove cover and add almonds. Stir until 290° - DON'T SCRAP SIDES WHILE STIRRING. (Toffee is done between 280° and 300° when brown streaks occur.) Pour on 2 buttered cookie sheets. Quickly spread thin. When cool, break into small bite-size pieces. Melt chocolate in double boiler over hot water. Stir chocolate until melted, let cook slightly. Dip toffee pieces into chocolate and then into finely chopped nuts.

CHOCOLATE TRUFFLES

Preparation: 2 to 3 hours   *Can be frozen*   *Yield: 2 to 3 dozen*
Chill: 2 to 3 hours

7 ounces semi-sweet baking
  chocolate
1 ounce unsweetened baking
  chocolate
2 tablespoons strong coffee
¼ cup bourbon, dark rum or
  Cognac
¼ pound unsalted sweet butter,
  cut in 1-inch pieces

1 tablespoon pure vanilla
  extract
6 ounces good quality
  gingersnaps, crushed to
  make ¾ cup
¾ cup unsweetened cocoa
  powder
Paper or foil candy cups

In small saucepan, place squares of chocolate, coffee and liqueur. Cover. Set pan in a larger pan of boiling water and turn off heat. When the chocolate is melted and smooth (about 5 minutes) beat in the butter piece by piece using an electric mixer. Stir in vanilla and pulverized gingersnaps. Chill, covered, for several hours. Sprinkle the cocoa powder on a plate. With a teaspoon, dig out a lump of chocolate mixture and form into a ball and roll in cocoa. Place in candy cups. Refrigerate in covered container.

Alternative: If a coffee flavor is preferred, roll chocolate balls in a mixture of ½ cup unsweetened cocoa powder and ¼ cup instant powdered coffee.

MOM'S BREAD AND BUTTER PICKLES

Preparation: 1 hour
Stand: 3 hours

4 quarts sliced cucumbers	5 cups sugar
6 medium onions, sliced	1 ½ teaspoons turmeric
1 green pepper, chopped	1 ½ teaspoons celery seed
1 red pepper, chopped	2 tablespoons mustard seed
4 stalks celery, chopped	3 cups vinegar
⅓ cup pickling salt	Cracked ice

Slice cucumbers. Add onions, green pepper, red pepper and celery. Add salt. Mix well in roaster pan. Cover with cracked ice and let stand 3 hours. Remove ice and drain vegetables well in colander. Combine sugar, turmeric, celery seed, mustard seed and vinegar in roaster pan and bring to boil. Add vegetables and bring to boil. Spoon into pint or quart jars that are heated. Seal by processing 10 minutes in boiling water bath.

APPLE BUTTER

Preparation: 15 minutes
Cook: 6 hours

3 (6 pound 12 ounce) cans applesauce	2 (9 ½ ounce) bags cinnamon drops
6 pounds sugar	1 teaspoon oil of cinnamon

Put applesauce and sugar in big electric roaster. Mix sugar, applesauce and cinnamon drops. Let cook at 350°, covered, for 2 hours. Remove lid and let mixture cook down allowing moisture to evaporate for about 4 hours. After turning off heat add 1 teaspoon oil of cinnamon. Put in jars and seal.

Note: Recipe may be halved and cooked in a large soup kettle over medium to low heat.

HINT: *If candy is too sweet, add a touch of salt.*

GIFTS FROM THE KITCHEN

CRANBERRY—WINE JELLY

Preparation: 1 hour   *Yield: 6 to 8 small glasses*

3 cups sugar
1 cup cranberry juice

1 cup claret
½ of a 3 ounce bottle pectin

Mix sugar, juice and wine in top of double boiler. Stir over rapidly boiling water until sugar is dissolved. Remove from heat and stir in pectin. Skim off foam, if any. Pour into sterile glasses and cover with paraffin.

GRAPE CONSERVE

Preparation: 1 hour
Cook: 50 minutes

5 pounds Concord grapes
3 pounds sugar

2 pounds raisins
1 pound English walnuts

Separate pulp from skins of grapes and cook separately. Cook skins 15 to 20 minutes, adding enough water to prevent sticking. Cook pulp without water until soft, then press through a sieve or food mill to remove seeds. Combine skins, juice and pulp with sugar and cook 20 minutes. Add raisins and cook slowly for 5 to 10 minutes. Stir often to prevent sticking. Add nuts last 5 minutes. Pour boiling hot into sterilized jars.

JALAPEÑO JELLY

Preparation: 30 minutes
Cook: 10 minutes

¾ cup diced green bell pepper
¼ to ¾ cup diced Jalapeños
1 cup cider vinegar

5 cups sugar
1 bottle Certo
Green food coloring (optional)

Chop bell peppers and Jalapeños. Place peppers, vinegar and sugar in large saucepan; bring to a boil. Boil for 5 minutes. Remove from heat and add Certo and coloring. Cool. Pour into sterilized baby food jars and seal with ⅛ inch paraffin.

Note: Delicious appetizer when spooned over a block of cream cheese and served with crackers. Also good served with meats, especially lamb.

GIFTS FROM THE KITCHEN

PEACH MARMALADE

Preparation: 1 hour
Cook: several hours

1 cup drained, crushed,
  canned pineapple
1 (6 ounce) jar maraschino
  cherries, drained
1 pound seedless white grapes

24 peaches
Grated peel of 1 orange
Juice of 2 oranges
9 cups sugar
Pectin, if needed

Grind pineapple, cherries and grapes. Peel peaches and slice. Add all other ingredients and cook in large pan until thick. If after cooking 2 hours the mixture does not thicken, add a packet of pectin for thickening. Bottle in sterile jar.

GREEN OR RED PEPPER JELLY

Preparation: 40 minutes
Cook: 15 minutes

2 large green or red peppers,
  cored and seeded
2 long green or red chili
  peppers, cored and seeded

1 ½ cups cider vinegar
5 ½ cups sugar
Green or red food coloring
1 (3 ounce) bottle liquid food
  pectin

Cut green peppers and chili peppers in small bowl. Place half in electric blender with ½ cup vinegar. Chop. Pour in very large kettle. Do other half of peppers with ½ cup vinegar. Chop. Pour in kettle. Pour ½ cup vinegar in blender to wash out. Add sugar to mixture. Stir well. Bring to a full rolling boil, stirring constantly. Boil one minute after it comes to boil. Remove from heat and skim top for one minute. Add food coloring. Add pectin. Stir. Skim foam again. Ladle into hot sterilized jars. Cool. Seal with paraffin, or seal with sealer jars while still hot.

HINT: *Coat your pan with butter to prevent candy from boiling over sides of pan.*

GIFTS FROM THE KITCHEN

WATERMELON PICKLES

Preparation: 1 hour
Stand: 3 days

3 quarts watermelon rind,
  trimmed
Boiling water
7 cups sugar
2 cups vinegar

½ teaspoon oil of cinnamon
¼ teaspoon oil of cloves
1 small unpeeled orange
1 unpeeled lemon

Trim off green skin and any pink flesh from melon. Cut rind into one inch cubes. Place in large saucepan and cover with boiling water. Boil until tender but not soft, about 20 minutes. Drain well. In saucepan combine sugar, vinegar and oils of cloves and cinnamon. Bring to boil and pour over rind. Let stand overnight at room temperature. Next morning drain syrup from rind, heat to boiling and pour back over rind. Let stand overnight. Third morning, slice orange and lemon and quarter each slice, add to watermelon rind in syrup. Heat to boiling and pack, boiling hot, into sterilized jars.

HINT: The weather is a big factor in candymaking. On a hot humid day it is advisable to cook candy 2° higher than in cold, dry weather.

Kids in the Kitchen

KIDS IN THE KITCHEN

EGG WITH A HOLE IN IT!

Preparation: 5 minutes   *Yield: 1 serving*

1 generous pat of butter <u>or</u>   1 slice bread (white <u>or</u>
  margarine   wheat bread)
1 egg

Melt butter in pan. This is important: You must bite the middle out of the
bread, making a hole. Brown on one side. Break egg into hole. When egg
starts to fry turn over and cook to your desired taste.

SPECIAL FRENCH TOAST

Preparation: 10 minutes   *Yield: 1 serving*

1 egg   2 slices "day old" bread
2 tablespoons milk   A dash of cinnamon
1 tablespoon orange juice   Butter and syrup

Beat egg in small bowl. Add milk and orange juice. Beat. Soak bread on both
sides. Place bread in a greased frying pan over medium high heat. Sprinkle
with cinnamon and fry. Turn, sprinkle with cinnamon and cook until golden
brown. Serve hot with butter and syrup.

MINI PIZZAS

Preparation: 10 minutes   *Yield: 4 servings*
Cook: 8 to 10 minutes

1 can refrigerated biscuits   1 can tomato <u>or</u> pizza sauce
  (any size depending on how   Pepperoni slices (1 per biscuit)
  many you're going to serve)   Shredded cheese
                                     Oregano

Preheat oven to 400°. Flatten each biscuit into a 4-inch circle on cookie sheet.
Spread tomato sauce on biscuit. Add pepperoni. Sprinkle on a pinch of
oregano. Top with cheese. Bake 8 to 10 minutes or until edges are lightly
browned.

SEA CREATURE SALAD

Preparation: 30 minutes   *Can do ahead*   *Yield: 4 servings*

2 (6 ½ ounce) cans tuna,
  drained
⅔ to 1 cup grated carrots
Grated onion to taste
2 tablespoons lemon juice
⅔ to 1 cup mayonnaise
Chow mein noodles for texture
Lettuce

Possible additions:
¼ to ½ cup chopped celery
¼ cup chopped water chestnuts
Black **or** stuffed olives

Mash drained tuna with a fork. Mix grated carrots and onions with tuna. Mix other additions of your choice with the tuna mixture. Stir in the lemon juice and the mayonnaise. Just before serving, stir in the noodles. Serve on top of lettuce leaves.

TUNA BURGERS

Preparation: 20 minutes   *Can do ahead*   *Yield: 4 to 8 servings*
Cook: 10 minutes

2 (6 ½ ounce) cans tuna,
  drained
1 small onion, chopped
1 hard boiled egg, chopped

Mayonnaise to taste
4 to 6 ounces shredded
  Cheddar cheese
4 hamburger buns

Preheat oven to 350°. Mix tuna, egg and celery together. Add mayonnaise to moisten. Spread tuna mixture on split buns. Sprinkle with cheese. Bake 8 to 10 minutes until cheese melts.

Note: You may prepare this ahead, but wait until you are ready to bake to put the tuna mixture on the buns.

HINT: *Substitute cornflakes for nuts in pecan pie - they will rise to the top like nuts - gives new flavor.*

KIDS IN THE KITCHEN

BANANAS ON A STICK

Preparation: 30 minutes   *Can do ahead*   *Yield: 8 servings*
Freeze: Several hours   *Can be frozen*

4 ripe bananas, peeled   **1 tablespoon shortening**
8 wooden popsicle sticks   **Chopped peanuts (optional)**
1 (6 ounce) package milk
  chocolate morsels

Cut bananas in half crosswise. Insert wooden stick in flat end. Wrap in aluminum foil and freeze. Melt milk chocolate morsels over hot (not boiling) water in double boiler pan. Coat each banana with chocolate mixture. Roll immediately in nuts if desired. Wrap each banana in aluminum foil and store in freezer.

FROZEN BANANAS FOR CHILDREN

Preparation: 30 minutes   *Can do ahead*   *Yield: 4 servings*
Freeze: 24 hours

4 ripe bananas   **Honey**
Cinnamon   **Granola**
Nutmeg   **Chopped peanuts**

Peel the bananas and place each one on a sheet of aluminum foil. Sprinkle one banana with cinnamon, sprinkle one with nutmeg, brush one with honey and roll it in granola, and brush one with honey and roll in chopped peanuts. Wrap the foil around each banana. Freeze for 24 hours. Unwrap a little at a time and eat as you would a popsicle.

HINT: *Shave colored gumdrops and decorate white frosted cakes.*

298

FROZEN FRUIT CUPS

Preparation: 30 minutes   *Freeze ahead*   *Yield: 30 servings*

6 ripe bananas, cut into pieces
1 (1 pound 4 ounce) can
 crushed pineapple, <u>not</u>
 drained
2 (1 pound 13 ounce) cans
 apricots, cut into pieces
 and drained

2 tablespoons lemon juice
2 cups sugar
1 (6 ounce) can frozen orange
 juice, undiluted
1 can water measured by
 orange juice can

Combine all ingredients. Place in muffin tins with paper liners (cupcake holders). Freeze in the pans. Remove from muffin pans after frozen and store in plastic bag in freezer.

BUTTERSCOTCH COOKIES

Preparation: 30 minutes   *Can do ahead*   *Yield: 3 to 4 dozen*
Refrigerate several hours   *Can be frozen*

2 (6 ounce) packages
 butterscotch morsels

½ cup peanut butter
6 cups cornflakes

Melt butterscotch and peanut butter together in heavy saucepan over very low heat. Add cornflakes and mix well until flakes are coated. Drop from teaspoon on waxed paper. Refrigerate for several hours.

CHOCOLATE BIT CAKE

Preparation: 30 minutes   *Can do ahead*
Bake: 35 minutes   *Can be frozen*

1 (3 ¾ ounce) box chocolate
 pudding mix, not instant
2 cups milk for pudding

1 (18 ¼ ounce) box chocolate
 cake mix
1 cup semi-sweet chocolate
 morsels

Preheat oven to 350°. Grease and flour 9 x 13 inch cake pan. Prepare pudding according to package directions. Combine with cake mix. Batter will be thick. Spread into pan and top with chocolate bits. Bake according to directions on cake mix.

CREAM CHEESE BARS

Preparation: 15 minutes *Can do ahead* *Yield: 36 bars*
Bake: 35 minutes *Can be frozen*

1 (18 ¼ ounce) box yellow
  cake mix
½ cup margarine, melted
1 egg

1 (1 pound) box powdered
  sugar
1 (8 ounce) package cream
  cheese, softened

Preheat oven to 350°. Mix cake mix, melted margarine and egg together. Put in bottom of greased 9 x 13 inch pan. Mix together powdered sugar and softened cream cheese. Pour over cake batter. Bake 35 minutes. Sprinkle with powdered sugar.

HOMEMADE GRANOLA

Preparation: 15 minutes *Can do ahead* *Yield: 8 cups*
Bake: 15 minutes

4 cups oats
1 cup chopped pecans
1 cup coconut
1 cup wheat germ
1 cup sesame seed

½ teaspoon cinnamon
⅓ cup brown sugar
⅓ cup vegetable oil
⅓ cup honey
1 cup raisins

Preheat oven to 275°. Combine oats, pecans, coconut, wheat germ, sesame seed, cinnamon and brown sugar. Combine oil and honey, mix well. Pour over granola and stir until well mixed. Put in long, shallow pan and bake for 15 minutes. Stir several times. Remove from oven and cool for 15 minutes, then add raisins. When cold store in airtight container.

HINT: *Rub scissors with butter to cut up marshmallows.*

PUDDING COOKIES

Preparation: 20 minutes   *Yield: 2 ½ to 3 dozen*
Bake: 8 minutes

1 cup buttermilk baking mix   1 (3 ½ ounce) package vanilla
¼ cup salad oil   instant pudding mix
                                              ½ cup chocolate chips

Preheat oven to 350°. Mix all ingredients together. Shape dough by teaspoonfuls into balls and place on cookie sheet. Bake about 8 minutes.

Note: You may substitute chocolate or butterscotch pudding for vanilla. Substitute peanut butter or butterscotch chips for chocolate.

BAKED CARAMEL CORN

Preparation: 30 minutes   *Can do ahead*   *Yield: 8 quarts*
Cook: 15 minutes

1 cup margarine   ½ teaspoon baking soda
2 cups brown sugar   1 teaspoon vanilla
½ cup molasses   8 quarts popped corn
1 teaspoon salt

Preheat oven to 250°. Melt margarine, stir in sugar, molasses and salt. Boil 2 minutes without stirring. Remove from heat, add soda and vanilla. Pour over popcorn. Place in two 9 x 13 inch pans. Bake 15 minutes. Stir every 5 minutes. Cool; break apart and store in airtight containers.

PEANUT BUTTER POPCORN

Preparation: 30 minutes   *Yield: 4 quarts*

4 quarts popped corn   1 cup sugar
½ cup honey   1 teaspoon vanilla
1 cup corn syrup   1 cup peanut butter

Spread waxed paper on 2 cookie sheets. Bring honey, syrup and sugar to boil. Boil 2 minutes. Add peanut butter and vanilla. Pour over popped corn. Spread onto cookie sheets. When cool, break into bite sized pieces.

CRACKER JACKS

Preparation: 30 minutes   *Can do ahead*   *Yield: 6 quarts*
Cook: 1 hour

6 quarts popped corn
1 cup margarine
½ cup maple syrup
2 cups brown sugar

10 ounces peanuts
1 teaspoon almond extract
½ teaspoon baking soda

Preheat oven to 250°. Mix margarine, syrup and brown sugar and bring to boil. Add peanuts and boil 5 minutes. Remove from heat and add almond extract and soda (mixture will be foamy). Pour over popcorn and bake 1 hour, stirring every 15 minutes.

POPCORN BALLS

Preparation: 45 minutes   *Can do ahead*   *Yield: 24 balls*

4 quarts popped corn
1 cup corn syrup
1 cup sugar

¼ teaspoon salt
Miniature gumdrops

Heat syrup, sugar and salt until sugar is dissolved. Pour over popped corn and gumdrops. When cool enough to handle, grease hands with butter and form into balls. Wrap in plastic wrap and tie with yarn bow.

RAISED WAFFLES

Preparation: 15 minutes   *Can do ahead*   *Yield: 6 servings*
Stand: 8 hours or overnight

½ cup lukewarm water
1 package dry yeast
2 cups lukewarm milk
½ cup melted butter or oil
1 teaspoon salt

1 teaspoon sugar
2 cups flour
2 eggs
Pinch of baking soda

Combine yeast and warm water in a large bowl. Let stand five minutes. Add milk, melted butter or oil, salt and sugar. Beat in flour. Cover bowl and let chill overnight or at least 8 hours. When ready to cook, add eggs and baking soda. Beat well. Grill on waffle iron until brown.

TABLE OF SUBSTITUTIONS

If you don't have: **You may substitute:**

If you don't have:	You may substitute:
1 cup sweet milk	½ cup evaporated milk plus ½ cup water
1 cup sour milk	1 tablespoon vinegar or lemon juice plus milk to make 1 cup - let stand 10 minutes
1 cup light cream	⅞ cup milk plus 3 tablespoons butter
1 cup heavy cream	¾ cup milk plus ⅓ cup butter
1 cup butter or margarine	⅞ cup oil plus ½ teaspoon butter
1 cup honey; 1 cup corn syrup	¾ cup sugar plus ¼ cup water
1 cup molasses	1 cup honey or 1 cup dark corn syrup
1 tablespoon minced fresh herbs	1 teaspoon dried herbs
1 teaspoon dry mustard	1 tablespoon prepared mustard
1 pound fresh mushrooms	6 or 8-ounce can or 3 ounces, dried
1 cup sifted all-purpose flour	1 cup plus 2 tablespoons sifted cake flour
1 cup sifted cake flour	1 cup minus 2 tablespoons sifted all purpose flour
1 cup self-rising flour	1 cup all-purpose flour plus 1 ½ teaspoons baking powder and ½ teaspoon salt
1 cup all-purpose flour	1 cup self-rising flour minus baking powder and salt called for in recipe; or 1 cup fine whole grain flour
1 tablespoon cornstarch	2 tablespoons flour or 4 teaspoons quick-cooking tapioca
⅓ cup dry bread crumbs	1 slice bread or ¾ cup soft bread crumbs
¾ cup cracker crumbs	1 cup bread crumbs
Confectioners sugar (approx. 1 cup)	1 cup granulated sugar plus 1 tablespoon cornstarch mixed in a blender 2 minutes
1 tablespoon tapioca	1 ½ tablespoons all-purpose flour
2 large eggs	3 small eggs
1 egg	2 egg yolks (for custard)
1 egg	2 egg yolks plus 1 tablespoon water (for cookies)
1 cup commercial sour	1 tablespoon lemon juice plus evaporated milk to equal 1 cup; or 3 tablespoons butter plus ⅞ cup sour milk
1 cup yogurt	1 cup buttermilk or sour milk
1 cup fresh milk	3 to 5 tablespoons nonfat dry milk solids in 1 cup water
1 square (1-ounce) unsweetened chocolate	3 tablespoons cocoa plus 1 tablespoon butter or margarine
1 clove fresh garlic	1 teaspoon garlic salt or ⅛ teaspoon garlic powder
1 teaspoon onion powder	2 teaspoons minced onion

UNCOMMON EQUIVALENTS

⅓ of ¼ cup = 1 tablespoon plus 1 teaspoon
⅓ of 5 tablespoons = 1 tablespoon plus 2 teaspoons
⅓ of ⅓ cup = 1 tablespoon plus 2 ⅓ teaspoons
⅓ of ½ cup = 2 tablespoons plus 2 teaspoons
½ of ¾ cup = 6 tablespoons
½ of 1 tablespoon = 1 ½ teaspoons
⅛ of 1 cup = 2 tablespoons or 1 ounce

EQUIVALENTS

1 pound sugar = 2 ¼ cups
1 pound powdered sugar = 4 to 4 ½ cups, sifted
1 pound brown sugar = 2 ¼ cups, packed
1 pound rice = 6 cups, cooked, or 2 cups raw
1 pound all-purpose flour = 4 cups, sifted
1 pound cake flour = 4 ½ cups, sifted
1 pound grated cheese = 4 to 5 cups
1 pound potatoes, whole = 2 cups, cooked and mashed
5 eggs = 1 cup
8 egg whites = 1 cup
1 pound green shrimp = 12 ounces, dressed
1 pound fresh shrimp, cooked and cleaned = 1 (5 ounce) can
1 fifth wine = about 5 (5 ounce) servings
1 quart punch = about 10 (3 ounce) servings

MEASUREMENTS

Pinch	As much as can be taken between tip of finger and thumb
Dash	Less than ⅛ teaspoon
60 drops	1 teaspoon
3 teaspoons (½ fluid ounce)	1 tablespoon
⅛ cup (1 fluid ounce)	2 tablespoons
¼ cup (2 fluid ounces)	4 tablespoons
⅓ cup	5 tablespoons plus 1 teaspoon
½ cup (4 fluid ounces)	8 tablespoons
⅔ cup	10 tablespoons plus 2 teaspoons
¾ cup (6 fluid ounces)	12 tablespoons
1 cup (8 fluid ounces)	16 tablespoons
2 cups (16 fluid ounces)	1 pint
4 cups (32 fluid ounces)	1 quart
2 pints	1 quart
2 pints	4 cups
2 quarts	½ gallon
4 quarts (liquid)	1 gallon
8 quarts (dry)	1 peck
4 pecks	1 bushel
16 ounces (dry measure)	1 pound
1 ounce	28.35 grams
1 pound	453.6 grams

INDEX

INDEX

INDEX

INDEX

INDEX

INDEX

INDEX

INDEX

INDEX

**The Junior League of
Huntington, West Virginia, Inc.**
617 Ninth Avenue
Huntington, West Virginia 25701

Please send me _____ copies of **ALMOST HEAVEN** at $9.95 plus
$1.55 postage and handling. (W. Va. residents add 50¢ sales tax.)

Enclosed is my check or money order for $ _____

Name _____

Address _____

City _____ State_____ Zip_____

Gift wrapping available $1.50 per book _____

**The Junior League of
Huntington, West Virginia, Inc.**
617 Ninth Avenue
Huntington, West Virginia 25701

Please send me _____ copies of **ALMOST HEAVEN** at $9.95 plus
$1.55 postage and handling. (W. Va. residents add 50¢ sales tax.)

Enclosed is my check or money order for $ _____

Name _____

Address _____

City _____ State_____ Zip_____

Gift wrapping available $1.50 per book _____

**The Junior League of
Huntington, West Virginia, Inc.**
617 Ninth Avenue
Huntington, West Virginia 25701

Please send me _____ copies of **ALMOST HEAVEN** at $9.95 plus
$1.55 postage and handling. (W. Va. residents add 50¢ sales tax.)

Enclosed is my check or money order for $ _____

Name _____

Address _____

City _____ State_____ Zip_____

Gift wrapping available $1.50 per book _____